ENGLISH WORKSHOP

SECOND COURSE

HOLT, RINEHART AND WINSTON
Harcourt Brace & Company

Austin • New York • Orlando • Atlanta • San Francisco
Boston • Dallas • Toronto • London

ACKNOWLEDGMENTS

We wish to thank the following teachers who reviewed materials for *English Workshop*, either in manuscript or in field tests.

Gail Craig
LaSalle Springs Middle School
Glencoe, MO 63038-2201

Melanie Demoranville
Joseph Care Junior High School
Swansea, MA 02777

Janet Peña-Davis
Dodge School
Chicago, IL 60612

Loreen Schallon
Redwood Middle School
Napa, CA 94558

Mary Schultz
Our Lady of the Greenwood
Greenwood, IN 46143

Executive Editor: Mescal Evler
Managing Editor: Robert R. Hoyt
Project Editor: Suzanne Thompson
Editorial Staff: Laura Britton, Tara Ellis, Karen Forrester, Karen Hoffman, Guy Holland, Christy McBride, Michael Neibergall, Marie Price, Patricia Saunders, Amy Simpson, Atietie Tonwe
Editorial Support Staff: Carla Beer, Stella Galvan, Margaret Guerrero, Ruth Hooker, Pat Stover
Editorial Permissions: Ann Farrar
Design, Photo Research, and Production: Pun Nio, *Senior Art Director;* Rebecca Byrd-Bretz, *Cover Design;* Debra Saleny, *Photo Research Manager;* Mavournea Hay, *Photo Researcher;* Carol Martin, *Electronic Publishing Manager;* Deborah Fey, Maria Homic, *Electronic Publishing Staff;* Beth Prevelige, *Production Manager;* Joan Eberhardt, *Production Assistant;* Linda Moyer, *Production Coordinator*

ISBN 0-03-097175-6
19 20 21 179 08 07 06

TABLE OF CONTENTS

LANGUAGE AND STYLE

GRAMMAR, USAGE, AND MECHANICS

PREWRITING: FINDING IDEAS FOR WRITING

Your writing begins when you explore your imagination and your memories of important events. Here are some techniques that many writers use to find and explore ideas.

WRITER'S JOURNAL

Set aside a notebook or a file folder to use as a *writer's journal*. It can serve as a record of your experiences, feelings, ideas, questions, and thoughts.

- Keep your journal handy, and write in it every day.
- Let your imagination run free. Jot down your dreams and feelings. Write lines from songs or poems, ideas for stories. Include your own sketches.
- Don't worry about spelling or grammar.

FREEWRITING

Freewriting is thinking about a subject and then writing whatever ideas pop into your head.

- Set a time limit of three to five minutes, and keep writing until the time is up.
- Start with a subject that's important to you—music, sports, a favorite person, an exciting experience.
- Jot down all the ideas that come to you. If you get stuck, just write anything. But keep your pen or pencil moving.

EXERCISE 1   Using Prewriting Techniques

Write a paragraph about a person who is important to you. It might be a friend, a family member, or a famous person. To find and develop your ideas, use the journal or freewriting techniques described above.

BRAINSTORMING

To *brainstorm*, write down a topic. Then list any related ideas that come to mind. You can brainstorm alone, but it's often more fun and more helpful to brainstorm in a group. That way, everyone can share different ideas. Often, one person's good idea suggests a good idea to another person.

- Write the subject at the top of a large piece of paper or on the chalkboard.
- Have one person jot down all the ideas shared in the group. Keep going until everyone runs out of ideas.
- Don't stop to discuss or make judgments about any of the ideas.

CLUSTERING

Clustering is a way to organize ideas as you brainstorm. You connect all the ideas in a diagram with circles and lines to help show how the ideas are related.

- Write your subject in the center of a sheet of paper, and circle it.
- Around the subject, write related ideas. Circle each idea, and draw a line to connect each one to the subject.
- Keep writing down ideas. Circle them, and draw lines connecting them to the ideas that they are related to.
- Keep adding and connecting ideas until your paper is filled.

EXERCISE 2   Brainstorming and Clustering

With a partner, choose one of the topics below. Brainstorm together, taking notes as you talk. Then work alone to make a cluster diagram on the topic. Add any other ideas you may think of. Meet with your partner to compare your clusters.

a historical event	a great story
an important invention	a place we'd like to visit
a great movie	a person we'd like to know
a favorite song	an unusual pet

PREWRITING: ASKING QUESTIONS

5W-HOW? QUESTIONS

Asking questions that begin with *who, what, where, when, why,* and *how* can help you think of facts and details you'll need as you write about most topics.

Recycling in Our City	
• *Who?*	Who in our city is in charge of recycling efforts?
• *What?*	What materials could we recycle?
• *Where?*	Where should the recycled materials be sent?
• *When?*	When should we begin the recycling project?
• *Why?*	Why is recycling important?
• *How?*	How have recycling projects helped the environment?

"WHAT IF?" QUESTIONS

Asking "What if?" questions can give a writer many new and different creative ideas. Your questions might look like these.

- *What if a character on the television screen stepped into my room?*
- *What if I grew eyes in the back of my head?*
- *What if the President of the United States came to visit me?*

EXERCISE 3 Using *5W-How?* Questions

Write an article about a river, a mountain, or another landmark in your area. On your own paper, write *5W-How?* questions that will help you gather the information you need. Jot down possible sources for each answer.

EXERCISE 4 Using "What if?" Questions

Work with a partner to develop the plot of a story. Choose one of these situations: (1) On a hike in a forest, two eighth-graders find a treasure chest filled with gold coins. (2) Two eighth-graders board a subway car; all the people on the car look exactly alike. With your partner, write ten "What if?" questions to gather ideas for the story. Then meet with another set of partners who chose the same plot. Discuss the paths that this story might take, based on the "What if?" questions each group produced.

PREWRITING: ARRANGING IDEAS

After gathering your ideas for a piece of writing, the next step is to arrange those ideas in an order that makes sense.

METHODS FOR ARRANGING IDEAS		
Type of Order	**Type of Writing**	**Definition**
Chronological	Narration	Presents events in the order in which they happen in time
Spatial	Description	Presents objects according to location
Importance	Evaluation	Presents details from the least important to the most important, or the reverse
Logical	Classification (Comparison and Contrast)	Groups related details together

EXERCISE 5   Arranging Ideas

On your own paper, identify which type of order would be most effective for arranging ideas for each of the following topics. Then list five ideas related to each topic, and put them in the order you would use for your draft.

1. You are describing and identifying the stores that are located in a row along one city block.

2. You are writing a report that compares and contrasts butterflies and moths.

3. You are writing a summary of the main events in a short story.

4. You are writing a report titled "How to Make Pizza."

5. You are writing an essay about why swimming alone might be dangerous.

WRITING A FIRST DRAFT

Once you've completed all the prewriting steps, it's time to start writing.

- Use your prewriting plans as a guide.
- Write freely. Focus on expressing your ideas clearly.
- As you write, keep your mind open for new ideas. Include these new ideas in your draft.
- Don't worry about spelling and grammar errors. You can correct them later.

Below is a draft of a paragraph about Sarah Vaughan, a famous jazz singer. Notice the brackets that the writer used to make notes. Later she will find the information she needs to fill those holes. The writer will correct spelling errors and rework awkward sentences at a later stage in the writing process.

> By chance, Sarah Vaughan [spelling?] agreed to sing at an amateur night in Harlem. By chance, a band leader heard her and signed her on as a vocalist. Her work has been admired by jazz lovers ever since. When Vaughan died in 1990, she was an internationally known and respected jazz musician. You can bet that <u>that</u> doesn't happen by ~~accident~~ chance. [check 1990 magazines for catchy quotes]

EXERCISE 6   Writing a First Draft

Use what you have learned about chronological order to write a draft of a paragraph to read out loud to a kindergarten class. In your draft, explain to the children how to complete a simple process, such as tying shoelaces or planting a seed. Don't worry about spelling errors as you write. Let your ideas flow onto the paper in an order that makes sense. When you are finished, get together with a partner and compare your drafts.

EVALUATING AND REVISING

EVALUATING

After you finish a first draft, *evaluate* it, using these five standards.

- The writing has a clearly stated main idea.
- The main idea is supported with details.
- The order of the ideas makes sense.
- The connections between ideas and sentences are clear.
- The writing is interesting. It grabs and holds the reader's attention.

Evaluating your own writing can be difficult. Ask a peer—a friend or a fellow writer—to evaluate your work, too. Here are some guidelines to follow when you evaluate a piece of writing.

Self-Evaluation	Peer Evaluation
1. Set your draft aside for a while before evaluating it. 2. Read your paper at least three times. First, read to check its *content*. Next, read to check its *organization*. Finally, read to check its *style*. 3. Read your draft aloud. Listen for awkward or unclear spots that need attention.	1. Tell the writer something good about the paper. 2. Focus on the content and organization. 3. Ask helpful questions and make suggestions—"Can you explain this point more clearly?" or "Can you add more details or examples to emphasize this point?"

EXERCISE 7 Practicing Peer Evaluation

On your own paper, write an evaluation of the paragraph below. Use the five standards for good writing. Also use the tips for peer evaluation.

If you go to the Ingleside Diner, you'll think you're in an old movie. The diner was built in 1946, and it looks it. It has metal tables. The metal seats have pink plastic cushions. The counter is wooden, and there are little dents in the wood where customers have rested their elbows for almost fifty years. There are things on the menu that only my grandmother makes, like vegetable soup and homemade blueberry muffins. Whenever my grandfather comes to visit, he always takes me to the Ingleside.

REVISING

After you've evaluated a piece of writing, it's time to revise it. Four techniques are involved: *adding, cutting, replacing,* and *reordering*.

Revision Techniques	
Add	Add words, phrases, sentences, or paragraphs.
Cut	Take out repeated or unnecessary words and ideas.
Replace	Replace weak or awkward words with more precise and vivid words.
Reorder	Move words, phrases, sentences, and paragraphs into a more logical order.
Example	

Edward Kennedy

⋀"Duke" Ellington was a famous American ~~writer of music~~ *composer*, pianist, and orchestra leader. He was only nineteen years old when he formed ~~and created~~ his first band in 1918. At the ~~most important~~ *height* ~~part~~ of the jazz age, he was known all over the world. He became one of the true leaders of American jazz music. Ellington's most famous songs are considered standards of the jazz age. They include such ~~ones~~ *hits* as "Satin Doll" and "Mood Indigo."

EXERCISE 8   Revising a Piece of Writing

Read the paragraph you wrote for Exercise 6 on page 5. Evaluate it carefully as you read it. Then revise it, using the techniques in the chart above. Rewrite your revised paragraph on your own paper.

PROOFREADING AND PUBLISHING

PROOFREADING

When you *proofread*, you carefully reread your writing to find mistakes in grammar, spelling, capitalization, and punctuation. It's helpful to put your work aside for a while first, so that you can read your paper with a fresh eye. It also helps to trade papers with a partner to check for errors in each other's papers. As you proofread, use these guidelines.

Guidelines for Proofreading

- Is every sentence a complete sentence?
- Are capitalization and punctuation correct throughout?
- Are there errors in subject-verb agreement?
- Are verb forms and verb tenses correct?
- Are adjective and adverb forms used correctly?
- Are pronouns used correctly?
- Is each word spelled correctly?

Symbols for Revising and Proofreading

Symbol	Example	Meaning
∧	*was* I ∧working	Insert
ℛ	It is is raining	Delete (take out)
≡	on madison Avenue	Capitalize
/	a call from my Friend Bilal	Lowercase
∪	my huose	Change order
⊙	He isn't here today⊙	Add a period
∧̧	apples⸴oranges, and pears	Insert a comma
¶	¶Monday we will, . . .	Begin a new paragraph

EXERCISE 9 Proofreading a Paragraph

Use proofreading symbols to mark the errors in the paragraph below. Also, replace informal language with standard English by writing your change above the original words or phrases.

When my Cousin Nicole came to visit form Texas, I took to the Brandywine river. We rented a canoe and paddle for about three ours. By the time we got to to the bridge at Route 44, we was hot and tired. So it was a great surprise to see my mother standing on the bridge, wiating for Nicole and I. By luck, it was her lunch hour. So she had left work to bring us sandwiches fruit, and a jug of lemonade.

PUBLISHING

After you proofread, you're ready to publish, or share, your writing.

Guidelines for Manuscript Form

- Use only one side of a sheet of paper.
- Write in blue or black ink, type, or use a word processor.
- Leave margins of about one inch at the top, the sides, and the bottom of each page.
- Follow your teacher's instructions for placing your name, the date, and your class on the paper.
- If you write, skip every other line. If you type, double-space the lines.
- Indent the first line of each paragraph.

Suggestions for Publishing

- Read your paper to the class or to a group of friends.
- Submit your writing to your school newspaper or magazine.
- Enter a writing contest. Your teacher or librarian may know of some contests you might wish to enter.

EXERCISE 10   Finding Ideas for Publishing

Read the following descriptions of types of writing. On your own paper, list one or two publishing ideas for each piece.

EX.   1. a poem about birds
   1. *school literary magazine; a writing contest*

1. a letter urging students to attend a bowling tournament
2. a story about the time your grandmother took you fishing
3. a review of the new movie at the local theater
4. an essay on what freedom means to you
5. an article about finding a summer job

EXERCISE 11   Preparing a Final Copy

Use the **Proofreading Guidelines** on page 8 to make corrections on the draft you wrote for Exercise 8. Next, use the **Manuscript Guidelines** on page 9 to prepare a clean, final copy of your paper. Then, meet with a small group of your classmates to share your work and to discuss ways to publish your writing.

Drawing by H. Martin; © 1985 The New Yorker Magazine, Inc.

" 'What I Did This Summer.' This summer, I went to camp. I hated it. I hated every minute of it. I hated my counsellor. I hated the food. I hated the woods. I hated the nature walks and the nature talks. I hated the outings. I hated the campfires. I hated the overnights. I hated . . ."

MAIN IDEAS AND TOPIC SENTENCES

Most paragraphs have a *main idea,* the big idea around which the paragraph is organized. A *topic sentence* often states this main idea. Though a topic sentence may come anywhere in a paragraph, it is often the first or second sentence in a paragraph.

> My grandparents came from four different countries. My mother's mother arrived from Spain. She married Grandpa da Silva, who moved here from Portugal. My father's mother came from Russia, and his father moved here from Poland.

However, many paragraphs have no topic sentence. For example, narrative paragraphs that tell about a series of events usually do not have a topic sentence.

> The tornado was headed right toward us, and the sirens sounded a little after noon. People who were inside ran to their basements. People who were on the streets poured into stores and offices, seeking shelter. Within minutes, the town looked deserted.

Although this paragraph has no topic sentence, you can still figure out the main idea. Because a tornado is coming, people are seeking shelter.

EXERCISE 1   Identifying Main Ideas and Topic Sentences

On the lines below each of the following paragraphs, write the main idea in your own words. If the paragraph has a topic sentence, underline that sentence.

1.   Our guesthouse served callaloo every day. The restaurant down the street served curried banana soup and pumpkin soup. The cold carrot soup is famous, as is the conch chowder. In Tortola, we could try a different soup every day of the week.

Main Idea _____

_____

2.   A surprising number of foods get their names from people. Both melba toast and peach melba get their names from the singer Nellie Melba. Graham crackers are named after Sylvester Graham, a minister and reformer. He believed that a good, wholesome diet could prevent many ills. The popular Bing cherry is named for a Chinese orchardist, while the less well known Napoleon cherry is named for the former French head of state.

Main Idea _____

_____

3.   As George de Mestral climbed the mountain, burs stuck to his clothing. When the climb was finished, he tried to pull them off. At first he was irritated. Then he was fascinated. Perhaps he could create a fastener that stuck as well as the burs did. De Mestral worked on the idea for years. He finally produced a model made of a row of hooks that fastened into a row of eyes. He called his fastener *locking tape*.

Main Idea _____

_____

4.   The Statue of Liberty is impressive by any standards. Standing more than one hundred fifty feet high, Liberty is made from more than three hundred separate sections. Its right arm alone extends more than forty feet. And the torch is so large that a dozen people can stand inside.

Main Idea _____

_____

UNITY AND COHERENCE

UNITY

When a paragraph has *unity*, all the sentences relate to the main idea. For instance, in a paragraph about the design of sports wheelchairs, every sentence should give some information about these chairs. A sentence about rocking chairs might destroy the unity. The sentence would not be about the main idea: the design of sports wheelchairs. Notice how all the sentences in the following paragraph relate to one idea.

> The tallest animals of all are the giraffes They live in the hot African grasslands called the savannah. A full-grown giraffe may be three times as tall as a tall man. Their long legs and long necks make it easy for them to eat leaves from high branches on trees. Acacia trees, which are found in the savannah, provide good food for giraffes.

COHERENCE

A good paragraph has *coherence.* In other words, readers can easily see how ideas in the paragraph are related. One way to create coherence is to use transitional words or phrases to connect ideas. The following chart shows some common transitional words and phrases.

Comparing Ideas	also, and, another, moreover, similarly, too
Contrasting Ideas	although, but, however, in spite of, instead, nevertheless, on the other hand, still, yet
Showing Cause and Effect	as a result, because, consequently, for, since, so, so that, therefore
Showing Time	after, at last, at once, before, eventually, finally, first, meanwhile, next, then, thereafter, when
Showing Place	above, across, around, before, behind, beyond, down, here, in, inside, into, near, next to, over, there, under
Showing Importance	first, last, mainly, more important, then, to begin with

Notice the transitional words in the following paragraph.

> This bee builds its nest <u>in</u> the ground. <u>Above</u> the ground you can see only a small dirt mound. <u>However</u>, a tunnel leads <u>down</u> from the mound to the brood cells <u>under</u> the soil.

EXERCISE 2   Identifying Sentences That Destroy Unity

Each paragraph below has one sentence that doesn't support the main idea. Find that sentence and draw a line through it.

1.   A quilt is a warm bedcover, but it may also tell a story. Some old quilts have sections that depict special events in the history of a family. Quilts are made of layers. One section might show the arrival of a new baby in the family; another section might show a wedding.

2.   Family camping can be a low-cost vacation. You and your family can enjoy the good weather and the taste of food cooked over the fire. Hiking and sightseeing are fun, yet inexpensive activities. You may need to buy some special camping equipment.

EXERCISE 3   Identifying Transitional Words and Phrases

Underline the transitional words and phrases in the following paragraph. Use the chart on the previous page as a guide.

You can prove that warm air expands. Before you begin, you will need to find a balloon, a measuring tape, and a blunt marker. First, blow up the balloon, and tie it shut. Then draw a line around the widest part of the balloon. Measure and record the length of this line. Next, place the balloon in a warm spot above a radiator or near a sunny window. Then wait twenty minutes and measure the line again. When you do, you will see that the line is longer. The balloon is larger because the air inside it has expanded.

USING DESCRIPTION AND NARRATION

DESCRIPTION

Description is one way of organizing a paragraph. You use description to tell what something is like or what it looks like. For example, you would use description to tell what a coyote looks like. Descriptions contain *sensory details*, details about what you see, hear, smell, taste, or touch.

Descriptive details are often arranged in *spatial order*—near to far, left to right, top to bottom—to show location. The following paragraph uses details of sight to describe an early invention called a parachute fire escape. The details in this paragraph are arranged in spatial order—from top to bottom.

> The picture showed a man wearing this so-called safety device. Above his head floated an open parachute. The parachute had thin metal bands inside it to keep it open. The open parachute was then attached to two other bands that held a strange headgear in place. One piece ran around the man's head, and one ran under his chin. The device included thick, bouncy pads, which the man wore under his feet.

EXERCISE 4   Arranging Details

Choose one of the subjects below. On your own paper, list details that you could use to describe it. Try to think of details that you can see, hear, smell, taste, or touch. Then arrange your list of details in spatial order.

1. a strange costume worn by a musical performer
2. a food that tastes better than it looks
3. a customized car or truck
4. a display in a mall or store window
5. a mythical creature from folklore

Fred Basset reprinted by permission: Tribune Media Services.

NARRATION

You are using *narration* when you tell someone what you did last Saturday or when you give someone directions. In other words, *narration* tells how something changes over a period of time. You can use narration to tell a story, explain a process, or explain causes and effects.

When you narrate, you often use *chronological order*. That is, you arrange events and actions in the order in which they occur.

STORY

When Kwan stepped up to the plate, the crowd was quiet. He smashed the first ball and sent it soaring over the left fielder's head. Before the crowd realized what had happened, Kwan had trotted around the bases and had reached home plate.

PROCESS

Installing tile is quite simple. First, use a ridged trowel to spread the adhesive over the plasterboard. Next, push the tiles firmly into the adhesive. Wait until the adhesive sets, and then spread the grout over the tile. Use a rubber trowel for this step, and push the grout into the spaces. Finally, wipe off the extra grout with a damp cloth.

CAUSE AND EFFECT

As the river rushes along, it picks up sand and silt. When the river reaches the ocean, the ocean blocks its path and causes it to slow down. Because the river is not moving as quickly, the solid material starts to settle to the bottom. The sand and silt then build up, so that the river has to flow around them. This buildup continues until a delta is formed.

EXERCISE 5   Arranging Details in Chronological Order

Choose one of the following topics. On your own paper, list several details you would include if you were going to write about the topic: story events, steps in the process, or causes and effects. Finally, arrange the details in chronological order.

1. endangered animals (causes)
2. finding a famous person's wallet (story)
3. how to get a summer job (process)
4. making your favorite sandwich (process)

USING COMPARISON/CONTRAST AND EVALUATION

COMPARISON AND CONTRAST

When you write about two or more subjects, you may want to compare and contrast them. You *compare* things when you show how they are alike. You *contrast* them by telling how they are different. You can develop a paragraph by comparing only, by contrasting only, or by both comparing and contrasting. In the paragraph below, the writer compares two kinds of popcorn and then contrasts them.

COMPARISON | Today popcorn is a popular snack. It doesn't matter whether the popcorn is microwaved or air cooked: Both types taste good. Another reason both types of popcorn are popular is that they are easy to cook. However, the number of calories in each type is
CONTRAST | different. Microwaved popcorn is higher in fat than the air-cooked variety. In fact, some brands have as much fat as a tablespoon of peanut butter!

EXERCISE 6 Comparing and Contrasting Features

Work with a partner on this exercise. First, choose a pair of topics to compare and contrast. Then, make two headings on your own paper: *Similarities* and *Differences.* Next, brainstorm with your partner to identify features of the subjects that are alike (similar) and those that are different. Finally, list the features you've identified under the correct headings.

1. video games and board games
2. ice-skating and roller-skating
3. tacos and egg rolls
4. lions and pet cats
5. a book and a movie

EVALUATION

Did you think the film *The Fugitive* was exciting and suspenseful? When you answer that question, you are *evaluating*. You are telling whether you think it is good or bad—how valuable it is. It's not enough just to tell your opinion, though. You also need to give reasons, or support, for your opinion.

One good way to organize reasons is to use order of importance, starting with the most important reason. You could also reverse this process and end with the most important reason, as in the following paragraph.

EVALUATION	School starts much too early for most students. It should start later for several reasons. First, a later start
REASON	would allow students to wait for their buses during daylight. At present, many students wait in the dark.
REASON	Second, a later hour would help students stay in step with the rest of the world. Many jobs (except teaching)
REASON	start later than school. The most important reason to change the starting time, however, is health. Most students simply cannot get enough sleep if they have to get up this early. Also, they have no time for the good breakfast that their parents want them to eat.

EXERCISE 7 Evaluating Ideas

Read the following topics, and choose two to evaluate. For each topic, write a sentence on your own paper that expresses your evaluation, or opinion. Then provide two or three reasons as support for your opinion. Arrange your reasons in order of importance.

EX.   1. Evaluation: Quebec is a great city for a vacation.
Reason 1: It's close and easy to reach.
Reason 2: It feels as exotic as any foreign country.
Reason 3: It offers a variety of activities and places to stay.

1. dress codes (Should schools have them?)
2. the arts in school (Should they be required courses in every school?)
3. movie prices (Should students pay lower prices than adults?)
4. music censorship (Should song lyrics ever be censored?)

PLANNING A COMPOSITION

Writing a composition takes careful planning. First, you decide on a main idea. Then you gather details or facts related to the main idea. Finally, you put the ideas together in a way that will make sense to your readers. A good plan will make your job easier.

EARLY PLANS

An *early plan,* also called an *informal outline,* is one way of sorting your ideas. First, put the related details into groups. Then arrange the groups in some order.

GROUPING.   After you have listed all the details you can think of about your topic, separate them into groups so that each group has only items that have something in common. Write a heading that shows how the items in each group are related.

ORDERING.   Decide how to order the items in your groups. You might use *chronological* (time) *order* to explain the step-by-step process of making pizza dough or of planting flower seeds. *Order of importance* presents details by going from the most important to the least important, or from the least important to the most important. For example, in a persuasive speech on recycling, you could give a list of reasons to explain why recycling is important. You could begin or end with your most important reason—to preserve natural resources for future generations. And you would probably use *spatial* (space or location) *order* to describe a sports arena or a view from a window.

EXERCISE 1   Creating an Early Plan

Here is a list of notes for a composition on hot-air ballooning. On your own paper, organize the notes into groups under these three headings: description of hot-air balloons, beginnings of hot-air ballooning, and hot-air ballooning today.

bag made of nylon, polyester

propane tank with fuel line to burner

world championships every other year

one of first successful flights, June 4, 1783, in France

basket of aluminum or wicker

a duck, a rooster, and a sheep—first balloon passengers

national championships, annually in Iowa

Montgolfier brothers made hot-air balloons, late 1700s

more than 2,000 hot-air balloonists in U.S. today

FORMAL OUTLINES

A *formal outline* uses letters and numbers to show the relationships of ideas. You can use a formal outline to plan a clear, well-organized composition. A formal outline can also be a helpful table of contents for someone reading your composition.

There are two kinds of formal outlines. A *topic outline* states ideas in words or brief phrases. A *sentence outline* states ideas in complete sentences. Here is a topic outline for a composition:

Title: The Life of Charles Richard Drew, African American Physician

Main Idea: Charles Drew was one of the most important physicians of modern medicine.

I.   His life

   A.   Born (1904) and raised in Washington, D.C.
   B.   Outstanding athlete
   C.   Educated at Amherst College and McGill University Medical School
   D.   Died in 1950

II.   His medical achievements

   A.   Conducted blood research
   B.   Developed method for preserving and storing blood
   C.   Advocated use of plasma instead of whole-blood transfusions on battlefield
   D.   Became first director of Red Cross program that collected plasma for use by U.S. soldiers, 1941
   E.   Founded American Red Cross blood bank

III.   His other achievements

   A.   Professor of surgery at Howard University
   B.   Received Spingarn Medal, 1944
   C.   Chief of staff, Freedmen's Hospital

EXERCISE 2   Creating a Formal Outline

Using the early plan you made in Exercise 1, create a formal outline of your composition on your own paper.

WRITING INTRODUCTIONS

Readers get their first ideas about a composition through the *introduction*. You can use your introduction to do two important things:

1. CAPTURE THE READERS' INTEREST. Your introduction should hook your readers and make them want to keep reading.

2. STATE THE MAIN IDEA. You'll usually state your main idea in your introductory paragraph. The main idea lets your readers know what to expect in your composition.

WAYS TO WRITE INTRODUCTIONS

Here are three techniques you can use to write interesting introductions:

- **Ask a question.** You can begin with a question and immediately answer it.

  What do smoke signals, wax tablets, the telegraph, and the telephone all have in common? They are all tools used for communication. Some of these tools are clearly more sophisticated than others, but all of them serve the same purpose. They allow people to communicate with one another.

- **Tell an anecdote.** An *anecdote* is a short, interesting story. Since most people enjoy a good story, an anecdote is often a good way to begin your composition.

  The young man with the hammer hoisted himself onto the top of the wall. All around him on the wall and on the ground, people chanted and cheered. The young man knelt down, with his hammer, and began to chip at the cold, gray concrete. Little by little, the wall began to crumble. The Berlin Wall was coming down.

- **State an intriguing or startling fact.** A surprising or unusual fact makes your readers curious. They can't wait to read on.

  It may give you a stomachache just to think about it, but a wild African elephant can eat more than seven hundred pounds of food a day. It can drink as much as forty gallons of water a day. In fact, everything about an African elephant seems to be gigantic.

EXERCISE 3   Identifying Types of Introductions

On the line below each paragraph, write the technique used in each of these attention-getting introductions.

1.   As a young child, Mary McLeod Bethune worked on her father's farm under the hot South Carolina sun. As she worked, she thought, "I'm going to read! I'm going to read!" Learning to read may be something that children today take for granted. But in the late 1800s, very few African Americans in the South were educated. Very few learned how to read or count.

    _____

2.   Where does our drinking water come from? Some people get theirs from water systems maintained by their cities and towns. Other people get theirs from their own wells. However, much of our drinking water, whether people get it from a city water system or from a home well, comes from the ground.

    _____

3.   The woman spotted the footprints in the damp ground and knelt down for a closer look. Using a ruler, she carefully measured the size of the first print and noted it in her journal. She counted the number of toes in the print and also noted the depth of the claw marks. The distance between each footprint, as well as the width of the pattern the tracks made, also interested her. After jotting down this information, she began to sketch the footprint and the pattern. This young woman, like naturalists everywhere, used footprint clues to identify the location of different species of wild animals.

    _____

4.   If there were an Olympics for animals, the pronghorn would be favored to win a gold medal in track and field. The fastest mammal in North America, the pronghorn can sprint more than fifty miles an hour.

    _____

WRITING CONCLUSIONS

The *conclusion* is the last part of your composition. In it, you sum up your ideas and tie up any loose ends. The conclusion lets your readers know that your composition has come to an end.

WAYS TO WRITE CONCLUSIONS

- **Refer to your introduction.** One technique is to refer to something in your introduction. Notice how the following conclusion refers to an idea in the introduction—the size of African elephants.

   Introduction: It may give you a stomachache just to think about it, but a wild African elephant can eat more than seven hundred pounds of food a day. It can drink as much as forty gallons of water a day. In fact, everything about an African elephant seems to be gigantic.

   Conclusion: One of the most famous African elephants was a seven-ton elephant named Jumbo. Jumbo was a star attraction first at the London Zoo and then in P. T. Barnum's circus. Because of Jumbo's fame and his enormous size, the word *jumbo* is now used to describe anything that is gigantic—even if that thing is not as huge as an African elephant.

- **Restate your main idea.** One way to end a composition is to restate your main idea in different words. In the following conclusion, the writer restates the idea that smoke signals, wax tablets, the telegraph, and the telephone all have something in common.

   How can smoke signals and the telephone be related? What do wax tablets and the telegraph have in common? Through the years, all of these tools have given people the power to communicate with each other. As technology progresses, people will develop other methods of communication. One thing is certain, however. People will always find ways to get their messages across.

- **Close with a final idea.**   Leaving the reader with one last thought can pull your composition together. Here, the writer explaining the impact of television ends with a hopeful thought.

> Television has had a tremendous influence on people all over the world. Let's hope the people who decide what should or shouldn't be on the air keep the best interests of viewers in mind.

EXERCISE 4 Writing a Conclusion

Read the introduction and body of the composition below. On your own paper, write a conclusion, using one of the techniques on the previous page. Then get together with a small group of your classmates and discuss your conclusions. Why did you choose one particular technique over another? What are the strengths and weaknesses of each conclusion?

Have you ever wished that you could climb inside a time machine and travel to some strange, exotic place in the distant past? Unfortunately, time machines exist only in science fiction stories. However, you can get a feeling of what it was like to live long ago by visiting the ruins of a city like Pompeii, Italy.

Pompeii was a Roman city on the western coast of Italy. About twenty thousand people lived there—as many as those living in a small U.S. city of today. The people of Pompeii worked as hide tanners, bakers, wine merchants, fabric dyers, fruit sellers, carpenters, mule drivers, and government administrators. Pompeii was a busy and prosperous city. It was a city with a future, or so it must have seemed.

Then, on August 24, A.D. 79, disaster struck Pompeii. The nearby volcano, Mount Vesuvius, suddenly erupted. Several million tons of rock and ash fell on the city and buried it beneath six to twelve feet of stone and dirt. Underneath this rubble were the city's shops, homes, theaters, temples, forum, and people.

In the eighteenth century, Pompeii was rediscovered. Since then, archaeologists have dug out the buildings of Pompeii from their volcanic tomb. Today if you visit Pompeii, you can walk down its streets and go into its homes and bakeries and theaters. The pouring of ash from Vesuvius preserved much of the city.

A FRIENDLY LETTER

A *friendly letter* is one written to a friend or a relative. You write the letter to say hello. You also share your experiences, thoughts, and feelings. In the following letter, the writer tells about an experience that was important to her.

1311 West Jordan Street
Chicago, IL 60610
November 30, 1993

Dear Kimi,

Thanks for your last letter. It was wonderful to hear that you like your new school. And you made the honor roll! That must have taken a lot of hard work, and I'm proud of you.

Remember the time we went to the animal park together? My science class just came back from a field trip there, and you won't believe how it's changed—no more small cages with lions and tigers pacing up and down. Now they're out in a large field that looks like their home in Africa. The guide told us it's a "savanna." You can ride around it in a small train.

The most exciting part is the new indoor rain forest. It's huge, and you can walk through part of it. It's so much like a real rain forest that it even feels damp and misty. The guide said that hidden water nozzles make it that way. I almost ran into a bat hanging upside down in a tree. You wouldn't believe its funny, human-looking face. And the birds come in almost every color of the rainbow. Squawking at all those visitors, they make all kinds of noises.

I really miss you, Kimi. When you come for a visit, we'll go back to the animal park together. Remember to bring a heavy jacket. It's already getting cold here.

Your friend,

Leah

Thinking About the Model

How does the writer express herself in the model letter? Now that you've read the letter, think about how the writer created it. Answer the following questions on the lines below.

1. You write friendly letters to friends and relatives, people who care about you and want to share your experiences. What experience does the writer share with her friend? Why might this experience be especially interesting to the reader?

    _____

    _____

    _____

2. Experiences are made up of details about people, places, and events. *Sensory details* appeal to the senses: sight, hearing, taste, smell, and touch. These details help readers share the writer's experiences. One sight detail from paragraph 3 of the model letter, page 25, is the "funny, human-looking face" of the bat. What is another sight detail from paragraph 3?

    _____

    What is a hearing detail from paragraph 3?

    _____

    What is a touch detail from paragraph 3?

    _____

3. Friendly letters share thoughts and feelings as well as experiences. What thoughts and feelings does the writer of the model letter share with her reader?

    _____

    _____

    _____

4. Friendly letters show that the writer cares about the reader. How does the writer show that she has her friend in mind?

    _____

    _____

 ## ASSIGNMENT: WRITING A FRIENDLY LETTER

Think of an experience you would enjoy sharing with one of your friends or relatives. Then write a friendly letter to that person. Use sensory details to make the experience seem real to the person reading your letter.

 ## Prewriting

What experience(s) will you share with your reader? How will you recall sensory details? The following steps will help you discover ideas for your letter.

Step 1:   In the space below, brainstorm for some experiences you can share with your reader. For three minutes, think about recent happenings at home, at school, and in your neighborhood. Perhaps you've been to the beach or to the lake. Or perhaps your school has recently had a field day, and you won second prize in a race. For now, write down every idea you can think of. Later, you can sort them out and decide which ideas will be most useful.

_____

_____

_____

_____

_____

_____

Step 2:   Choose one or two experiences from your brainstorming list to include in your letter. Choose experiences that

- you remember well
- are important to you and your reader
- you are willing to share with your teacher and classmates

Step 3:   Collect details about your experience by reliving it. One way to relive an experience is by visualizing. Imagine yourself having the experience. Think about where you were, what you did, what you saw, heard, tasted, smelled, and touched. Then fill out the chart below by listing as many details as you can. For example, if you've been to a basketball game, you might visualize the bright blue and gold banners, the basketball pounding as it's dribbled down the court, and the hot dogs and cold drinks. Remember to record your thoughts and feelings about the experience and to include details that show you care about the reader.

Actions:
Sights:
Smells:
Sounds:
Tastes:
Textures:
Thoughts and Feelings:

 **Writing**

Write your friendly letter on your own paper. Use the ideas you gathered in **Prewriting** to help you write your draft. Before you begin, study the guidelines for friendly letter form given below.

Friendly Letter Form

A friendly letter has a simpler form than a business letter. Study the parts of a friendly letter.

1. **Heading.** Imagine that the letter is divided in half vertically. Begin the heading to the right of the middle. The heading includes three lines:
   - your street address
   - your city, state, and ZIP Code (A comma follows the name of the city.)
   - date of your letter (A comma separates the day of the month from the year.)

   Note: Be certain that the ZIP Code you use is correct. The ZIP Code follows the two-letter state abbreviation. Do not use any punctuation between the state abbreviation and the ZIP Code.

2. **Salutation.** The salutation is your greeting. Leave about a one-inch margin at the left of the letter, and begin your salutation at that margin. Follow the salutation with a comma. The first word and all nouns should be capitalized.

3. **Body.** The body is the main part of your letter. If you are typing your letter or are composing on a computer, begin the body at the left margin and leave a blank line between paragraphs. If you are writing your letter by hand, you should indent each paragraph. It isn't necessary then to leave extra space between paragraphs.

4. **Closing and Signature.** Write the closing so that it is aligned with the heading. The closing may be very informal, such as *Your friend*. Always hand-sign your name, even if you type or word-process your letter. The closing is followed by a comma. Only the first word should be capitalized.

 # Evaluating and Revising

When you evaluate your paper, you decide on its strengths and weaknesses. Use the following **Questions for Evaluation** to help you evaluate your friendly letter.

Questions for Evaluation
1. Does this letter identify an experience and give details about what happened? If not, what experience might be identified and what details might be added?

_____

_____

_____

2. Does the letter include details about people, places, and events? If not, what sensory details might be added?

Sights: _____

_____

Smells: _____

_____

Sounds: _____

_____

Textures: _____

_____

Tastes: _____

_____

3. Does the letter include details about thoughts and feelings? If not, what details might be added?

_____

_____

4. Does the letter show that the writer cares about the reader? If not, what details might be added or changed?

_____

_____

Peer Evaluation

Exchange rough drafts with a classmate. Then follow these steps.

Step 1: Read the rough draft carefully. As you read, imagine that you're the friend or relative who will receive the letter. Look for strengths as well as weaknesses.

Step 2: Complete the **Questions for Evaluation** on pages 30–31. Be as helpful as possible by making specific suggestions for changes. For example, don't just tell your classmate that the letter needs more sensory details. Suggest some specific sensory details that your classmate might add.

Self-Evaluation

Step 1: Try to be as objective as possible as you reread your rough draft.

Step 2: Read your classmate's evaluation of your letter. Put a check next to any comments that you plan to use when you're revising the letter.

Step 3: Use the **Questions for Evaluation**. In the margins and between the lines of your rough draft, make notes about changes you plan to make.

Now revise your draft until you can answer *yes* to each of the **Questions for Evaluation**. Use your classmate's evaluation and your own evaluation of your letter.

Proofreading and Publishing

Step 1: Use the **Proofreading Guidelines** on page 8 to find and correct errors in your paper.

   a. Check first for spelling errors. If you are not one hundred percent certain that a word is spelled correctly, look it up.

   b. Check for errors in grammar, usage, and spelling. [Hint: Try proofreading from the bottom of your paper upward, one line at a time. Or proofread from the right margin of your paper to the left. This way, you are more likely to spot errors.]

Step 2: Make a clean copy of your revised and proofread letter.

Step 3: Check that you have used the correct letter form. Refer to the **Friendly Letter Form** on page 29.

Step 4: Publish your letter by giving it or mailing it to your friend or relative.

FOR YOUR PORTFOLIO

On a separate sheet of paper, write the answers to these questions. Keep the answers with a copy of your letter.

1. What was the easiest part of writing your friendly letter? What was the hardest part?

2. Look for collections of letters that have been published. For example, letters by historical figures, such as former presidents, are often collected and published. Check under the heading *Letters* in your library's card or on-line catalog. Find and make a copy of an interesting letter.

A CHILDREN'S STORY

You probably know many stories. You've read them in books and magazines and have seen them on TV and at the movies. The following selection is a children's story, written for nine- to ten-year-old children. As you read the story, think about what might make the story appeal to children.

The Friend

"Don't go past the boundary," the twins' parents warned them. "Remember that your oxygen pack is only good for two hours."

"We'll be OK," Sara and John promised as they zipped themselves into their silver spacesuits. The suits allowed them to walk naturally. Without the suits, the twins would have floated in the moon's low gravity field.

At the boundary, Sara and John sat watching the earth in the distance. It seemed like a giant, shiny ball hanging above them.

"What do you suppose Tom's doing now?" sighed John. "I really miss our friends."

"Yeah, me too," Sara joined in. "It's so boring here."

At first the moon had been an exciting place to live. The twins had enjoyed exploring its rocky landscape. After six months, however, they were tired of being the only children in the first earth colony.

"I know," Sara suggested. "Let's explore those rocks over there. Maybe a moon monster is hiding behind them."

"Quit trying to scare me, Sara. You know we're not supposed to leave the compound."

"Oh, come on. We've got plenty of oxygen." With that, Sara turned down the gravity-force mechanism in her spacesuit. She began bounding across the moon's surface. John hurried to catch up.

Hand in hand the twins covered a great distance, totally unaware of the time. Suddenly, John gripped Sara's hand harder. "Help, Sara, I can't get my breath!"

Sara quickly realized what was happening. They were running out of oxygen. And the base was two hours away. "What will we do?"

At that moment the twins noticed flashing lights coming toward them. Then, across the distance, they saw an amazing sight. A robot shaped like a flat metal box was hurrying toward them. On top of the robot's head, two stalks stuck out into the air. Attached to the top of each stalk was a large eye that glowed like a fiery-hot coal. The robot's deep mechanical voice resounded in their headsets. "Do you need some help?"

Desperately, the twins nodded. "We're humans from the earth compound. We're running out of air."

"Hop on," beeped the robot. "I'll have you back in a few minutes."

John and Sara climbed onto the robot, clinging to the stalks that the robot's eyes were on. The robot began to roll forward. Then it suddenly leaped into the air. The children could see the moon's craters streak by below them. They were flying!

Each minute seemed like an eternity to Sara and John. They were getting weaker and weaker from lack of oxygen. Finally, the compound came into view. The robot took them right to their front door. John and Sara rushed inside and gulped the fresh air that filled their house.

Gasping for air, they begged their parents for forgiveness. "We are so sorry, Mom and Dad. We lost track of time, and we were so bored, and we wanted to see what was over there and . . . ."

"Hold on there, kids. We know that you are very sorry for what you did. You don't have to explain. And everything will go back to normal, except that the robot that brought you home will be with you every time you step out of this house, just in case anything like this ever happens again. Not that it will, though, right?"

"Right, Dad. Thanks for not being mad. We love you. Now I think I'm going to take a long nap," sighed Sara. "What about you, John?"

"I think I'll take a nap too. I've had about all the excitement I can stand for one day."

The twins gave their parents hugs and slowly walked to their rooms. They were asleep the minute their heads hit their pillows.

Thinking About the Model

A children's story has all the same *elements*, or parts, as a story for older readers. Now that you've read the children's story on pages 33–34, think about the way the writer combined the elements to create a story. Answer the following questions on the lines provided.

1. Stories have *characters* that may be people, animals, or even robots. Who are the main characters in the model story?

   _____

   _____

2. The *setting* is the time and place of the story. The setting can help to create a *mood*, or atmosphere. The setting can also cause a problem for the characters. What is the setting of the model story?

   _____

   _____

   How does the setting create a problem for the characters?

   _____

   _____

3. A story has a *plot*, which consists of a series of events. These events usually involve a central problem called a *conflict*. For example, a character might be hiking in the mountains when a blizzard hits. The character might then have to struggle against the blizzard to survive. What is the conflict in the model story?

   _____

   _____

   What are the events in the plot? _____

   _____

   _____

   _____

4. Events in a story usually build in excitement until they reach a *high point* of mystery, danger, or suspense. What is the high point of the model story on pages 33–34?

    _____

    _____

    _____

5   What happens after the high point of a story is called the *outcome.* The outcome shows how the conflict is solved. What is the outcome of the model story?

    _____

    _____

    _____

6. A children's story differs in certain ways from a story for older readers. The model story, for example, has younger characters. What is another way in which the model story differs from a story for older readers?

    _____

    _____

    _____

Frank & Ernest reprinted by permission of NEA, Inc.

ASSIGNMENT: WRITING A CHILDREN'S STORY

Write a story that is suitable for children nine to ten years old. Use the basic elements of a story—characters, setting, and plot. Make sure the content, vocabulary, and sentence length are all appropriate for younger readers.

Prewriting

Where do story ideas come from? The following steps will help you think of some ideas.

Step 1:   A story idea includes a main character and a central conflict, or problem, that the character must face. Here are some examples of characters and conflicts you might use for a children's story.

> CHARACTER: Heidi, a fourteen-year-old German shepherd who has lived with a family for ten years
>
> CONFLICT/PROBLEM: *What if* the family moves far away from its old home, and Heidi becomes lost on the journey?
>
> CHARACTER: Han-Ling, a ten-year-old Chinese American girl who is planning a Chinese celebration for her friends
>
> CONFLICT/PROBLEM: *What if* Han-Ling's invitations to her friends get lost in the mail?
>
> CHARACTERS: Nine-year-old Alicia and ten-year-old Alberto, who are sent to spend the summer on their grandparents' farm in Mexico
>
> CONFLICT/PROBLEM: *What if* the brother and sister dislike the farm at first, but by the end of the summer they enjoy it so much that they don't want to go home?

You can start planning your children's story by thinking about a character. This may be a character you see often, such as a family pet, a relative, or someone who lives in your neighborhood. Or it may be someone who comes from your imagination, such as a space alien. Ask yourself "What if?" questions to think of a problem, or conflict, that the character might face. Choose one of the story ideas given above, or create one of your own. Make sure that the character and the conflict will be interesting to third- and fourth-grade students. Describe your story idea on the lines on the following page.

Character(s): _____

What happens: _____

_____

Step 2: Good storytellers create vivid word pictures so the reader can see the characters in his or her mind's eye. In the model story, for example, the twins go bounding across the moon's surface. John grips Sara's hand when his oxygen supply runs low. The robot has eyes that glow like fiery-hot coals. Think about how your main character looks and behaves. What specific words will help readers picture your character? Gather details about your character by making a list of the character's qualities, or characteristics, on your own paper. Describe your character's age, appearance, habits, background, likes and dislikes, activities, and anything else that seems important to an understanding of him or her. You may wish to use a character like the robot in the model story. If you do, create a description for this character also.

Step 3: In the model story, the setting is the surface of the moon, some time in the future. Where and when will your story take place? Explain the setting of your story on the lines below.

_____

_____

Step 4: What happens in the story? Events in a story happen when characters struggle to overcome, or solve, a central conflict. The events build to a high point of excitement just before the problem is solved. The outcome shows how the central conflict ends. For example, Anna and her friends want to go to summer camp, but they don't have any money (conflict/problem). They organize a neighborhood carnival with food, games, and prizes (events). They count their money to see if they have made enough for camp (high point). The carnival earns enough money for Anna and her friends to go to camp (outcome).

Plan your children's story by filling out the story map on the following page. Use your notes from Steps 1–3. On the story map, list details to describe your setting, main character, and plot.

SETTING

Time:_____

Place:_____

Details That Describe

Setting:_____

_____

_____

_____

MAIN CHARACTER

Name:_____

Details That Describe

Character:_____

_____

_____

_____

_____

STORY
MAP

PLOT

Conflict:_____

_____

Events:_____

_____

_____

_____

_____

_____

High Point:_____

_____

Outcome:_____

_____

Step 5: The dialogue, or words characters say, helps to make a story and its characters seem real. Dialogue is usually written in informal English, as in this example from the model story. Notice the sentence fragment "Yeah, me too" and the informal expression *yeah*.

"What do you suppose Tom's doing now?" sighed John. "I really miss our friends."

"Yeah, me too," Sara joined in. "It's so boring here."

On the lines provided, write some dialogue that might take place in your story. Be sure to show who is speaking and to start a new paragraph when the speaker changes.

_____

_____

_____

_____

_____

_____

_____

_____

_____

_____

_____

_____

 Writing

The story map is the plan for your story. Use it to guide you as you write your first draft. The following suggestions will help you create a strong beginning, middle, and ending.

Beginning
- Grab your reader's interest from the beginning by introducing your conflict early. You can start in the middle of things. Or you might describe the setting. (In the model story, the twins' parents warn the twins that they have only a two-hour supply of oxygen.)

Middle
- Use vivid, specific details to make characters and actions seem real.
- Build actions and events to a high point of excitement.
- Use dialogue to reveal emotions and personalities.

Ending
- Show the outcome of, or solution to, the central conflict. Satisfy your reader's curiosity by clearing up any loose ends.

Now, begin to write the first draft of your children's story on your own paper. Use your prewriting notes and ideas, along with the suggestions given above.

Evaluating and Revising

You've finished writing a draft of your story, and you deserve some credit for your effort. But now you have a chance to make your story better. First, you can **evaluate** it by looking for its strengths and weaknesses. Then you can **revise** it to get rid of the weaknesses.

   You can use the following **Questions for Evaluation** when you evaluate your story or a classmate's story.

Questions for Evaluation

1. Does the beginning of the story introduce the conflict and grab the reader's attention? If not, what could be added?

2. Are the story and the words used in it appropriate for children aged nine to ten? If not, what would appeal to children in that age group?

3. Is the setting clear? Does it help create a mood? If not, what might be added or changed?

4. Are the characters believable? If not, what could be added or changed?

5. Is the dialogue informal? Does it sound natural? If not, how could it be made more informal and natural?

6. Do the events in the story build to a high point? If not, what could be added or changed to build the excitement?

7. Is the ending (outcome) satisfying? Does the ending show how the central conflict, or problem, is solved? If not, what could be added or changed to make the ending stronger?

Peer Evaluation

Exchange rough drafts with a classmate. Then follow these directions.

Step 1: Read your classmate's rough draft carefully. Remember, you are not checking for grammar and mechanics. You are evaluating the story for content.

Step 2: Answer the **Questions for Evaluation** on page 42. Try to give specific suggestions for revision. For example, don't just tell your classmate that his or her story needs a more interesting beginning. Suggest specific details that your classmate might add.

Self-Evaluation

Step 1: Reread your rough draft. Try to imagine that you are reading the story for the first time. Ask yourself, "Is the story interesting? Will it appeal to children?"

Step 2: Read your classmate's evaluation of your story. Put a check mark beside any comments that you plan to use when you revise.

Step 3: Complete the **Questions for Evaluation** on page 42. On your first draft, make notes about changes you plan to make.

Now, revise your draft until you can answer *yes* to each of the **Questions for Evaluation**. Use both your own and your classmate's evaluation of your story.

 ## Proofreading and Publishing

Step 1: Use the **Guidelines for Proofreading** on page 8 to find and correct errors in your story. Start by checking your spelling throughout the story. If you are not positive about the spelling of a word, look it up in a dictionary. Remember to check your spelling even if you are using a word processor that will check your spelling for you. Look for problems with sentence structure, usage, capitalization, and punctuation. Double-check your use of quotation marks and commas in your dialogue.

Step 2: Make a clean copy of your revised and proofread story.

Step 3:   See if your local library has a Story Hour. If it does, publish your story by going to Story Hour and reading it to the children there. You may want to collect all the stories written in your class and make a book to donate to a school or to the public library.

FOR YOUR PORTFOLIO

You might want to keep some of the answers and ideas below in your portfolio with your children's story.

1. On a separate sheet of paper, write the answers to the following two questions, and keep them with a copy of your story. What part of this assignment did you like the best? What part did you like the least?

2. Look around your home or the library for stories that you used to read when you were nine or ten. Reread these stories. Make a copy of your favorite story for your portfolio.

3. Draw a picture of one of the scenes from your story. If you are feeling especially creative, illustrate the whole story with five or six drawings. Add your pictures to your portfolio.

The purpose of a news story is to share information. A reporter chooses a topic, then tries to answer the *5W-How?* questions—*Who? What? When? Where? Why?* and *How?* The opening paragraph, called the **lead**, introduces the topic. The rest of the story provides details in the order of their importance.

HMS Welcomes Foreign Student
By Shavon Austin

Felicia Ramírez-Rebori is used to rain forests, hot Christmases, and cattle ranches. But this year her life promises to be completely different. Felicia, who usually lives in Paraguay, in South America, is spending one year in Massachusetts.

The new eighth-grader at Hamilton Middle School said she was really excited when she found out that her family would be moving to the United States. Her parents, who are both computer scientists, will be working for one year with computer companies in Boston.

"We all talked it over and decided it would be a great adventure for everyone," Felicia said. Felicia has a sister and a brother who will both be students at Hamilton High School this year.

So far, she said, she thinks life in Massachusetts is "interesting, fun, and only a little bit strange." She has studied English for ten years, so language is not a problem. She also speaks Spanish and Guaraní, which is the language spoken by most people in Paraguay.

She said she and her family have been visiting the historical sites of Boston and learning about the history of the United States. Her biggest thrill, however, has been going to the ocean. Paraguay is a landlocked country, and Felicia had only seen the ocean once before coming to Massachusetts.

Before they go back to Paraguay next summer, Felicia said, her family would like to visit Chicago and New York and possibly drive across the United States.

Thinking About the Model

You've read the model news story. Now think about how the writer created
it. Answer the following questions on the lines below.

1. The most important information in a news story is placed at the
    beginning. This section of the story is called the *lead*. Based on what
    you know about reading newspapers, why do you think the most
    important information is located at the beginning?

    _____

    _____

    _____

2. To gather information, reporters use the *5W-How?* questions listed
    below. In the lead of the model news story, the writer answers most
    of these questions for the reader. Read the lead of the model news
    story, and answer the following questions. If you can't find an
    answer in the lead, continue reading until you can find it.

    Who? _____

    _____

    What? _____

    _____

    When? _____

    _____

    Where? _____

    _____

    Why? _____

    _____

    How? _____

    _____

3. News stories are informative. They include facts, not opinions.

    FACT   Felicia and her family have been learning about the
            history of the United States.

    OPINION   Felicia and her family should learn about the history of
              the United States.

    List at least four facts included in the model news story.

    a. _____

    b. _____

    c. _____

    d. _____

4. To gather information, reporters often interview people who
    witnessed or took part in the event or activity. The model news story
    includes quotations from one person who was interviewed. Who
    was interviewed?

    _____

5. Many people read only the first few paragraphs of a news story.
    They want the main facts, but not too many details. What
    information does the writer of the model news story include in the
    last paragraph?

    _____

    _____

    _____

6. Why would this information be less important to most readers than
    the information in the first one or two paragraphs?

    _____

    _____

 **ASSIGNMENT: WRITING A NEWS STORY**

Choose a topic, and write your own news story. Be prepared to share your story with your teacher and your classmates.

 **Prewriting**

Step 1:   Brainstorm with a classmate to come up with possible topics for a news story. As you try to think of topics, remember this: Readers are most interested in local events and people. Did one of your classmates win a service award? Has the tennis team had a winning streak? Was the Fire Department's annual fund-raiser a success? Look at school and local bulletin boards or calendars for ideas. Write your topic ideas on the lines below.

_____

_____

_____

_____

Step 2:   Think about the topics you've listed in Step 1. Which one would you most like to share with readers? Which is most current? Which one would make the most interesting news story? Write your topic on the line below.

_____

Step 3:   What do your readers want to know about your topic? First, they want the basic information, or the main points of the story. Then they may also want some related facts and details. To start collecting that information, ask yourself the *5W-How?* questions. You may not know all the answers at this point, but on the lines below, write the answers you do have.

Who? _____

_____

What? _____

_____

Where? _____

_____

When? _____

_____

Why? _____

_____

How? _____

_____

Step 6: What information is still missing? Whom could you interview to get that information? On the lines below, identify one or two people you could interview.

_____

_____

Step 7: Interview one person you identified in Step 6. Follow these strategies for interviewing.
1. Set up an appointment for the interview.
2. Write out your questions in advance. (Remember the *5W-How?* questions, especially the ones you couldn't answer yourself.)
3. Take notes during the interview. Use a notebook or 4- × 6-inch note cards. If you think you may want to use the person's exact words in your article, be sure to take notes accurately.

Step 8: On the lines below, write the information you gathered from your interview.

_____

_____

_____

_____

_____

Writing

Using your prewriting questions as a guide, begin to draft your news story on your own paper. Here are some points to keep in mind as you write.

- Summarize the main points, or the most important information, in a one- or two-sentence lead.
- Put the most important facts and details in the first two or three paragraphs. Save the least important information for the end.
- Keep your paragraphs short—no more than two or three sentences.
- If you are using someone's exact words, be sure to put quotation marks around them.
- Stick with the facts. Don't include your opinions or feelings.

After you finish your draft, write a *headline*, or title, for your news story. Here are some tips for writing headlines.

- Focus on a subject and a strong verb.
- Avoid unnecessary articles and prepositions such as *a, an, the, to,* and *from.*

> WEAK   The Jazz Band Provides a Dazzling Performance in Lincoln
> STRONG   Jazz Band Dazzles Lincoln

Evaluating and Revising

Once you have finished your draft, evaluate it to determine its strengths and weaknesses. To evaluate your news story, use these **Questions for Evaluation**.

Questions for Evaluation

1. Does the news story contain a headline with a subject, a strong verb, and no unnecessary articles or prepositions? If not, what should you add or change?

2. Does the story contain a lead that is interesting and that answers most of the *5W-How?* questions? If not, what can you revise or add?

3. Is the important information presented in the first two or three paragraphs? If not, how might you rearrange your ideas?

4. Do the paragraphs contain no more than two or three sentences? If not, what needs to be cut or replaced?

5. Does the story present facts, not opinions? If not, what do you need to revise, add, or delete?

Peer Evaluation

Exchange rough drafts with a classmate. Ask your classmate to follow these steps.

Step 1:   Read the news story carefully. Do not focus on grammar, usage, spelling, or punctuation errors at this point.

Step 2:   On a separate sheet of paper, answer the **Questions for Evaluation** on page 50. Make specific, positive suggestions.

Self-Evaluation

Next, evaluate your rough draft yourself. Follow these steps.

Step 1:   Reread the rough draft of your story. Put yourself in the place of the person who is reading about this topic for the first time. Is the story clear? Are all the essential facts presented?

Step 2:   Read your classmate's evaluation. Circle any comments that you plan to use as you revise.

Step 3:   Answer the **Questions for Evaluation** for your own rough draft.

Use your classmate's suggestions and your own answers to the **Questions for Evaluation** to revise your rough draft.

Proofreading and Publishing

Step 1:   First, check for errors in spelling. If you aren't completely sure about the spelling of a word, look it up in the dictionary. Make sure the names of people and places are spelled correctly.

Step 2:   Proofread your story for errors in grammar, usage, punctuation, and capitalization. Refer to the **Guidelines for Proofreading** on page 8. Double-check your use of capital letters for proper nouns and adjectives. If you have used direct quotations, double-check your use of commas and quotation marks. Use the rules in Chapter 22 to correct capitalization errors in your paper.

Step 3:   Showing your news story to classmates, teachers, and family is one way to publish your work. You can reach an even larger audience by trying to publish your work in the school newspaper.

FOR YOUR PORTFOLIO

If you are keeping a portfolio, you might want to include some of these suggestions.

1. What part of news writing did you enjoy most? What part did you enjoy least? Write your answers on a separate sheet of paper, and keep them in your portfolio.

2. Read some school, local, and national newspapers. Find several news stories that you consider interesting, and think about what you like about them. Photocopy the stories, and put them in your portfolio.

3. Some reporters cover only stories that deal with a particular field of activity, such as politics, crime, or sports. Would you enjoy being a medical reporter? A reporter who covers art news? Make a list of subject areas and story ideas. Keep the list in your portfolio.

A PUBLIC SERVICE ANNOUNCEMENT

Do you have a message for people in your community? Do you want people to attend your school play or to support the baseball team? One good way to get your message out is to write a public service announcement, or PSA.

A *public service announcement* is similar to an advertisement. But it is played free of charge or at low rates by radio and television stations. The following public service announcement is meant to be sent to a radio station.

Contact: Hector Salinas, 555-2333

Hurricane Dave was the worst storm to hit our coast in one hundred years. It destroyed the homes and belongings of many people in our town. Many families are facing a winter without BASIC NEEDS such as clothes and blankets. Your neighbors need your help.

The students of Brookwood Middle School ASK you to join them in their efforts to help the victims of Hurricane Dave. If you can donate new or used clothing, shoes, bedding, cooking utensils, or appliances, please bring them to the Brookwood School parking lot on Saturday, October 9, between 9 A.M. and 2 P.M. That's Saturday the 9th at the Brookwood School parking lot. For more information, call 555-2636. Again, that number is 555-2636. PLEASE help us make sure that everyone in our community has a warm, comfortable winter.

Thinking About the Model

Often, the purpose of a public service announcement, or PSA, is to persuade. The writer wants the audience's support for a project, an event, or an idea. In addition, the writer usually shares some basic information. Think about what the writer is doing in the model. Then answer the following questions.

1. What is the writer of this PSA trying to persuade the audience to do?

   _____

   _____

2. A PSA should begin with a hook—something that catches the attention of listeners. How does the writer of the model PSA capture the audience's attention?

   _____

   _____

3. A radio PSA is meant to be heard by the audience, not read by them. Therefore, it should use simple words, short sentences, and a personal, conversational tone. What words does the writer of the model use to create a conversational tone?

   _____

   _____

4. One way to persuade an audience to do something is to convince them that there are benefits. In other words, the results will be good for them or someone they care about. According to the model PSA, what are the benefits of donating goods to the hurricane relief drive?

   _____

   _____

   _____

5. In addition to persuading the audience, a PSA must include information such as time, date, and location. The most important pieces of information are usually repeated. In the model, what important details are mentioned twice? What does the writer tell the audience to do for more information?

   _____

   _____

   _____

ASSIGNMENT: WRITING A PUBLIC SERVICE ANNOUNCEMENT

Write a public service announcement to persuade adults in your community to attend an event or a program at your school. It's your job to ensure good attendance at the event. Perhaps your class or club will make money selling tickets or concessions. Or perhaps you need a large crowd at the tennis match to cheer for the team. Write your announcement to be read aloud.

Prewriting

Step 1:   What event or program could you write about? It might be an upcoming play, rally, club meeting, sports activity, or fund-raiser. If you can't think of a real event you would like to write about, brainstorm for some possible events you might want people to attend. Jot your ideas on your own paper. Then review your list, and choose the event that interests you the most.

Step 2:   Now think about the basic facts related to the event. These are facts your audience will need to know in order to attend the event. You can use the *5W-How?* questions to gather the information. On your own paper, write the information you gather.

- *Who* is in charge of, or sponsoring, the event?
- *What* is the event?
- *When* is it being held?
- *Where* will it take place?
- *Why* is the event taking place? (What is its purpose?)
- *How* can the audience get more information?

Step 3:   People who write ads try to include "benefits" in order to persuade the audience. In other words, how will the listener benefit from attending? How will someone else benefit? Here are some examples.

Audience/Listener Benefit:
- Be one of the first fifty people to purchase a ticket. You'll receive an autographed photograph of the team.
- Please your tastebuds. Sample the foods of many countries— tamales, sushi, moussaka, sauerkraut, and more.

Benefit to Others:
- Fifty percent of the ticket sales will be donated to the YMCA.
- Your donation will keep one child warm for the whole winter.

On your own paper, list two or three ways in which people will benefit from the event you are promoting in your PSA.

Step 4: Now that you have gathered information and details, you need to think of a hook. A *hook* is an interesting way to grab the audience's attention at the beginning of the PSA. In the model on page 53, the writer begins with a startling fact—that the hurricane was the worst storm to hit in one hundred years. On your own paper, try these three ways of creating a hook:

- A startling fact
- A question
- Sound effects (such as screeching tires)

Review the three hooks you have written. Put a check mark beside the one you think will work best.

 ## Writing

Now use your prewriting notes to write a 60-second public service announcement. Here's a framework you can follow. Draft your PSA on your own paper.

- Start with a hook.
- Use conversational language, short sentences, and simple words.
- Identify the event.
- Include two or three benefits for the listener or other people.
- Give the listener all the essential information: date, time, place, and a phone number to call for more information.
- Repeat the most important information.
- End with a call to action; ask your listeners to attend your event.

 ## Evaluating and Revising

Even though you now have a draft of your PSA, it's probably not as good as it could be. The following **Questions for Evaluation** will help you decide how to improve your writing.

Questions for Evaluation

1. Does the PSA begin with an interesting hook? If not, what could be added to grab the listeners' attention?
2. Is the event clearly identified? If not, what should be added?
3. Does the PSA identify at least two or three benefits of attending the event? If not, what benefits could be included?
4. Does the PSA provide all of the information the listeners need in order to attend the event or find out more about it? If not, what should be added?
5. Does the PSA repeat the most important information? If not, what should be repeated?
6. Does the PSA sound conversational? What words or sentences can be changed to make the PSA more appropriate for radio?
7. Does the PSA end with a call to action? If not, what could be added or changed?
8. A 60-second public service announcement will run about 100 words. Is this PSA about the right length? If not, what can be cut or added to the announcement to make it fit a 60-second spot?

Peer Evaluation

Before exchanging your draft of your PSA with that of a classmate, read your drafts aloud to each other. Ask your classmate to follow these steps.

Step 1:   Listen to the rough draft carefully as it is read aloud.

Step 2:   Answer the **Questions for Evaluation** on a separate sheet of paper. Make specific suggestions for changes.

Self-Evaluation

Now complete your self-evaluation. Follow these steps.

Step 1:   Reread your rough draft. Read it aloud and, if possible, tape and replay your reading. Listen to the sounds of the words and sentences. Are they easy to understand? Do they flow smoothly?

Step 2:   Answer the **Questions for Evaluation** for your draft.

Step 3:   Think about the suggestions you made for your classmate's work. Which suggestions apply to your own draft?

Using your classmate's suggestions and your own answers to the **Questions for Evaluation**, revise your rough draft. Don't stop revising until you can answer *yes* to each of the questions.

Proofreading and Publishing

If your public service announcement reads well, a radio station is more likely to use it. Prepare your announcement carefully, following these steps.

Step 1:   Check each word for correct spelling. Check in a dictionary if you are not sure how a word is spelled.

Step 2:   Carefully check the grammar, usage, capitalization, and punctuation.

Step 3:   Make a clean, final copy that includes all your corrections. Keep in mind that you are preparing the copy for someone else to read aloud. Here are some suggestions for making the copy easy to read.

- Double-space the lines.
- Provide a pronunciation guide for any difficult names.
- Underline words that you want the reader to stress, or write the words in all capital letters. For example, you might want the reader to stress some of your "benefit" words.
- In the upper right-hand corner, print the word *Contact*, followed by a colon and your name and telephone number.

Step 4:   If your announcement is about an upcoming event, send it to some radio stations that might use your PSA.

Step 5:   If your teacher approves, set up a microphone in class. With your classmates, take turns reading the PSAs aloud.

FOR YOUR PORTFOLIO

Answer the following questions. Place the answers with your drafts in your writing portfolio.

1. Think about other radio announcements that you've heard. Why do you remember them?

2. How is writing for radio different from writing for readers?

SENTENCE FRAGMENTS

8a   A *sentence fragment* is a part of a sentence that has been punctuated as if it were a complete sentence.

FRAGMENT   Were preparing for Tet, the Vietnamese New Year. [The subject is missing. *Who* were preparing for Tet, the Vietnamese New Year?]

SENTENCE   **Mai and her sister Li** were preparing for Tet, the Vietnamese New Year. [The compound subject completes the meaning of the verb phrase.]

FRAGMENT   Two large sea gulls. [The verb is missing. *What about* the sea gulls?]

SENTENCE   Two large sea gulls **circled** in the sky above the fishing boat. [The verb completes the meaning of the subject.]

FRAGMENT   After the lights went out. [This group of words has a subject and a verb, but it does not express a complete thought. *What happened* after the lights went out?]

SENTENCE   After the lights went out, **we searched the house for candles and matches**. [The independent clause completes the meaning of the subordinate clause.]

Use this simple, three-part test to identify word groups as sentence fragments or complete sentences.

1. Does the group of words have a subject?
2. Does it have a verb?
3. Does it express a complete thought?

 NOTE   If you are in a hurry, you might accidentally end a sentence too soon by putting in a period and a capital letter. You can correct such a fragment by attaching it to the rest of the sentence.

EXERCISE 1   Identifying Sentence Fragments

On the line before each of the following groups of words, write *sent.* if the group is a sentence or *frag.* if the group is a fragment. [Note: A complete sentence can have the unstated subject *you*.]

EX.   ___frag.___   1. A courageous journey across the ocean.

_____   1. Amelia Earhart showed great skill and daring.

_____ 2. Left college to take flying lessons.

_____ 3. Also served as a social worker while in Boston.

_____ 4. The first woman to cross the Atlantic Ocean by air.

_____ 5. When the plane set down in Burry Port, Wales.

_____ 6. Her book, *The Fun of It*, was an instant success.

_____ 7. Earhart and her publisher, George Putnam, married shortly after the publication of the book.

_____ 8. Set out with Fred Noonan from Miami, Florida, in 1937.

_____ 9. Since she never reached her destination.

_____ 10. No trace of the plane or its crew.

EXERCISE 2   Identifying and Revising Sentence Fragments

On your own paper, revise each fragment below by adding a subject, by adding a verb, or by attaching the fragment to a complete sentence. You may need to change the punctuation and capitalization, too.

EX. 1. Although the work was hard.

    1. Although the work was hard, we enjoyed the challenge.

1. My best friend, Luis.
2. After the band performed.
3. Books, magazines, photographs, and souvenirs.
4. Flooded its banks and covered Interstate 90.
5. Because of the most recent crisis in the flood plain.
6. The animals in the wildlife park.
7. Because of the hole in the ozone layer.
8. During the intense heat wave.
9. While I was at the beach.
10. Running with my new dog.

RUN-ON SENTENCES

8b   A *run-on sentence* is two complete sentences run together as if they were one sentence.

Run-ons are confusing because the reader can't tell where one idea ends and another begins. A comma marks a brief pause in a sentence, but it does not show the end of a sentence. If you use just a comma between two complete sentences, you create a *comma splice*. To revise run-on sentences or comma splices, you can make two sentences, or you can use a comma and a coordinating conjunction such as *and, but,* or *or*.

RUN-ON	Michael Jordan played for the Chicago Bulls he was the team's star player.
CORRECT	Michael Jordan played for the Chicago Bulls. He was the team's star player.
RUN-ON	Michael was a member of the 1984 Olympic basketball team, that year the U.S. team won a gold medal.
CORRECT	Michael was a member of the 1984 Olympic basketball team, and that year the U.S. team won a gold medal.

NOTE   To spot run-on sentences, read your writing aloud. A natural, distinct pause in your voice usually marks the end of one thought and the beginning of another. If you pause at a place where you don't have any end punctuation, look carefully to make sure you haven't written a run-on sentence.

EXERCISE 3   Identifying and Revising Run-on Sentences

On your own paper, revise each of the following run-on sentences by breaking it into two separate sentences or by using a comma and a coordinating conjunction. If a sentence is correct, write *C*.

EX.   1.   Storms can be quite powerful some of the most powerful storms are called hurricanes.

   1.   Storms can be quite powerful. Some of the most powerful storms are called hurricanes.

1.   Hurricanes are storms with fierce winds they often form over the Atlantic Ocean and parts of the Caribbean Sea.

2.   The storms have a circular shape they can be hundreds of miles across.

3. A calm area is located in the middle of a hurricane this area is called the *eye.*

4. People living along the Gulf of Mexico and the Atlantic coast of the United States have witnessed the power of hurricanes.

5. High waves from the storm batter the coast they can cause heavy damage to beaches and oceanfront property.

6. High winds destroy trees and power lines heavy rains cause flooding of roads and highways.

7. Problems occur when a hurricane moves over land.

8. After they reach land, hurricanes sometimes cause tornadoes.

9. During hurricane season, the National Weather Service keeps a close watch on the Caribbean Sea the Weather Service issues warnings to people in any storm's path.

10. People in threatened areas leave their homes they seek shelter in a safe place away from the coast.

EXERCISE 4   Identifying and Revising Run-on Sentences

The paragraph below is confusing because it contains fragments and run-ons. On your own paper, rewrite the paragraph, correcting the errors.

EX.   1 Have you ever heard of Doodyville it is the
       2 hometown of a well-known puppet.

Have you ever heard of Doodyville? It is the hometown of a well-known puppet.

1   *Howdy Doody* was a popular children's television show, it aired

2   during the 1950s. The program featured Howdy Doody and

3   "Buffalo" Bob Smith they told about their adventures in

4   Doodyville. Howdy was a marionette which is a kind of puppet

5   an operator above the stage controlled his movements with

6   strings. The show featured contests and sing-alongs it also had an

7   audience of children who were referred to as "The Peanut Gallery."

8   Another character on the show was Clarabell the clown whenever

9   Clarabell got hit with a pie in the face, The Peanut Gallery laughed

10   and screamed. I always wondered about Clarabell's voice an

11   automobile horn was used to make it.

COMBINING BY INSERTING WORDS AND PHRASES

COMBINING BY INSERTING WORDS

8c One way to combine two short sentences is to take a key word from one sentence and insert it into the other sentence.

Inserting Without a Change	
ORIGINAL	A brown bear flattened the tent. The bear was hungry.
COMBINED	A **hungry** brown bear flattened the tent.

Inserting With a Change	
ORIGINAL	The bear's visit was a **surprise**. It woke the campers.
COMBINED	The bear's **surprising** visit woke the campers.

 NOTE When you change the forms of words, you often add endings such as *–ed*, *–ing*, and *–ly* to make adjectives and adverbs.

EXAMPLES brilliant   elect   excite   happy
          brilliant**ly**   elect**ed**   excit**ing**   happi**ly**

 REFERENCE NOTE: For information on spelling with suffixes, see pages 283–285.

EXERCISE 5   Combining Sentences by Inserting Words

Combine each of the following sentence pairs by taking the italicized word from the second sentence and inserting it into the first sentence. Follow the hints in parentheses for changing the forms of words. Write the new sentences on your own paper.

EX. 1. Sarah Bernhardt was a French actress. She had *talent*. (Add *–ed*.)
     1. *Sarah Bernhardt was a talented French actress.*

1. Bernhardt had a clear voice. Her voice was *rich*. (Use a comma.)
2. Critics applauded her movements onstage. She moved with *grace*. (Add *–ful*.)

3. She performed for audiences on both sides of the Atlantic. The audiences certainly did *admire* her. (Drop the *e* and add *–ing.*)

4. In 1907, she toured the United States. The tour was *triumphant.* (Add *–ly.*)

5. The "Divine Sarah" wrote a book about acting. Her book was *truly interesting.* (Add with no change.)

COMBINING BY INSERTING PHRASES

8d   You can combine sentences by taking a phrase from one sentence and inserting it in another sentence.

A *phrase* is a group of words that doesn't have both a subject and a verb.

ORIGINAL   An inspector visited the restaurant. She was from the Health Department.

COMBINED   An inspector **from the Health Department** visited the restaurant.

EXERCISE 6   Combining Sentences by Inserting Phrases

Combine each pair of sentences below by taking the italicized words from the second sentence and inserting them into the first sentence. Add commas where needed. Write the sentences on your own paper.

EX.   1. Fiestas are important occasions. They play a key role *in Mexican American culture.*

    1. Fiestas are important occasions in Mexican American culture.

1. Celebrations are held day and night. The celebrations occur *in public squares and in private homes.*

2. During fiestas, people celebrate. They celebrate *by dancing, playing music, and cooking wonderful meals.*

3. Numerous fiestas take place within a nine-day period. They take place *from the sixteenth to the twenty-fourth of December.*

4. In many houses a decorated container, a piñata, is filled with treats and hung from the ceiling. It is hung *with a piece of string.*

5. A person wearing a blindfold smashes the piñata. The person smashes it *with a stick.*

COMBINING BY USING AND, BUT, OR OR

8e Sentences can be combined with the conjunctions *and, but,* and *or.* These connecting words can form a *compound subject,* a *compound verb,* or a *compound sentence.*

ORIGINAL   The players are on the field. The coaches are on the field.

COMBINED   **The players and the coaches** are on the field. [compound subject]

ORIGINAL   Would the pitcher throw a fastball? Would the pitcher decide to throw a curveball?

COMBINED   Would the pitcher **throw a fastball or decide to throw a curveball**? [compound verb]

ORIGINAL   Harry hit a long drive to right field. The ball was caught.

COMBINED   Harry hit a long drive to right field, **but the ball was caught.** [compound sentence]

NOTE   When you form a compound subject, make sure that it agrees with the verb in number.

ORIGINAL   Elie jogs every morning. Lanie jogs every morning.

REVISED   **Elie and Lanie jog** every morning.

EXERCISE 7 **Combining Sentences by Forming Compounds**

On your own paper, combine each of the sentence pairs below by forming a compound subject, a compound verb, or a compound sentence.

EX. 1. A keyboard instrument can have plucked strings. A keyboard instrument can have hammered strings.

      1. A keyboard instrument can have plucked or hammered strings.

1. Violins are stringed instruments. Cellos are stringed instruments.

2. Stringed instruments can be plucked. Stringed instruments can also be played with a bow.

3. Players can pluck the strings with their fingers. They can use small pieces of wood, metal, or plastic.

4. The clavichord has hammered strings. The dulcimer also has hammered strings.

5. One instrument that depends on wind currents for its sound is the aeolian harp. It is rarely played in an orchestra.

COMBINING BY USING A SUBORDINATE CLAUSE

8f   **If two sentences are closely related but unequal in importance, they may be combined with a subordinate clause or other introductory words.**

You can make a short sentence into a subordinate clause by inserting *who, which,* or *that* in place of the subject. You can also make a subordinate clause by adding a word that tells time or place. Words that tell time or place include *after, before, where, wherever, when, whenever,* and *while.*

ORIGINAL   A newsmagazine is a special type of magazine. It summarizes the weekly news.

COMBINED   A newsmagazine is a special type of magazine **that summarizes the weekly news.**

NOTE   If you put a subordinate clause at the beginning of the sentence, you'll need to put a comma after the clause.

ORIGINAL   Mother watched the game. I went to make popcorn.

COMBINED   **While Mother watched the game,** I went to make popcorn.

EXERCISE 8   Combining Sentences by Using Subordinate Clauses

Combine each of the sentence pairs below by making the second sentence a subordinate clause and attaching it to the first sentence. The hints in parentheses will tell you what words to use at the beginnings of the clauses. Write the sentences on your own paper. You may need to delete some words from the second sentence.

EX.   1.   Many stories were reprinted as books. The stories appeared in *The New Yorker.* (Use *that.*)

1.   Many stories that appeared in <u>The New Yorker</u> were reprinted as books.

1.   One of the first magazines in the English-speaking world was *Gentleman's Magazine.* It was published in Great Britain. (Use *which.*)

2.   Samuel Johnson wrote for this magazine. He was a famous author and critic. (Use *who.*)

3.   The colonies were still under British control. The first American magazine was published in Philadelphia. (Use *when.*)

4.   Edgar Allan Poe edited several magazines. He is a famous writer of short stories. (Use *who.*)

5.   The *Atlantic Monthly* is a long-respected magazine. It specializes in high-quality literature. (Use *that.*)

IMPROVING SENTENCE STYLE

REVISING STRINGY SENTENCES

8g *Stringy sentences* **have too many independent clauses strung together with words like** *and* **or** *but*. **Stringy sentences are confusing because they don't show the relationships between the ideas.**

To fix a stringy sentence, you can

- break the sentence into two or more sentences
- turn some of the independent clauses into phrases or subordinate clauses

STRINGY   Lucia baited the hook, and she cast the line into the water, and she watched the float bob up and down, and the float suddenly disappeared beneath the surface, and she had hooked a fish and it was a big one!

REVISED   After Lucia baited the hook, she cast the line into the water. As she watched the float bob up and down, it suddenly disappeared beneath the surface. She had hooked a big fish!

 NOTE When revising a stringy sentence, you may decide to keep *and* or *but* between two independent clauses. If you do, add a comma before the *and* or *but* to show a pause between the two thoughts.

REVISING WORDY SENTENCES

8h *Wordy sentences* **use more words than are really needed.**

You can revise wordy sentences in three different ways.

- Replace a group of words with one word.

WORDY   The passengers fastened their seat belts because of the fact that the plane was about to land.

REVISED   The passengers fastened their seat belts **because** the plane was about to land.

- Replace a clause with a phrase.

WORDY   After we had eaten our breakfast, we packed our gear and headed for the slopes.

REVISED   **After** breakfast, we packed our gear and headed for the slopes.

- Take out a whole group of unnecessary words.

WORDY   What I said was that the car sped down the street, which was the kind of street that was busy.

REVISED   What I said was that the car sped down the busy street.

EXERCISE 9   Revising Stringy and Wordy Sentences

On your own paper, revise the following stringy and wordy sentences. The hints in parentheses will help you.

EX.   1.   Annie Oakley became famous because of the fact that she starred in Buffalo Bill's Wild West Show. (*Take out words.*)

1.   Annie Oakley became famous because she starred in Buffalo Bill's Wild West Show.

1.   Annie was young, and she entered a shooting match with Frank Butler, and Butler was a professional sharpshooter, and Annie won the match. (*Use "when" to create a subordinate clause, and break into two sentences.*)

2.   Annie was not very tall and, in fact, was only five feet tall. (*Take out words.*)

3.   In the show, Annie ran into the ring, and she picked up a gun, and she shattered glass balls in midair, and this feat showed her great skill. (*Change into phrases, and break into two sentences.*)

4.   In her performances that she gave, Annie flipped a playing card into the air, and it fell, and she riddled it with bullets as it fell. (*Take out words.*)

5.   Frank Butler liked Annie and he wrote to her and visited her and later they were married. (*Take out words.*)

6.   For a period of seventeen years, Oakley was a member of the Wild West Show. (*Take out words.*)

7.   Annie was given the name "Little Sure Shot," which was a nickname. (*Take out words.*)

8.   She traveled to England and Germany and France and other countries in Europe. (*Take out words.*)

9.   A musical play that was called *Annie Get Your Gun* was written about Annie Oakley. (*Change into phrase.*)

10.   According to all reviews and reports written, the musical was and still is popular. (*Take out words.*)

CHAPTER REVIEW

A. Revising Sentence Fragments and Run-on Sentences

On your own paper, revise each fragment and run-on to make the paragraph below clearer.

EX. 1. Giant pandas are black-and-white, bearlike mammals they live in remote forest areas of China.

    1. Giant pandas are black-and-white, bearlike mammals. They live in remote forest areas of China.

1   Giant pandas eat mainly bamboo. Which grows in the
2 mountain forests, they have strong, wide teeth just right for
3 grinding tough shoots and roots. Their bodies, however, cannot
4 digest the bushy plant properly only a small portion of what they
5 eat gives them any nourishment. To get all the necessary
6 nutrients, must eat at least thirty pounds of bamboo each day.
7 Because they require such enormous amounts of food. Pandas
8 need vast areas of bamboo forest. In recent years many of the
9 forests in their native China have been destroyed therefore, the
10 population of giant pandas has also dwindled.

B. Revising Stringy and Wordy Sentences

On your own paper, revise the stringy and wordy sentences to improve the style of the following paragraph.

EX. 1. In our present day, shoes are mass-produced by machines operated by people working in factories, but in the early days of our country shoes were made by hand by skilled craftspeople who also fulfilled other roles in the communities of which they were a part.

    1. Nowadays shoes are mass-produced in factories, but in colonial America they were handmade by skilled craftspeople who also fulfilled other roles in their communities.

1   When the thirteen original states were still colonies,
2 shoemakers were highly trained and respected members of
3 society. They had no shops but what I mean to say is that instead
4 of working in shops, they traveled from home to home with their
5 tools. These craftspeople made new shoes or mended or fixed old

6 ones. Due to the fact that they traveled from place to place, the
7 shoemakers spread the latest news and gossip, and they also
8 performed another important service for the colonists, which was
9 that shoemakers also served as dentists for the colonists.
10 Shoemaking required great skill, but pulling teeth required no
11 particular skills all the shoemaker needed were a strong pair of
12 arms, a firm grip, and a good pair of one kind of tool which is
13 called pliers.

C. Revising Choppy Sentences

In the paragraph below, combine the choppy sentences by either inserting words and phrases, using *and, but,* or *or,* or using subordinate clauses. Write the revised paragraph on your own paper.

EX.   1. On the seabed, oysters attach to rocks. They also attach to shells or wooden posts.

    1. On the seabed, oysters attach to rocks, shells, or wooden posts.

1   Oysters belong to a large group of animals. This group of
2 animals is called mollusks. All oysters have soft bodies. They also
3 have hard, rough shells. These shells protect their bodies. Oysters
4 are like many other mollusks. They are found in shallow water on
5 the coasts. Oysters feed on plants and animals. When the oysters
6 are large enough, they are harvested. Then they are sold for food.
7 Sometimes a grain of sand gets inside an oyster's shell. When this
8 happens, the oyster may make a pearl. These kinds of oysters are
9 different. They are called pearl oysters. Mollusks that produce
10 pearls grow in fresh water and they grow in salt water. They grow
11 in many parts of the world. Pearls are made of the same material
12 that makes up the mollusk's shell. The material is called mother-
13 of-pearl. Pearls are used in jewelry. They can be very valuable.
14 Their value depends on their size. It also depends on their color
15 and on their shininess. Pearls can be white, gray, or black. They
16 can also be blue, yellow, lavender, or mauve. They can also be
17 green or cream.

CHOOSING YOUR WORDS I

FORMAL AND INFORMAL ENGLISH

Words communicate much more than information. They also express attitudes and feelings. Choose your words with care to adapt your language to different purposes, audiences, and situations.

Formal English and *informal English* are the two basic types of language in English. **Formal English** is used for business letters, public speeches, and serious papers and reports. Usually it includes long sentences, extremely precise words, and few or no contractions.

Informal English is used in everyday conversations and in such informal writing as personal letters and journal entries.

FORMAL ENGLISH   I am interested in certain forms of popular music.
INFORMAL ENGLISH   I'm way into rock and pop.

Informal English includes the categories of *colloquialisms* and *slang*. **Colloquialisms** are colorful, widely used expressions in written and conversational language.

EXAMPLE   She didn't have a ticket, so she was **booted out** the door.

Slang consists of made-up words and old words used in new ways. Most slang expressions are a special vocabulary for a particular group of people, such as teenagers or musicians. Many slang expressions that were used widely a year ago may already be out-of-date.

EXAMPLE   They needed more **dough** to pay for their tickets. [money]

EXERCISE 1 Identifying Informal Language

Underline the italicized word or phrase that is an example of informal language. Be prepared to explain your choices.

EX.   1. If you want to be a <u>*big shot*</u>, you will have to *develop* your skills.

1. Please *walk more slowly*; I want to *hang out* with you.

2. We were really *ticked off* when the concert was *canceled*.

3. The water in the pool was *ice-cold* and felt *awesome* after our hike.

4. That dog has been *barking*, and the noise is really *bugging* me.

DENOTATION AND CONNOTATION

Would you rather be described as *stingy* or *thrifty*? Both words have the same basic meaning, or **denotation.** However, they have different emotional associations, or **connotations.** The word *thrifty* has positive associations. The word *stingy* has negative associations.

Choose your words carefully when you write or speak. If you use a word with negative connotations, you may communicate a negative meaning to your readers or listeners.

 NOTE It's especially important to think about connotations when you are choosing among synonyms. Two words may mean the same thing, yet one may carry positive associations while the other has negative associations.

> EXAMPLES The judge **grinned** at the students.
> The judge **sneered** at the students.

Both of these words mean "smiled," but *grinned* has positive associations. The judge seems friendly. *Sneered*, on the other hand, has negative associations. The judge seems unfriendly and even mean.

EXERCISE 2   Identifying Positive and Negative Connotations

To complete each sentence below, underline the word in parentheses that has positive connotations.

EX.   1. His apartment was (<u>small</u>, *cramped*) but neat and comfortable.

1. I was (*alarmed, surprised*) when Jim called.

2. This tall cabinet is (*antique, old*).

3. A strong (*aroma, odor*) came from the kitchen.

4. We felt (*sleepy, worn-out*) after we cleaned the attic.

5. She (*requested, demanded*) that I help her with her homework.

6. His uncle's cooking was generally (*bland, mild*).

7. The police (*asked, interrogated*) them about the incident.

8. The fabric of the fancy dress was (*thin, sheer*).

9. Her mother was an example of (*pride, vanity*).

10. (*Gaudy, Ornate*) decorations bordered the walls.

CHOOSING YOUR WORDS II

TIRED WORDS AND EXPRESSIONS

How would you feel if you were forced to watch the same movie time after time? Probably you'd get tired of the same events and dialogue played repeatedly. The same thing happens to words when they are used too often. They become stale and tired, and they lose much of their meaning. Tired words and expressions are called *clichés*. Avoid them in your writing. Replace them with fresh, vivid details.

TIRED   We had **a very nice time** riding the roller coaster. [vague, tired]
FRESH   We found the roller coaster fast, wild, and thoroughly exciting.

TIRED   I'm as **hungry as a bear.** [overused, tired]
FRESH   I'm so hungry that my stomach is growling and I feel lightheaded.

EXERCISE 3   Revising Sentences to Eliminate Tired Words and Expressions

The sentences below contain clichés in italics. On the lines after each sentence, replace the tired word or expression with a word or expression that is not overused.

EX.   1.   He is a *fine* student.   As a student, he works hard, thinks creatively, and finishes his assignments on time.

1.   Her smile was *as bright as the sun.* _____

_____

2.   Your party was *really great.* _____

_____

3.   I felt *down in the dumps* when I heard the bad news. _____

_____

4.   The sunset last night was *beautiful.* _____

_____

5.   *As quick as a wink*, the subway car flew through the tunnel. _____

_____

JARGON

Jargon is special language that is used by a particular group of people who share the same occupation, sport, or hobby. A word can be used as jargon by several groups, with each group giving it a different meaning.

EXAMPLES   Kim **feathered** the paint edges after she scraped off the loose paint. [painters' jargon meaning "to make the edge very thin"]
We carefully **feathered** our oars in the strong breeze. [boating jargon meaning "to turn the oar so the flat side doesn't catch the wind"]
The emerald, which had a **feather**, wasn't very valuable. [jewelers' jargon describing a feather-shaped flaw]

Jargon can be practical and effective because it can reduce many words to one or two. However, jargon is inappropriate for a general audience that may not be familiar with the special meanings of the words.

 REFERENCE NOTE: For an example of how dictionaries label special uses of words, see pages 279–280.

EXERCISE 4   Translating Jargon

Each sentence below contains an example of jargon in italics. On your own paper, change the jargon into standard English. Use context clues to help you. Use a dictionary to check any definitions that you are unsure of.

EX.   1.   The manager was more interested in *the bottom line* than in improving job conditions.

1.   profit or loss

1. The software company is offering an *update* to its popular word-processing program that was introduced last year.
2. My uncle Fred wired our house; he once worked as a *gaffer* at Universal Studios.
3. If your sink isn't draining, you could use a *snake* to clear it.
4. Can you believe there were two *balks* in the baseball game?
5. "Change into this *johnny;* the doctor will be in shortly," said the nurse.

CHAPTER REVIEW

A. Revising Informal Language

The paragraph below is part of an eighth-grade student's report on the dinosaur velociraptor. The student included many examples of informal English. On your own paper, revise the paragraph. Replace all informal English with formal English.

EX. [1] All raptors had these really big claws on their hind legs that they used on the stuff they caught.

1. All raptors had huge claws on their hind legs that they used to attack and kill their victims.

[1] *Velociraptors* bit the dust around 76 million years ago. [2] A *velociraptor* was just about the size of a wolf, you know. [3] It was like six to nine feet long, and it weighed, oh, about sixty to one hundred forty pounds. [4] It had a really stiff tail that it could use for balance when tearing after other animals. [5] It could go pretty fast—about thirty-five to forty miles per hour. [6] Guys who study raptors say that raptors probably hunted in packs. [7] The group would zero in on a victim from all sides, working together to knock it off.

B. Analyzing Words for Negative and Positive Connotations

Each of the pairs below consists of two synonyms. One word in each pair has a negative connotation, and the other word has a positive connotation. In each pair, underline the word that has a negative connotation.

EX. 1. lean, scrawny

1. proud, snobby
2. choosy, picky
3. undistinguished, normal
4. rowdy, active
5. informative, talkative
6. glaring, shining
7. clever, tricky
8. argue, disagree
9. cheap, inexpensive
10. unique, weird

C. Revising Sentences to Replace Clichés and Tired Words

Each sentence below contains an overused word or a cliché in italics. On the lines following each sentence, revise the sentence. Replace the tired words with words or expressions that are not overused. You may wish to change the structure of the sentence, as shown in the example.

EX.   1. She is a *great* poet.   She writes poetry filled with vivid images.

1. He is a *terrific* athlete. _____

   _____

2. *In this day and age*, children grow up quickly. _____

   _____

3. Her singing is *second to none*. _____

   _____

4. Tara made a *last-ditch effort* to finish writing the paper. _____

   _____

5. Alice is *nice*. _____

   _____

D. Translating Familiar Jargon

Choose a favorite activity, hobby, sport, or interest such as dancing, coin collecting, basketball, or drama. On your own paper, write four examples of jargon related to your activity, hobby, sport, or interest. Then write a definition to help someone else understand each example of jargon.

EX.   Subject: drama

   1. aside: a line spoken by a character that is meant to be heard by the audience alone

Funky Winkerbean reprinted with special permission of North America Syndicate, Inc.

SENTENCE SENSE

10a A *sentence* is a group of words that expresses a complete thought.

A sentence begins with a capital letter and ends with a period, a question mark, or an exclamation point.

EXAMPLES The fans at the softball game cheered wildly**.**
Answer the telephone**.**
Did you read the newspaper this morning**?**
What a wonderful surprise this is**!**

When a group of words looks like a sentence but does not express a complete thought, it is called a *sentence fragment*.

SENTENCE The fruit in the bowl is too ripe.

SENTENCE FRAGMENT The fruit in the bowl. [This is not a complete thought. What about *The fruit in the bowl*?]

10b A *declarative sentence* makes a statement. It is always followed by a period.

EXAMPLES The trails can be steep and rocky**.**
Kareem Abdul-Jabbar played for the Los Angeles Lakers in the 1970s and the 1980s**.**

10c An *imperative sentence* gives a command or makes a request. It is usually followed by a period. A strong command is followed by an exclamation point.

The subject of a command or a request is always *you*, although *you* doesn't appear in the sentence. In such cases, *you* is called the *understood subject*.

EXAMPLES (You) Write your name on the top of the paper**.**
(You) Call the fire department**!**

10d An *exclamatory sentence* shows excitement or expresses strong feeling. It is followed by an exclamation point.

EXAMPLE What an amazing athlete Jackie Joyner-Kersee is**!**

10e An *interrogative sentence* asks a question. It is always followed by a question mark.

EXAMPLE What is your favorite restaurant**?**

EXERCISE 1   Identifying Sentences and Sentence Fragments

Identify each group of words below by writing *sent.* for *sentence* or *frag.* for *sentence fragment* on the line before each group.

EX.   _frag._ 1. whenever she rides her mountain bike
       sent. 2. Alana wears her helmet whenever she rides her mountain
                    bike

_____ 1. who wrote the screenplay for that movie

_____ 2. river rafting, a popular and exciting sport

_____ 3. gathering the elephants and herding them down to the Chao
           Phraya River

_____ 4. a colorful caterpillar crept along a branch of the tree

_____ 5. when compared to other creatures

_____ 6. the lead part in the play

_____ 7. a plumber repaired the leaking faucet in the kitchen

_____ 8. wonderful drawings full of interesting details

_____ 9. the paper in this book was once part of a tree

_____ 10. even though the coach and the players seemed ready for the
           game on Saturday

_____ 11. the man cleaned the carpets

_____ 12. after running as hard as she could for several minutes

_____ 13. tuck in your shirt

_____ 14. she left early to do her homework

_____ 15. for example, his long curly hair

EXERCISE 2   Classifying and Punctuating Sentences

On your own paper, write one of each of the four kinds of sentences (declarative, imperative, interrogative, and exclamatory). Use correct end punctuation, and label each sentence.

EX.   1. Which planet is closest to the earth?   (interrogative)

THE SUBJECT AND THE PREDICATE

A sentence is made up of two parts: the *subject* and the *predicate*.

10f   The *subject* tells whom or what the sentence is about. The *predicate* tells something about the subject. The *complete subject* consists of all the words needed to tell *whom* or *what* the sentence is about. The *complete predicate* consists of all the words that say something about the subject.

EXAMPLES   Ten Lipizzaner stallions | jumped over the fence.
             CMPL. S.   *CMPL. PRED.*

            CMPL. S.   *CMPL. PRED.*
            All of the clown's balloons | popped.

         CMPL. S.   *CMPL. PRED.*
         Bobby Ray | drew an ink sketch of the school.

Usually, the subject comes before the predicate. Sometimes, however, the subject appears elsewhere in the sentence. To find the subject of a sentence, ask *Who?* or *What?* before the predicate.

EXAMPLES   Flying as fast as it could, the **hawk** caught a small bird. [*What* caught a small bird? A *hawk* did.]
           Will **Janelle** play the trombone? [*Who* will play the trombone? *Janelle* will.]

 NOTE   Because a subject and a verb are the essential parts of a sentence, they are called the *sentence base*.

EXERCISE 3 Identifying Complete Subjects and Complete Predicates

In each of the following sentences, draw a line between the complete subject and the complete predicate.

EX.   [1] Native Americans | hold many festivals and celebrations.

[1] The sun dance festival was important to the peoples of the Great Plains. [2] The festival was celebrated in the summer. [3] Leaders chose the site for the ceremony. [4] Young warriors rode out to other villages and announced the location of the ceremony. [5] People came

together and built a large stucture of upright posts and rafters. [6] A tall pole stood in the middle of the area. [7] The people pitched their tepees in a circle facing each other. [8] The dancers painted their bodies and danced to the music. [9] The dancers faced the sun throughout the ceremonies. [10] The actual ceremonies lasted twelve days.

EXERCISE 4   Creating Sentences

Create five sentences by drawing a line to connect each complete subject with a complete predicate below. Then write the sentences on the lines provided. Use capital letters and end marks. Draw a line between the complete subject and the complete predicate.

EX.   1. a turtle yelling "Fire" —— scrambled out of the soup.

1. A turtle yelling "Fire!" │ scrambled out of the soup.

Complete subjects

the crowd of yellow-bellied frogs

two half-opened oysters

the blue dog named Yeller

a fat cat squinting in the sun

a fish with a small fishing pole
   under its fin

Complete predicates

scanned one dictionary page and
   turned to the next

argued over the peanuts

stands waiting for the school bus

politely asked me for the time

pushed the red panic button

1. _____

_____

2. _____

_____

3. _____

_____

4. _____

_____

5. _____

_____

THE SIMPLE SUBJECT AND THE SIMPLE PREDICATE

10g **The *simple subject* is the main word or words in the complete subject.**

EXAMPLES   A **poster** in the gym describes the contest. [The complete subject is *A poster in the gym.*]
The huge double **doors** slammed shut. [The complete subject is *The huge double doors.*]

The simple subject may consist of one word or several words. The simple subjects in these examples are both compound nouns.

EXAMPLES   A **home run** ended the game.
I Love Lucy was a popular television series.

NOTE   In this book, the term *subject* refers to the simple subject unless otherwise indicated.

EXERCISE 5   Identifying Complete Subjects and Simple Subjects

In each of the following sentences, underline the complete subject once and the simple subject twice.

EX.   1. <u>Many <u><u>immigrants</u></u> entered the United States through Ellis Island.</u>

1. The immigration station on Ellis Island opened on Saturday, January 1, 1892.

2. An immigrant's first look at the island was from the ferryboats.

3. A two-story brick building stood on the island.

4. Smaller buildings on the grounds included a hospital, a laundry, a dining hall, and a dormitory.

5. On the first floor of the main building was the Great Hall.

6. A large U.S. flag hung from the balcony of this hall.

7. Sitting on wooden benches were hundreds of immigrants.

8. Physical and dental examinations often required a two-day wait.

9. Most immigrants received a landing card after the examination.

10. The Ellis Island Immigration Station became a Coast Guard station in 1941.

10h   The *simple predicate* is the main word or group of words in the complete predicate.

The simple predicate may be a one-word verb, or it may be a verb phrase. A *verb phrase* consists of a main verb and its helping verbs.

EXAMPLES   *CMPL S.*   *CMPL. PRED.*
My brother | **sings** in the third act.

CMPL. S.   *CMPL. PRED.*
Ignacio | **is sorting** the mail.

CMPL. S.   *CMPL. PRED.*
Our group | **will be joining** the cleanup committee.

The words *not* and *never*, which are frequently used with verbs, are not part of a verb phrase. Both of these words are adverbs.

EXAMPLES   We | **did** not **listen** to the radio this morning.
Gordon | **has** never **played** football.

NOTE   In this book, the term *verb* refers to the simple predicate unless otherwise stated.

EXERCISE 6   Identifying Complete Predicates and Verbs

In each of the sentences below, underline the complete predicate once and the verb twice.

EX.   1. Your body <u>can repair</u> itself.

1. Even a small burn should not be neglected.

2. You should hold a minor burn under cold water for ten minutes.

3. Some skin cells are destroyed by the heat.

4. You should never put grease, butter, or cream on a burn.

5. Usually, a small blister forms over the hurt area.

COMPOUND SUBJECTS AND COMPOUND VERBS

10i A *compound subject* consists of two or more connected subjects that have the same verb. The usual connecting words are *and* and *or.*

EXAMPLES   **Lloyd, Flo,** and **I** collected all the rubbish.
Either **snow** or **showers** are predicted.
At the bottom of the trunk were some old **newspapers** and **magazines**.

10j A *compound verb* consists of two or more connected verbs that have the same subject. A connecting word—usually *and, or,* or *but*— is used between the verbs.

EXAMPLES   Tanya **stopped** and **stared** in disbelief.
You may **read** a book, **play** chess, or **watch** a movie.

EXERCISE 7   Identifying Compound Subjects

In each of the sentences below, underline the compound subject once and the verb twice.

EX.   1. Either sage or rosemary is a good choice for dry, stony ground.

1. Lila and Karl planted an herb garden last spring.

2. Parsley, chives, and horseradish are all common cooking herbs.

3. Roses and lilies are also included in the category of herbs.

4. Nurseries, hardware stores, and seed catalogs sell a wide variety of herb seeds.

5. Among herbs, chicory and flax make a fine show of blue flowers.

6. The different textures and colors of thyme leaves produce a beautiful pattern.

7. Karl and his parents dug a garden plot in their yard.

8. Watering and weeding kept Lila and Karl busy all May and June.

9. Basil and mint are the largest crops so far this year.

10. Collecting dill seed and harvesting licorice root will happen in late summer and fall.

EXERCISE 8   Identifying Compound Verbs

In each of the sentences below, underline the subject once and the compound verb twice.

EX.   1. The <u>runners</u> <u>fought</u> for position and then <u>settled</u> into a comfortable pace.

1. My cat sleeps behind the books in the bookcase and looks like a dust ball afterward.

2. The Oregon Trail started in Independence, Missouri, and ran for about 2,100 miles.

3. The photographers traveled to distant countries and took wonderful pictures of many strange animals.

4. Oprah Winfrey not only is a talk-show host but also runs her own television production company.

5. Father's Day was first celebrated in West Virginia, and was observed for the eighty-fourth time in 1993.

EXERCISE 9   Identifying Compound Subjects and Compound Verbs

In each of the sentences below, underline the subject once and the verb twice.

EX.   1. The <u>sun</u> <u>is</u> a star and <u>resembles</u> a ball.

1. Long ago, people gave names to the brightest stars and learned their locations.

2. These ancient stargazers saw patterns in the sky and named the constellations.

3. Among the brightest stars in the sky are Sirius and Rigel.

4. Sometimes stars explode and become much brighter.

5. Many mysteries or unanswered questions about such events remain.

CHAPTER REVIEW

A. Classifying Sentences

On the line provided, classify each of the sentences below by writing *dec.* for *declarative*, *inter.* for *interrogative*, *imp.* for *imperative*, or *excl.* for *exclamatory*. Add the appropriate end punctuation.

EX. __excl.__ 1. What a serious problem this is!

_____ 1. Trash litters beaches around the world

_____ 2. What terrible damage this litter causes

_____ 3. Why are plastic bags so harmful to sea creatures

_____ 4. Sea animals often mistake bits of plastic for food and choke on them

_____ 5. What can you do to help stop this problem

_____ 6. Take along a large garbage bag every time you go to the beach

_____ 7. Pick up litter and throw it in the bag

_____ 8. Every year, people all over the world get together and sponsor cleanup parties

_____ 9. Does that sound like fun

_____ 10. Write the Center for Marine Conservation in Washington, D.C., for more information

B. Identifying Subjects and Predicates

On the line before each sentence, label the italicized word group *cmpl. s.* for *complete subject* or *cmpl. pred.* for *complete predicate*.

EX. __cmpl. pred.__ 1. Claude Debussy *was born in France in 1862.*

_____ 1. *This important composer* was a gifted pianist.

_____ 2. His exceptional talent *was apparent by the time he was nine years old.*

_____ 3. Debussy *grew up in Paris in a very poor family.*

_____   4. *A Russian lady, von Meck, helped his career.*

_____   5. Von Meck *hired Debussy to play piano duets with her and her children.*

_____   6. *She* took him to her many palaces all over Europe.

_____   7. Debussy *traveled with the von Mecks during his summer vacations from the Paris Conservatory.*

_____   8. *Many of Debussy's works* were inspired by a singer whom he loved.

_____   9. *The new forms of music he developed* startled his contemporaries.

_____   10. He *believed that exploration was the basis of music.*

C. Writing a Journal Entry

You have been invited by NASA to witness the launch of a space shuttle from Cape Canaveral, Florida. On the morning of the launch, you can see the shuttle standing on a launch pad. The orbiter, which looks like an airplane, clings to a tank. At its side are two booster rockets. The scientists in the control room wait anxiously as the countdown begins. On the lines below, write a journal entry of at least five sentences describing the launch. Be sure each sentence has a subject and a predicate. Draw a line between the complete subject and the complete predicate.

EX.   July 30, 0:7:45 — I | could see the space shuttle on the launch pad.

_____

_____

_____

_____

_____

_____

_____

_____

NOUNS

The Eight Parts of Speech			
noun	pronoun	verb	conjunction
adverb	adjective	preposition	interjection

11a A *noun* is a word used to name a person, a place, a thing, or an idea.

Persons	teacher, Sandra Day O'Connor, woman, brother
Places	valley, Los Angeles, solar system, suburb
Things	piano, truck, pyramid, Eiffel Tower, bird
Ideas	happiness, bravery, honesty, health, anger

A *compound noun* is two or more words used together as a single noun. The parts of a compound noun may be written as one word, as separate words, or as a hyphenated word.

ONE WORD   birdhouse, fingerprints, Greenland
SEPARATE WORDS   Harry Truman; sea turtle; July 4, 1776; *The Hobbit*
HYPHENATED WORD   father-in-law, vice-president, thirty-one

NOTE   When you are not sure how to write a compound noun, look in a dictionary.

EXERCISE 1   Identifying Nouns

Underline all of the nouns in each of the following sentences.

EX.   1. <u>Liliuokalani</u> was the last <u>ruler</u> of <u>Hawaii</u>.

1. Lydia Kamakaeha was born a Hawaiian princess.

2. As a member of the royal family, Lydia received quite a complete education.

3. Her travels included a tour of Europe and of the United States.

4. A talented composer, she wrote the song "Aloha Oe."

5. King Kalakaua gave Pearl Harbor to the United States in 1887.

6. Lydia opposed the king's gift of Hawaiian land.

7. She wanted Hawaii to stay an independent kingdom.

8. Many foreign business leaders turned against the princess because of her concern for Hawaii.

9. When Lydia took the throne of Hawaii in 1891, she became Queen Liliuokalani.

10. Hawaii's foreign business leaders helped reduce her power as queen.

11. In January 1893, Sanford Dole and his political group asked the queen to step down from the throne.

12. President Grover Cleveland tried to keep Liliuokalani as ruler.

13. The first and only reigning queen of Hawaii abdicated in 1895.

14. During her short reign, Liliuokalani fought to make Hawaii as strong a nation as its neighboring nations.

15. In 1898, she wrote *Hawaii's Story by Hawaii's Queen*, a book about her life in the islands.

EXERCISE 2   Identifying Compound Nouns

Underline the compound nouns in the paragraph below. [Note: A sentence may contain more than one compound noun.]

EX.   [1] All the landholders pledged their support to the new king.

[1] William of Normandy was the cousin of King Edward of England. [2] The king had promised William the throne but changed his mind on his deathbed. [3] Instead, the king named his brother-in-law Harold as the successor to the throne. [4] Angry at this betrayal, William immediately set sail with his army across the English Channel to England. [5] He set up his headquarters near the coast. [6] Harold met the invaders on the outskirts of Hastings. [7] The fighting was furious, and the outcome of the battle was often in doubt. [8] Finally, in October 1066, William's forces defeated the Anglo-Saxons at the Battle of Hastings. [9] On Christmas Day, William was crowned king. [10] William I—frequently called William the Conqueror—would rule England with an iron hand for more than twenty years.

COMMON, PROPER, ABSTRACT, AND CONCRETE NOUNS

11b A *common noun* names any one of a group of persons, places, things, or ideas. A *proper noun* is a specific name for a particular person, place, thing, or idea. It always begins with a capital letter.

Proper nouns always begin with a capital letter. Common nouns begin with a capital letter only when they come at the beginning of a sentence.

Common Nouns	Proper Nouns
scientist	Marie Curie, Percy Lavon Julian
mountain	Matterhorn, Kilimanjaro
magazine	*National Geographic, Newsweek*
holiday	Thanksgiving, New Year's Day
short story	"The Last Leaf," "Shadows on the Rock"
team	Los Angeles Rams, Boston Red Sox

EXERCISE 3 Identifying Common and Proper Nouns

In the following paragraph, underline the common nouns, and circle the proper nouns.

EX. [1] (Mammoth Cave) in (Kentucky) has almost three hundred miles of passages.

[1] Thousands of years ago, many people used caves as shelters. [2] Archaeologists have uncovered fossil remains, stone tools, weapons, and paintings in caves in Europe, Africa, and western Asia. [3] A cave near Peking was occupied by people more than 200,000 years ago. [4] In a cave in Lascaux, France, artists during the Ice Ages painted images of horses, deer, and other animals on the rock wall. [5] In Aruba, caves contain drawings by American Indians. [6] Pueblo Indians lived in cave villages in what is now the southwestern United States. [7] In some

parts of the world, people still use caves as homes. [8] Caves in Africa, Europe, and Asia are still used as homes for some people. [9] Some members of a people called the Tasaday lived in caves in the Philippine Islands. [10] In Spain, some Gypsies still make their homes in caves near Granada.

11c A *concrete noun* names a person, place, or thing that can be perceived by one or more of the senses (sight, hearing, taste, touch, or smell). An *abstract noun* names an idea, a feeling, a quality, or a characteristic.

Concrete Nouns	lighthouse, Corazon Aquino, computer, athlete, Mount Hood, storm, statue
Abstract Nouns	love, hope, honesty, patriotism, independence, satisfaction, dream, freedom, justice

---

EXERCISE 4 Identifying Concrete Nouns and Abstract Nouns

Classify both italicized words in each sentence below. On the line before each sentence, write *con.* for *concrete* or *abs.* for *abstract*. Use a semicolon to separate your answers.

EX. _____con.; abs._____ [1] *Abraham Lincoln* had great [2] *hopes* for the future.

_____ Is your [1] *class* studying [2] *history*?

_____ In a [3] *speech* before the Virginia Convention in Richmond in 1775, Patrick Henry said, "Give me [4] *liberty* or give me death."

_____ The flag of the United States flying over Fort McHenry meant [5] *victory* for the [6] *country*.

_____ Francis Scott Key's [7] *poem* expresses the [8] *feelings* Key had when he saw the flag through the early morning mist.

_____ The Pledge of Allegiance ends with the [9] *words* "with liberty and [10] *justice* for all."

PRONOUNS

11d A *pronoun* is a word used in place of one noun or more than one noun.

Personal Pronouns	I, me, my, mine, we, us, our, ours, you, yours, he, him, his, she, her, hers, it, its, they, them, their, theirs
Reflexive Pronouns	myself, ourselves, yourself, yourselves, himself, herself, itself, themselves
Indefinite Pronouns	all, another, any, anyone, both, each, everybody, everything, few, many, most, no one, some, several

The word that a pronoun stands for is called the pronoun's *antecedent*.

EXAMPLES **Alicia** carried **her** umbrella to school.

Our **guests** served **themselves** at dinner.

NOTE Some authorities prefer to call possessive forms of pronouns (such as *my*, *his*, and *their*) adjectives. Follow your teacher's instructions.

EXERCISE 5 Identifying Pronouns

Underline all the pronouns in the sentences below.

EX. [1] Every week, Manuel forced <u>himself</u> to save part of <u>his</u> allowance.

[1] Mr. and Mrs. Hernández were celebrating their twenty-fifth wedding anniversary. [2] Manuel decided to take them to their favorite Italian restaurant. [3] The meal would be fairly expensive, but he had been saving for the occasion for a couple of months.

[4] "May I come, too?" Sophia asked her brother as she sat down.

[5] "Since I can't afford more than three dinners," Manuel responded, patting his sister on the arm, "you will have to pay for your meal yourself."

EXERCISE 6   Identifying Pronouns and Their Antecedents

In the sentences below, underline the pronouns once and their antecedents twice.

EX.   1. "I will prove to Pat what a good detective I am," Sean said.

1. "I went to Hawaii with my brother," said Irene.

2. Tommy and Aretha said that the sculpture is theirs.

3. "Pedro," asked Janice, "have you seen the art exhibit?"

4. The Durands bought themselves a new computer.

5. The children will take their sleeping bags with them.

6. Marcia said to Heidi, "I think this book is very entertaining."

7. Because Mr. Choy left his briefcase at home, he had to go back.

8. Tanya gave her speech for her entire class.

9. Mrs. Díaz told Aaron, "Your story is interesting, but you should add more details."

10. Felicia said she would meet Molly and Derrick at the library.

EXERCISE 7   Using Pronouns in Sentences

Replace one of the italicized nouns in each sentence below with a pronoun. Write your sentences on your own paper.

EX.   1. *Franklin* and *Denise* need a ride home.
      1. Franklin and she need a ride home.

1. *Katie* and *Tony* went hiking last Saturday.
2. *Perry* was looking for *Mr. Hall*.
3. *Friends* were traveling with *Mother* to the concert.
4. Did *students* attend the ceremony for *Ms. Rico*?
5. Later, *Raúl* asked *George* about the test.
6. *Chip* and *his team* set a new record.
7. The *committee* gave *our class* a set of encyclopedias.
8. How can *Franklin* help *Keith*?
9. Please ask the *neighbors* to call *Tomasa*.
10. *Darlene* and *Francesca* did well in the play.

ADJECTIVES

11e An *adjective* is a word used to modify a noun or a pronoun.

To *modify* a word means to describe the word or to make its meaning more definite. An adjective modifies a word by telling *what kind, which one*, or *how much* or *how many*.

What Kind?	*curly* hair, *narrow* path, *fresh* fruit, *heavy* rain
Which One?	*these* records, *first* row, *other* artists, *back* door
How Much? or How Many?	*twelve* birds, *much* help, *less* time, *some* marbles

NOTE Some authorities prefer to call possessive forms of pronouns (such as *my, his*, and *their*) and demonstrative pronouns (such as *this* and *these*) adjectives. Follow your teacher's instructions.

An adjective may come before or after the word it modifies.

EXAMPLES   **Many** sailboats gathered at the **harbor** entrance.

Michael sounded **cheerful** and **enthusiastic** on the telephone.

The most frequently used adjectives are *a, an*, and *the*. These adjectives are ***articles***. *A* is used before a word beginning with a consonant sound. *An* is used before a word beginning with a vowel sound. *The* indicates that a noun refers to someone or something in particular.

EXAMPLES   How is **a** frog different from **a** toad?
An artist displayed **an** example of her work.
The coat on **the** chair is mine.

EXERCISE 8   Identifying Adjectives and the Words They Modify

Underline the adjectives in the following sentences, and draw an arrow to the word each adjective modifies. Do not include *a, an*, and *the*.

EX.   1. Sharks are one of the oldest animals on this planet.

1. Some of the biggest and fiercest fish on earth are sharks.

2. A small number of species of sharks can be found in freshwater rivers, but most live in warm salt water.

3. The skeleton of a shark is made of a hard, elastic substance called cartilage.

4. Many species have torpedo-shaped bodies, while several other species have long, flat bodies.

5. Sharks can move through the water at speeds of up to forty miles an hour.

6. Some sharks can live several weeks without a single meal.

7. A shark usually has sharp teeth for cutting and rounded teeth for grinding.

8. A few sharks, though big, are slow and sluggish.

9. Several sharks, however, are fast and dangerous.

10. Larger sharks often eat smaller ones, including their own young.

EXERCISE 9   Using Adjectives to Revise

In each sentence below, add interesting adjectives to modify the nouns. Insert a caret (∧) where each adjective will appear. Then write your adjective above the caret.

EX.   1.   A ∧ turtle swam in the ∧ pond.
        large, green   *clear, blue*

1. A bear waited in the shadows.
2. Did the beachcomber collect shells and rocks?
3. The women in the town have started a business.
4. Divers searched the bottom of the ocean for treasure.
5. We watched a sunset on the beach.
6. The boys sat in the bleachers.
7. Down the road came a car.
8. Mr. Goldsohn went into the shop to buy a lamp for his collection.
9. The backpack had room for clothes.
10. The river was full after the storm.

PROPER ADJECTIVES

11f A *proper adjective* is formed from a proper noun and begins with a capital letter.

Proper Nouns	Proper Adjectives
France	**French** literature
Queen Victoria	**Victorian** furniture
Ohio	**Ohio** vacation
Asia	**Asian** ports
Robert W. Bunsen	**Bunsen** burner

EXERCISE 10   Identifying Proper Adjectives

In the sentences below, underline the proper adjectives, and draw an arrow to the word each proper adjective modifies.

EX.   1. Laurence Olivier was a great <u>Shakespearean</u> actor.

1. Students from school will be touring the Rio Grande valley.

2. Huge skyscrapers dominate the New York City skyline.

3. In July 1975, Russian and American astronauts conducted a joint mission in space.

4. British ships were close to the French coast.

5. We saw an exhibit of Mexican art at the museum.

6. The pianist played several Beatles songs.

7. The Greek and Canadian citizens checked their passports before they boarded the plane.

8. That French restaurant serves Italian bread with meals.

9. The debate focused on the Mideast situation.

10. What is your favorite Elizabethan drama?

EXERCISE 11   Using Proper Adjectives in Sentences

On the lines after each proper adjective and its noun, write a sentence using the pair of words correctly.

EX.   1.   African art   _We saw an exhibition of African art._

1.   Chinese vase _____

2.   Greek alphabet _____

3.   Diego Rivera painting _____

4.   Christian church _____

5.   Angora wool _____

6.   Sperry typewriter _____

7.   Pablo Neruda poem _____

8.   Muslim calendar _____

9.   Wagner opera _____

10.   Louisiana crayfish _____

11.   Betsy Ross flag _____

12.   Jewish synagogue _____

13.   Arthurian legend _____

14.   Navajo culture _____

15.   Danish furniture _____

16.   L'Engle novel _____

17.   German shepherd _____

18.   Buddhist temple _____

19.   French bread _____

20.   Colorado beetle _____

CHAPTER REVIEW

A. Identifying Pronouns, Adjectives, and Single and Compound Nouns

Identify each italicized word in the sentences below. On the line before each sentence, write *n.* for *noun*, *comp.* for *compound noun*, *pron.* for *pronoun*, or *adj.* for *adjective*. Separate your answers with semicolons.

EX. _____n.; adj._____ 1. The *earth* is an *active* planet.

_____ 1. The *rocky*, outermost layer of the earth is the *crust*.

_____ 2. *It* encloses the *other* layers the way an *eggshell* encloses an egg.

_____ 3. *Each* of the other *layers* is *thicker* than the crust.

_____ 4. *Three* kinds of *rock*—igneous, sedimentary, and metamorphic—make up the crust.

_____ 5. The *ocean crust* is dense and rather thin, while the *continental* crust is lighter and *thicker*.

_____ 6. Its average *thickness* is about *five* miles under the ocean's *waters*.

_____ 7. Over millions of years, the *crust* has been shaped into a *pattern* of *flatlands* and *high* mountains.

_____ 8. *Some* of the mountains in the *Himalayan* range soar more than five miles above *sea level*.

_____ 9. The *deepest* area of the *ocean* is at the *bottom* of the *Mariana Trench*, more than thirty-five thousand feet below the surface of the *Pacific Ocean*.

_____ 10. *No one* has ever gone below the crust of the *planet*.

B. Identifying Pronouns, Adjectives, and Abstract and Concrete Nouns

Identify each noun, pronoun, and adjective in the following sentences. Above the word, write *abs.* for *abstract noun*, *con.* for *concrete noun*, *pron.* for *pronoun*, or *adj.* for *adjective*. Do not include the articles *a*, *an*, and *the*.

       adj.   con.   pron. abs.   con.

EX. 1. Every woman had her reasons to travel to the West.

1. Jessie Ann Benton led a comfortable early life.

2. Her father, Thomas Hart Benton, was the Democratic senator from Missouri.

3. In 1841, she married John Charles Frémont, who was assigned to the Topographical Corps of the United States Army.

4. His first job was to map the Dakota country and find the best routes through the frontier.

5. Although Jessie could not accompany John on his journeys, she took a keen interest in them.

6. Jessie helped him turn his account into an interesting report.

7. Later, Jessie got the chance to see the American frontier for herself.

8. The Frémonts settled in California, where they built their first home.

9. In 1856, Jessie helped her husband run as the first Republican candidate for President of the United States.

10. Her personal memoirs and her magazine articles were her contributions to history.

C.   Writing a Poem with Nouns, Pronouns, and Adjectives

Write the letters of your first name vertically on your own paper. Beside each letter, write a line of poetry that begins with that letter and that describes one of your special qualities. Use two nouns, two pronouns, and two adjectives in your poem. Underline and label each noun, pronoun, and adjective. Write *n.* for *noun*, *pron.* for *pronoun*, and *adj.* for *adjective* above the word.

EX.   Dawn . . .

                    adj.
Dares to be <u>different</u>.
                  adj.   n.
Always asks <u>unusual</u> <u>questions</u>.
            pron.   adj. n.
Wonders if <u>she</u> will be admitted to the <u>drama</u> <u>club</u>.
            pron. n.   pron.
Never wants <u>her</u> <u>friends</u> to ignore <u>her</u>.

VERBS

12a A *verb* is a word that expresses an action or a state of being.

EXAMPLES   I **lost** the keys to the house. [action]
Andre **is** an engineer. [state of being]

An *action verb* may express physical action or mental action.

PHYSICAL ACTION   *greet, repair, drive, whisper, decorate*
Who **borrowed** the scissors?

MENTAL ACTION   *recognize, judge, remember, think*
Imagine his surprise!

A *transitive verb* is an action verb that expresses an action directed toward a person or thing.

EXAMPLES   Steve **helped** his brother. [The action of *helped* is directed toward *brother*.]
Please **carry** the boxes. [The action of *carry* is directed toward *boxes*.]

NOTE   Words that receive the action of a transitive verb are called *objects*.

EXAMPLE   The Chinese printed **books** from wooden blocks in A.D. 581.

An *intransitive verb* expresses action (or tells something about the subject) without passing the action to a receiver.

EXAMPLES   The bus **skidded** on the wet pavement.
The woman **spoke** softly to the children.

EXERCISE 1   Identifying Action Verbs

Underline the action verb in each of the following sentences.

EX.   1. Tina <u>bought</u> an airline ticket to Hawaii.

1. The artist creates clay objects.

2. Ernestine invited the twins to her birthday party.

3. Who forgot the picnic basket?

4. The children surprised their mother with balloons.

5. Robin Hood challenged the sheriff to a duel.

6. In 1932, Babe Didrikson broke three Olympic records.

7. Dad worries about you.

8. Think of a name for the puppy.

9. We locked the bicycles in the rack in front of the school.

10. Salvador likes the wild animals best.

EXERCISE 2   Identifying Transitive and Intransitive Verbs

On the line before each sentence below, identify the italicized action verb by writing *trans.* for *transitive* or *intr.* for *intransitive*.

EX.   _intr._ 1. The small boats *pulled* at their anchor lines.

_____ 1. A blanket of warm air *slid* over the mountains.

_____ 2. Thunderstorms *rumbled* along the edge of the storm front.

_____ 3. The wind *nudged* the smaller boats against the floating docks.

_____ 4. The harbor master *checked* the lines of the rowboats.

_____ 5. She *climbed* into one of the dinghies and started the motor.

_____ 6. The boat with its lone passenger *headed* out into the harbor.

_____ 7. Static hissed and *crackled* from the speaker of the boat's radio.

_____ 8. The harbor master *switched* to the channel used by fishing boats in the area.

_____ 9. The announcer *warned* everyone about the approaching storm.

_____ 10. Weather forecasters *predicted* gale-force winds by evening.

EXERCISE 3   Writing Sentences with Transitive and Intransitive Verbs

For each verb below, write two sentences on your own paper. In one sentence, use the verb as a transitive verb and underline its object. In the other, use the verb as an intransitive verb. Label each usage.

EX.   1. play
      1. My brother plays the oboe in the school orchestra. (transitive)
          On Saturday, Tanisha plays at Symphony Hall. (intransitive)

   1. drive   2. eat   3. leave   4. speak   5. begin

LINKING VERBS

12b A *linking verb* links, or connects, the subject with a noun, a pronoun, or an adjective in the predicate.

EXAMPLES Thomas Jefferson **was** the third president of the United States. [Thomas Jefferson = president]
The best hitter on the team **is** she! [hitter = she]
The grapefruit **tastes** sour. [sour grapefruit]
Maylin **appeared** hungry. [hungry Maylin]

Commonly Used Linking Verbs			
Forms of *Be*	am	be	being	was
	are	been	is	were
Other Verbs	appear	grow	seem	stay
	become	look	smell	taste
	feel	remain	sound	turn

Most linking verbs, except the forms of *be* and *seem*, may also be used as action verbs. Whether a verb is being used to link words or to express action depends on its meaning in a sentence.

LINKING   Yesterday, the weather **turned** colder.
ACTION   Jason **turned** the handle of the doorknob.

LINKING   Her voice **sounded** stern.
ACTION   The sentry **sounded** the alarm.

LINKING   Her hands **remained** steady throughout the ordeal.
ACTION   My brother **remained** in the car.

EXERCISE 4   Identifying Linking Verbs

Underline the linking verb in each of the following sentences. Then circle the words that the verb links.

EX.   1. The (variety) of animal life in the park is (remarkable).

1. Yellowstone National Park is home to many kinds of animals.

2. It was the first national park in the United States.

3. Wild animals remain free in this protected wilderness.

101

4. Lodgepole pine trees grow tall and thin, with few branches.

5. They are the most common trees in the park.

6. Visitors to the park are eager for a look at Old Faithful, the geyser.

7. Everyone seems awed by the display.

8. In winter, the buzz of snowmobiles sounds loud in the quiet forest.

9. Near the Gallatin River, a lone bull moose appears quite unconcerned.

10. The mountain air feels unusually raw and cold on this summer day.

EXERCISE 5 Identifying Action Verbs and Linking Verbs

Underline the verb in each of the following sentences. Then, on the line before each sentence, identify the verb as an action verb or a linking verb by writing *a.v.* for *action verb* or *l.v.* for *linking verb*.

EX.   _l.v._   1. The great horned owl <u>looks</u> fierce.

_____   1. The owl is one of nature's most unusual birds.

_____   2. Over five hundred species of owls live in the world.

_____   3. Owls often build nests in old barns and deserted buildings.

_____   4. Owls have sharp talons and short, hooked beaks.

_____   5. Their large eyes point almost directly forward.

_____   6. An owl turns its head completely around sometimes.

_____   7. The owl moves at the slightest noise.

_____   8. Like all birds of prey, they feed on small animals, insects, and other birds.

_____   9. During daylight hours, owls remain still.

_____   10. With the approach of darkness, owls grow more restless.

_____   11. Even total darkness is usually no problem for these birds.

_____   12. At night in the forest, their ears hear the sounds of scurrying animals.

_____   13. An owl can see in dim light.

_____   14. I know owls live in the woods near my house.

_____   15. They make noises after dark.

HELPING VERBS

12c A *verb phrase* consists of a main verb preceded by at least one helping verb (also called an *auxiliary verb*).

EXAMPLES   A storm **is approaching.** [The helping verb is *is*, and the main verb is *approaching*.]

Thunder **could be heard** in the distance. [The helping verbs are *could* and *be*, and the main verb is *heard*.]

The children **should have taken** their umbrellas. [The helping verbs are *should* and *have*, and the main verb is *taken*.]

The baseball game **will be canceled** because of the storm. [The helping verbs are *will* and *be*, and the main verb is *canceled*.]

Commonly Used Helping Verbs			
Forms of *Be*	am are	be been	being is	was were
Forms of *Do*	do	does	did	
Forms of *Have*	have	has	had	
Other Helping Verbs	can could	may might	must shall	should will	would

Some helping verbs may also be used as main verbs.

EXAMPLES   I can **be** ready in five minutes.
We **have** a new substitute teacher.

Sometimes the verb phrase is interrupted by another part of speech. In most cases, the interrupter is an adverb. In a question, however, the subject often interrupts the verb phrase.

EXAMPLES   The moon **will** completely **block** the sun.
Were you **listening** to the radio this morning?
He **did** not **know** the answer. [or **didn't**]

Notice that *not*, as in the last example, is never part of a verb phrase.

EXERCISE 6   Identifying Verb Phrases

Underline the verb phrases in each sentence in the paragraph below. Circle the helping verb or verbs in each phrase. [Note: Some sentences may contain more than one verb phrase.]

EX.   [1] The inventor of the match (had) stumbled onto an interesting idea.

[1] People have used fire for thousands of years. [2] The idea might seem strange, but until recent years, fire could not be made easily. [3] People would rub sticks together, or they would strike flint on metal. [4] Inventors had long been aware of the problem and had been working for years on a solution, but without much success. [5] Finally, in 1827, the match was invented. [6] Until the mid-1800s, matches were made by hand. [7] Not long after that, matchmaking machines were developed. [8] Today, wooden matchsticks are cut from poplar wood. [9] Then the tips of the matchsticks are dipped in chemicals. [10] Because the entire process takes only a few seconds, some factories can produce more than a million matches an hour.

EXERCISE 7   Writing Verb Phrases

On your own paper, write complete sentences, using the verb phrases below.

EX.   1. was cooking
      1. Rafael was cooking when his sister walked into the kitchen.

1. have walked
2. could be
3. were made
4. have been working
5. was born

6. has photographed
7. can mend
8. was making
9. has experienced
10. can be seen

ADVERBS

12d An *adverb* is a word used to modify a verb, an adjective, or another adverb.

An adverb tells *where, when, how,* or *to what extent* (*how much* or *how long*).

Where	When
The spider hid **nearby**.	I visited my aunt **today**.
The children stayed **inside**.	Nuru **often** takes the bus.
How	**To What Extent**
The horses moved **slowly** to the starting gate.	The boat **almost** sank.
The dancer twirled **gracefully**.	You should **rarely** talk with your mouth full of food.

MODIFYING VERBS	**Soon** everyone went **inside**. [The adverb *soon* tells *when* everyone went, and the adverb *inside* tells *where* everyone went.]
	Peter tried to work **alone**. [The adverb *alone* tells *how* Peter wanted *to work*.]
MODIFYING ADJECTIVES	The test was **rather** hard. [The adverb *rather* modifies the adjective *hard*, telling *how hard* the test was.]
	Too many students failed the test. [The adverb *too* modifies the adjective *many*, telling *how many* students failed the test.]
MODIFYING ADVERBS	**Quite** suddenly, the meeting ended. [The adverb *quite* modifies the adverb *suddenly*, telling *how suddenly* the meeting ended.]
	The cars moved **somewhat** sluggishly. [The adverb *somewhat* modifies the adverb *sluggishly*, telling *how sluggishly* the cars moved.]

Often an adverb is simply an adjective with *–ly* added.

ADJECTIVE	careful	easy	loud	real
ADVERB	carefully	easily	loudly	really

EXERCISE 8   Identifying Adverbs and the Words They Modify

Underline the adverbs in the following sentences, and draw an arrow to the word each adverb modifies.

EX. 1. Have you ever wanted to visit Puerto Rico?

1. Tomás and Rosa recently visited their aunt in Puerto Rico.

2. Because of the surrounding mountains, the plane had a fairly difficult approach path for its landing in San Juan.

3. The children were relieved when the plane landed safely.

4. Everyone on the plane clapped loudly for the pilot.

5. Rosa wanted to go quickly to the beach for a swim.

6. Tomás was quite excited about visiting Fort El Morro again.

7. "I want to do so many things with you," said their aunt.

8. For the first twenty-four hours of their visit, Rosa and Tomás decided to rest quietly.

9. During the rest of the trip, they usually did something different each day.

10. Everyone was completely satisfied with the vacation.

11. Tomás often reads books about Puerto Rico.

12. He searches everywhere for photographs of the country.

13. He and Rosa easily recognize photographs of San Juan.

14. Rosa really enjoys the mountains of Puerto Rico.

15. "Do you know what Puerto Rico's highest peak is?" Tomás asked yesterday.

16. "It is Cerro de Punta, and we saw it on our vacation," Rosa answered excitedly.

17. They thought it was more beautiful than other mountains.

18. It stands beautifully in Puerto Rico's central mountain range.

19. Puerto Rico is quite mountainous.

20. Tomás and Rosa can hardly wait to return.

REVIEW EXERCISE

A. Labeling Action Verbs and Linking Verbs

Underline the verbs and verb phrases in the sentences below. Then, on the line before the sentence, identify each verb or verb phrase by writing *a.v.* for *action verb* or *l.v.* for *linking verb*.

EX. ___l.v.___ 1. The book about cities looked interesting.

_____ 1. A city is a large settlement.

_____ 2. The first urban centers developed in Mesopotamia and then in the Nile Valley of Egypt.

_____ 3. Many of these early cities were centers of trade.

_____ 4. By the fifth century B.C., Athens, Greece, had become a powerful city-state.

_____ 5. Rome's population may have reached one million around A.D. 100.

_____ 6. Most Romans lived in shabby apartment buildings.

_____ 7. People made these dwellings out of wood and plaster.

_____ 8. During the Middle Ages, walls often surrounded the cities.

_____ 9. Since the Industrial Revolution, the number of cities has grown dramatically.

_____ 10. By the year 2000, cities will be home to the vast majority of people in developed countries.

B. Writing Adverbs

On each line in the following sentences, use the clues given in parentheses to write an adverb that completes the sentence.

EX. 1. In the afternoon, the beach was __quite__ (to what extent) crowded.

1. _____ (when) Sora and I went to the beach.

2. We found a _____ (to what extent) deserted spot near the dunes.

3. We _____ (how) looked over the area.

4. Nearby, some children were _____ (how) building a sandcastle.

5. In the bay, there were _____ (how much) high waves.

6. They pounded the shore _____ (how much).

7. _____ (to what extent) few swimmers stepped into the rough surf.

8. Some _____ (to what extent) large sea gulls stood on the rocks in the distance.

9. Other sea gulls soared_____ (how) on air currents.

10. Sora _____ (how) walked towards some sea gulls.

11. She _____ (to what extent) wanted to feed them.

12. She moved _____ (where), and the birds seemed to look at her.

13. They flew_____ (where).

14. "Birds are _____ (how often) timid," I told her.

15. The air was _____ (how) growing colder.

16. We _____ (how) zipped our jackets.

17. The tide moved in and_____ (how) knocked down the children's sandcastle.

18. "I wonder if it will rain_____ (when)," I said.

19. "The clouds are _____ (how much) grey, so it might," Sora said.

20. We _____ (how) headed home.

C. Writing a Report

Your club, Students for a Better Environment, has just completed its six-month project to clean up and beautify the community. You have been asked to write a brief report of the activities and results of the project. On your own paper, write ten complete sentences to include in your report. At least once, insert *be* as a helping verb and as a linking verb. Underline the verb or verb phrase in each sentence.

EX.   1. Valerie and Misha recycled their families' newspapers, glass bottles, and aluminum cans.

       2. Two maple trees were planted in front of the post office.

PREPOSITIONS

12e **A *preposition* is a word that shows the relationship of a noun or a pronoun to another word in the sentence.**

Notice how a change in the preposition changes the relationship between *cat* and *tree* in each of the following examples.

EXAMPLES   The cat **in** the tree is mine.
The cat **beside** the tree is mine.
The cat **in front of** the tree is mine.

Prepositions that consist of more than one word (for example, *in front of*) are called *compound prepositions*.

Commonly Used Prepositions				
aboard	because of	during	near	to
about	before	except	next to	toward
above	behind	for	of	under
according to	below	from	off	underneath
across	beneath	in	on	until
after	beside	in addition to	out	onto
against	besides	in front of	out of	up
along	between	inside	over	upon
along with	beyond	in spite of	past	with
among	but (except)	instead of	since	within
around	by	into	through	without
aside from	down	like	throughout	

Some words may be used as either prepositions or adverbs. To tell an adverb from a preposition, remember that a preposition is always followed by a noun or pronoun called its object.

ADVERB   Sheep grazed in the field **beyond.**
PREPOSITION   Sheep grazed in the field **beyond the fence.**

ADVERB   Walk **around** to the back of the store.
PREPOSITION   Walk slowly **around the track.**

EXERCISE 9 Writing Prepositions

Write a preposition on each line to complete the sentences below. Use a variety of prepositions.

EX. 1. A blizzard descended ___on___ the city ___without___ warning.

1. Early _____ the morning, the children raced _____ the window.

2. A heavy blanket _____ snow lay _____ the streets and sidewalks.

3. Adela shouted _____ joy _____ the sight.

4. Immediately, she turned _____ the television set and listened _____ the school cancellations.

5. The newscaster announced that school had been canceled _____ the day _____ the storm.

6. _____ breakfast, Adela and her brother Diego grabbed their jackets _____ the closet and raced _____ the stairs.

7. A snowplow was clearing away the snow _____ the street _____ their apartment building.

8. Parked cars were buried _____ an avalanche of snow.

9. Grim-faced pedestrians plodded _____ the drifts.

10. _____ the bitter cold and high winds, the children delighted _____ the first blizzard of the season.

EXERCISE 10 Writing Sentences with Adverbs and Prepositions

Use each of the words below in two sentences, first as an adverb and then as a preposition. Underline and label each use of the designated words. Write the sentences on your own paper.

EX. 1. behind
    1. I left my book behind. (adverb)
       Workers piled rocks behind the shed. (preposition)

  1. before   2. aboard   3. below   4. inside   5. up
  6. along   7. near   8. before   9. in   10. out

CONJUNCTIONS AND INTERJECTIONS

12f   A *conjunction* is a word used to join words or groups of words.

Coordinating conjunctions connect words or groups of words used in the same way.

Coordinating Conjunctions
and   but   or   nor   for   so   yet

EXAMPLES   Kai **or** Samuel will work in the booth. [two nouns]
My horse is slow **but** steady. [two adjectives]
We rode beyond the pasture **and** through the woods. [two prepositional phrases]
The baby was hungry, **so** Dad fed him. [two clauses]

For is used as a conjunction if it connects groups of words that are clauses. On all other occasions, *for* is used as a preposition.

CONJUNCTION   Everyone liked her, **for** she was kind and understanding.
PREPOSITION   Ruby reached **for** the apple.

Correlative conjunctions are pairs of conjunctions that connect words or groups of words used in the same way.

Correlative Conjunctions		
both . . . and	neither . . . nor	not only . . . but also
either . . . or	whether . . . or	

EXAMPLES   **Both** Jupiter **and** Saturn have rings. [two nouns]
Please drive me **either** to the bus stop **or** to the train station. [two prepositional phrases]
Not only did Luís drop the ball, **but** he **also** fell into the dugout. [two clauses]

EXERCISE 11   Identifying Coordinating Conjunctions and Correlative Conjunctions

Underline the conjunctions in the paragraph below. Then, above the underlined word, identify each conjunction as coordinating or correlative by writing *coor.* for *coordinating* or *corr.* for *correlative* above the chosen word.

EX.   1. Did Romans have toys *coor.* <u>or</u> games?

[1] Information about children's playthings in ancient Rome is interesting whether you still play with toys or consider yourself too old for them. [2] Not only did children in ancient Rome have toys to play with, but they also had many of the same kinds of toys youngsters play with today. [3] Did you know that babies played with squeaky animals and that Roman children had miniature carts and horses? [4] We also know that board games were popular, for many have been found in the ruins of Roman dwellings. [5] *Robbers* and *Twelve Lines* were two of the most popular board games.

12g   An *interjection* is a word used to express emotion. It does not have a grammatical relation to other words in the sentence.

An *interjection* is set off from the rest of the sentence by an exclamation point or a comma.

EXAMPLES   **Yikes!** That water is cold.
Aha! I knew you were hiding there.
Oh, you always know the answer.

EXERCISE 12   Writing Interjections

On your own paper, write five sentences to describe your reaction to the news that you have just won a million dollars. In each sentence, use a different interjection from the list below.

EX.   1. Great!
Great! I have a lot of ideas about how to spend this money.

1. Wow!   2. Hurrah!   3. My,   4. Oh,   5. Surprise!

CHAPTER REVIEW

A. Identifying Different Parts of Speech

Identify each italicized word or word group in the following sentences. Write *v.* for *verb, adv.* for *adverb, prep.* for *preposition, conj.* for *conjunction,* and *intj.* for *interjection* on the line before each sentence.

EX. <u>v. ; prep.</u> 1. We *have* been reading a collection *of* fables.

_____ 1. The bus *never* arrived, *and* we were late for class.

_____ 2. *Well,* my friend, your troubles are *finally* over.

_____ 3. The light above the table was *neither* old *nor* valuable.

_____ 4. *Both* Mac *and* his brother were hiding *behind* the shed.

_____ 5. *Yikes!* I *should* not *have taken* that advanced course.

_____ 6. *According to* scientists, the earliest forms of life before the dinosaurs *possibly* were in the sea.

_____ 7. The sailboat capsized, *but* fortunately no one *drowned.*

_____ 8. Which *is* fiercer, the leopard *or* the lion?

_____ 9. Last night, local painters and sculptors *were* honored *at* the museum's opening.

_____ 10. The fruit were *carefully* inspected *for* bruises.

B. Identifying Action Verbs and Linking Verbs

In the paragraph below, underline the action verbs and verb phrases once. Underline the linking verbs and verb phrases twice.

EX. [1] According to the story, the coyotes <u><u>seemed</u></u> happy that Pecos Bill <u>lived</u> with them.

[1] They say that one day Bill was riding in a wagon when it hit a rock.

[2] The jolt sent him up in the air, but he did not become frightened. [3] He landed in the middle of a pack of coyotes, but he remained calm. [4] After that, Bill stayed with the pack and joined them in their hunts. [5] To most people the coyotes appeared wild, but to Pecos Bill they were gentle.

C. Identifying Adverbs and Prepositions

Underline the adverbs and prepositions in the following sentences. Above each underlined word, write *adv.* for *adverb* and *prep.* for *preposition*.

EX. 1. Today manatees are on the endangered species list.

[adv. is written above "Today"; prep. is written above "on"]

1. Manatees usually live in shallow water, among thick sea grasses.

2. They regularly feed on shallow-water plants and vegetation beneath the water.

3. Manatees are very important because of their eating habits.

4. They often keep waterways clear of thick vegetation.

5. Generally, manatees move slowly along the surface of the water.

6. They often live alone or in herds of fifteen to twenty.

7. Tired sailors would mistake manatees for mermaids, in spite of a manatee's somewhat odd appearance.

8. A manatee has two small flippers, as well as one large flipper at the end of a rather round body.

9. This animal also has a square snout with whiskers.

10. Many manatees are injured yearly by motor boats.

D. Writing Sentences

On your own paper, write two sentences in which each of the words below is used as the part of speech given in parentheses. Underline the words in the sentences, and write their parts of speech after the sentences.

EX. 1. wish (*noun* and *verb*)
    After you blow out the candles, make a wish. (noun)
    I wish David were here. (verb)

1. on (*adverb* and *preposition*)
2. taste (*noun* and *verb*)
3. well (*interjection* and *adverb*)
4. my (*interjection* and *pronoun*)
5. few (*pronoun* and *adjective*)
6. for (*conjunction* and *preposition*)
7. long (*adjective* and *adverb*)
8. green (*noun* and *adjective*)
9. down (*adverb* and *preposition*)
10. run (*noun* and *verb*)
11. over (*adverb* and *preposition*)
12. catch (*noun* and *verb*)
13. house (*noun* and *adjective*)
14. terrific (*adjective* and *interjection*)
15. ring (*noun* and *verb*)
16. off (*adverb* and *preposition*)
17. swim (*noun* and *verb*)
18. water (*noun* and *adjective*)
19. loud (*adjective* and *adverb*)
20. below (*adverb* and *preposition*)

DIRECT OBJECTS

A *complement* is a word or a group of words that completes the meaning of a verb.

Every sentence has a subject and a verb. Often a verb also needs a complement to make the sentence complete. A complement may be a *noun*, a *pronoun*, or an *adjective*.

13a A *direct object* is one type of complement. It is a noun or a pronoun that receives the action of the verb or shows the result of the action. A direct object tells *what* or *whom* after an action verb.

EXAMPLES   Ryan smelled **gasoline**. [The noun *gasoline* receives the action of the verb *smelled* and tells *what* Ryan smelled.]
Did the horse jump the **fence**? [The noun *fence* receives the action of the verb *Did jump* and tells *what* the horse jumped.]
Benjamin saw **us** at the pottery exhibit. [The pronoun *us* receives the action of the verb *saw* and tells *whom* Benjamin saw.]

Direct objects may be compound.

EXAMPLES   Mrs. Bradley washed the **car** and the **trailer**.
We brought our **paper**, our **pencils**, and our **books**.

A direct object is never in a prepositional phrase.

DIRECT OBJECT   Juan wrote a long **letter**.
OBJECT OF A   Juan wrote with a gold **pen**.
PREPOSITION

EXERCISE 1   Identifying Action Verbs and Direct Objects

In the following sentences, underline the action verbs once and the direct objects twice.

EX.   1. These animals <u>make</u> <u>nests</u> in hollow trees.

1. The tornado took the roof off our house.

2. Will you put the groceries on the counter?

3. The singer gave free tapes to several lucky people.

4. Payat will organize the class into four equal teams.

5. Have the workers cleaned the recreation hall yet?

6. In the dark, owls catch mice and other small animals.

7. In short races, Paula always outruns us.

8. Ryan photographed a huge flock of pink flamingos.

9. During the summer, my teacher writes mystery novels.

10. At graduation, the coach distributed awards to six players.

11. On his vacation, my neighbor Ben met the Queen of England.

12. At the restaurant last night, we ate our favorite dinner.

13. Four hundred soldiers protected the island all week.

14. Did she really swim the channel?

15. My brother would always read us scary stories.

EXERCISE 2   Writing Direct Objects

On your own paper, add a different direct object and any other words you might need to make a complete sentence of each of the groups of words below. Underline the direct objects.

> EX. 1. men asked
>   1. The men asked several <u>questions</u>.

	SUBJECT	VERB		SUBJECT	VERB
1.	class	built	14.	Mona	heard
2.	runner	wore	15.	they	bought
3.	crowd	cheers	16.	nobody	believed
4.	hurricane	destroyed	17.	Alfredo	cooks
5.	gardener	planted	18.	teacher	counted
6.	Domingo	installed	19.	brother	returned
7.	Val	repairs	20.	bear	climbed
8.	animals	know	21.	song	began
9.	guide	followed	22.	team	won
10.	we	met	23.	submarine	sunk
11.	lumberjack	swung	24.	Sharon	writes
12.	Simon	thanked	25.	everyone	likes
13.	knife	cuts			

INDIRECT OBJECTS

> **13b** An *indirect object* is a noun or a pronoun that comes between the action verb and the direct object and tells *to what* or *to whom* or *for what* or *for whom* the action of the verb is done.
>
> EXAMPLES   I showed the **class** my invention. [The noun *class* tells *to whom* I showed my invention.]
> Will the farmer pick **us** some fresh strawberries? [The pronoun *us* tells *for whom* the farmer will pick strawberries.]
>
> A sentence with an indirect object always has a direct object. Like a direct object, an indirect object may be compound. And, like a direct object, an indirect object is never in a prepositional phrase.
>
> EXAMPLES   Josh sent **Tim** and **me** invitations. [compound indirect object]
> Josh sent invitations to **Tim** and **me**. [object of a preposition]
>
> **REFERENCE NOTE:** For more information on prepositional phrases, see page 125.

EXERCISE 3 Identifying Direct Objects and Indirect Objects

In the following sentences, underline the direct objects once and the indirect objects twice.

EX. 1. The pitcher threw <u><u>her</u></u> the <u>ball</u>.

1. On Tuesday afternoons, Tranh teaches my sister juggling.

2. The audience gave the performer a standing ovation.

3. Two officers told us the good news.

4. My brother ordered Lenore and me some lemonade.

5. Later, the teacher will hand you a reading list.

6. The aide brought us several calculators.

7. My mother sends her friends birthday cards every year.

8. Sometimes my cousin Minnie cooks us a wonderful dinner.

9. Will loaned me his binoculars for the game.

10. Our coach taught my sisters the dance step.

11. A local business gave the school two computers.

12. My swimming teacher tossed me a towel.

13. Mrs. Thundercloud sent Pedro and me pictures of her family.

14. The Parent-Teacher Association bought the school new bleachers for the gym.

15. Our principal, Ms. Chong, showed everyone the new mural.

16. Before next week our teacher will tell us the names of the winners.

17. Will you hand Mara and me the new spoons?

18. After school I brought Kelly her assignment and her books.

19. Yes, Michaela mailed her sister the poster.

20. In study hall I loaned Zeke some notebook paper.

EXERCISE 4   Revising Sentences to Include Indirect Objects

On your own paper, rewrite each sentence below so that it includes the italicized information as the indirect object. Underline the indirect object in your revised sentence.

EX.   1. Michael will teach his song *to the chorus*.
   1. Michael will teach the chorus his song.

1. Uncle Diego bought the concert tickets *for my sister and me*.
2. The assistant brought the sheet music *to the pianist*.
3. The program director told the main story line *to our group*.
4. My uncle promised a backstage tour *to us*.
5. The tour guide gave bowls of poi *to us* to sample.
6. Many people gave advice *to my father*.
7. The neighbors brought salad *to Barbara and Bill* at the barbeque.
8. An admirer in the audience sent flowers *to Rita*.
9. The grocer sold the eggs *to my aunt* at a lower price.
10. We traded our boat *to Joe* for his cabin.

PREDICATE NOMINATIVES

A *subject complement* completes the meaning of a linking verb and identifies or describes the subject. There are two kinds of subject complements—the *predicate nominative* and the *predicate adjective*.

☞ **REFERENCE NOTE:** For more information about linking verbs, see page 101.

13c **A *predicate nominative* is a noun or a pronoun that follows a linking verb and identifies the subject or refers to it.**

EXAMPLES   His best-known invention was the braille **alphabet**. [The noun *alphabet* follows the linking verb *was* and identifies the subject *invention*.]

My cousin has become a **wife**, a **mother**, and a **doctor**. [The nouns *wife, mother,* and *doctor* follow the linking verb *has become* and identify the subject *cousin*.]

Like subjects and objects, predicate nominatives never appear in prepositional phrases.

EXAMPLE   My favorite was the **story** about the chopsticks. [The noun *story* identifies the subject *favorite*. The noun *chopsticks* is the object of the preposition *about*.]

EXERCISE 5   Identifying Predicate Nominatives

In the sentences below, underline the linking verbs once and the predicate nominatives twice.

EX.   1. The Great Wall of China is an amazing creation!

1. Marco Polo was an Italian explorer.

2. Polo became a friend of the emperor Kublai Khan.

3. Kublai Khan was an extremely powerful ruler.

4. He was Genghis Khan's grandson.

5. Marco Polo became a government official in Yang-chau.

6. He was once mayor of a city in China.

7. One surprise for Polo was China's paper money.

8. Marco Polo was also a writer.

9. His journey must have been a great adventure!

10. Marco Polo is one of my favorite characters from history.

11. My mother was not a good student in high school.

12. In college she and a geology student became classmates and good friends.

13. Later on, Mother was a teaching assistant.

14. My mother is now a geologist for the state.

15. My father is a mathematician for a computer company.

16. My father always has been a fan of computers.

17. I am becoming a competent programmer.

18. Dad and I are friendly rivals in several computer games.

19. Next year I will be a member of our school's computer club.

20. I will become a biologist someday.

21. Both of my parents are scientists.

22. They have been constant readers all their lives.

23. My parents became husband and wife twenty years ago.

24. Our family is always the first at the science fair.

25. My name is Frederick.

PREDICATE ADJECTIVES

> **13d** A *predicate adjective* is an adjective that follows a linking verb and describes the subject.
>
> EXAMPLES   The storm is **weaker** today. [The adjective *weaker* follows the linking verb *is* and describes the subject *storm*.]
> Hisako appeared **tired** yesterday. [The adjective *tired* follows the linking verb *appeared* and describes the subject *Hisako*.]
>
> Predicate adjectives may be compound.
>
> EXAMPLE   One cat seemed **older** and **quieter** than the other. [The adjectives *older* and *quieter* follow the linking verb *seemed* and describe the subject *cat*.]

EXERCISE 6   Identifying Predicate Adjectives

Underline the predicate adjectives in the sentences below.

EX.   1.   The fish looks very <u>fresh</u> today.

1.   Saburo became quite hungry last evening.

2.   This restaurant seems clean and airy.

3.   The smoke from the fire smelled spicy to us.

4.   The fish in lemon sauce tastes tart and sweet at the same time.

5.   Latrice appeared surprised but pleased by the variety of food.

6.   My fingers were sticky and slightly stained from the stuffed grape leaves.

7.   The toppings for the curry in those ceramic bowls look delicious.

8.   That thick soup will stay hot for a long time.

9.   The voices in the next booth sounded happy.

10.   After such a big meal, we were full and sleepy.

EXERCISE 7 Identifying Linking Verbs and Predicate Adjectives

In the sentences below, underline the linking verbs once and the predicate adjectives twice. Predicate adjectives may be compound.

EX.   1. The hikers <u>were</u> <u><u>eager</u></u> to begin their climb up the mountain.

1. The scenery along the trail was beautiful.

2. The shade of the trees felt cool and wonderful.

3. The trail mix and spring water tasted great.

4. Above the timberline, the rocks were almost completely bare.

5. The hikers felt proud when they reached the summit.

6. The wilderness around the mountain appeared endless.

7. The view from the top was spectacular.

8. The clouds swirling among the pine trees seemed magical.

9. As the hikers returned to camp, their backpacks grew heavier, or so they thought.

10. At the end of the climb, they were all quite tired.

11. Our counselor was experienced at telling scary tales to campers.

12. By the campfire, he looked ghostlike himself.

13. His voice sounded weird.

14. "The Monkey's Paw" was really frightening.

15. The plot seemed real.

16. Our eyes grew wider and wider.

17. Even the night appeared darker.

18. Suddenly we all seemed chilled to the bone.

19. We felt sure something terrible would happen.

20. Later, we were ready to climb snugly into bed.

CHAPTER REVIEW

A. Identifying Complements

Underline the complement in each sentence below. On the line before the sentence, write *d.o.* for *direct object*, *p.n.* for *predicate nominative*, or *p.a.* for *predicate adjective*. Complements may be compound.

EX.   _p.a._   1. The islands in the Caribbean are <u>beautiful</u> this time of year!

_____ 1. *Carnaval* appears very lively this year.

_____ 2. The music sounds loud and exciting tonight!

_____ 3. Marchers in the parade throw treats to the crowd.

_____ 4. February is the best month for a visit.

_____ 5. We visited the museum and an old castle on Saturday.

_____ 6. This hotel is a landmark for travelers.

_____ 7. Our tour guide brought a delicious fruit salad.

_____ 8. Ocean currents are dangerous on this side of the island.

_____ 9. Oscar and Than played water polo during their vacation.

_____ 10. Their friend Paula is one of the best swimmers on the island.

_____ 11. Scuba divers sometimes find interesting relics in nearby caves.

_____ 12. It is usually too hot for tennis here.

_____ 13. Roger and Jimmy toured the ancient fortress.

_____ 14. Seashells were more plentiful last year.

_____ 15. This is definitely the island of my dreams!

B. Writing with Complements

For each of the following descriptions, write a sentence on your own paper that contains the complement described. Then underline that complement.

EX.   1. a question with an indirect object
1. Did you give <u>Brynna</u> the book?

1. an exclamatory sentence with a predicate nominative

2. a declarative sentence with a direct object
3. a declarative sentence with a compound direct object
4. a question with a predicate adjective
5. an imperative sentence with an indirect object

C.   Writing a Letter About the First Thanksgiving Feast

You were present at the first Thanksgiving feast at Plymouth Colony. The people you met, including Chief Massasoit and his friends, were unforgettable. The food was, too. Now, on your own paper, write a friendly letter about the event to a friend in England.

1. Use an encyclopedia or history book to research the first Thanksgiving. List people who attended, and jot down notes about each person. Discover what food was served. Describe how it might have looked, smelled, and tasted.

2. Write fifteen sentences to describe the first Thanksgiving as if you had been there. Underline the direct objects, the indirect objects, and subject complements that you use.

EX.

> December 1, 1621
>
> Dear Mary,
>
>   Our Thanksgiving was a great success! Massasoit and a large number of his people arrived. They were very generous to us. They brought several deer, which gave us enough meat for a month.
>
>   Your friend,
>
>   Susan

PREPOSITIONAL PHRASES

A *phrase* is a group of related words that is used as a single part of speech and does not contain a verb and its subject.

VERB PHRASE   might have been seen [no subject]
PREPOSITIONAL PHRASE   across the dirt road [no subject or verb]

14a   A *prepositional phrase* is a group of words consisting of a preposition, a noun or pronoun that serves as the object of the preposition, and any modifiers of that object.

EXAMPLES   Vanessa and her brother walked **in front of the stage**. [The noun *stage* is the object of the preposition *in front of. The* is an adjective modifying *stage*.]
The children **on the bus** waved **to us**. [The noun *bus* is the object of the preposition *on. The* is an adjective modifying *bus*. The pronoun *us* is the object of the preposition *to*.]
Inside the small cabin the hikers found shelter. [The adjectives *the* and *small* modify the object *cabin* and are part of the prepositional phrase.]

The object of a preposition may be compound.

EXAMPLE   Francis stood **between Max and me**. [*Max* and *me* are both objects of the preposition *between*.]

EXERCISE 1   Identifying Prepositional Phrases

Underline all the prepositional phrases in the following paragraph.

EX.   [1] In April of 1992, new guidelines for our daily diets were released by the Department of Agriculture.

[1] The Cirque du Soleil, or Circus of the Sun, came to our town.

[2] It came from its home in Montreal. [3] Unlike other circuses, this circus had no animal acts. [4] But you could see an acrobat on a tightrope, a clown with a painted face, and jugglers with colorful costumes. [5] During its two-year North American tour, the circus

stopped at twelve cities. [6] Once the circus reached a new city,

organizing everything under the tent took a week. [7] In addition, the

manager found sleeping quarters for the forty-two members. [8] He

also provided meals for them throughout their stay. [9] Keeping the

performers in good health was important. [10] On some tours,

performers needed extra rest between performances.

EXERCISE 2   Identifying Prepositions and Their Objects

Find the prepositional phrase in each of the following sentences. Underline
the prepositional phrase once and the object of the preposition twice.

EX.   1.   Studies show that exercise along with a nutritious diet promotes
good health.

1.   Everyone benefits from exercise.

2.   The most beneficial exercise for the heart is aerobic exercise.

3.   Recently, many studies have been conducted about the benefits
of exercise.

4.   According to these studies, exercise apparently slows the
aging process.

5.   One study at Boston's Harvard Medical School demonstrated
this fact.

6.   Researchers in California studied the effects of exercise on six
hundred women.

7.   These researchers announced in February 1991 that moderate
exercise can lower blood pressure.

8.   Besides high blood pressure, exercise can also help prevent a form
of diabetes.

9.   People of all ages should include exercise in their schedules.

10.   Before each workout, people should perform flexibility exercises.

ADJECTIVE PHRASES

14b An *adjective phrase* is a prepositional phrase that modifies a noun or a pronoun.

Adjective phrases answer the same questions that adjectives answer: *What kind? Which one? How many? How much?*

EXAMPLES   A book **of jokes** might make a good gift. [The phrase modifies the noun *book*, telling *what kind* of book.]

Those three musicians are the ones **on the magazine cover.** [The phrase modifies the pronoun *ones*, telling *which* ones the three musicians are.]

The young boy **in that picture on the wall** is my grandfather. [The phrase *in that picture* modifies the noun *boy*. The phrase *on the wall* modifies the object *picture*.]

Is that your car **with the flat tire in the driveway?** [The phrases *with the flat tire* and *in the driveway* modify the noun *car*.]

EXERCISE 3 Identifying Adjective Phrases

Underline all adjective phrases in the following paragraph.

EX.   [1] The lights <u>in the hall</u> and <u>in the theater</u> flickered and dimmed.

[1] The members of the orchestra took their places on the stage and began tuning their instruments. [2] One woman with a violin began playing musical scales. [3] The other musicians around her also made sure their instruments were tuned and ready. [4] When the conductor rapped his baton, the people in the audience immediately grew quiet. [5] Soon, the lovely strains of a composition by Kimi Itoh, a music student from Westfield Music Conservatory, filled the air. [6] The first concert of her music had begun. [7] When the music stopped, there was a moment of silence. [8] Then Kimi heard the loud applause

from the crowd. [9] Her professional career in music had started.

[10] She has never forgotten that special day in her life.

EXERCISE 4   Identifying Adjective Phrases and the Words They Modify

In the sentences below, underline each adjective phrase once. Then draw an arrow from each phrase to the word it modifies.

EX.   1. A representative from the park service gave a lecture about sea turtles.

1. One beach in South Carolina is a nesting place for sea turtles.

2. The nest at a high spot on the beach interested many people.

3. The people in the cottage beside the dunes saw turtle tracks.

4. Tracks from the sea meant a turtle had made a nest.

5. The nest under the sand had a batch of one hundred eggs.

6. Six species of sea turtles have bony shells.

7. The waves from the crashing sea bring the turtles ashore.

8. Female sea turtles on land are almost helpless.

9. The sea turtles in Canadian waters are probably leatherbacks.

10. The hornlike formations on sea turtles' backs are called scutes.

EXERCISE 5   Writing Sentences with Adjective Phrases

Use each adjective phrase below in a sentence of your own. Write the sentence on your own paper. Then underline the phrase, and put brackets around the word it modifies.

EX.   1. under our porch
    1. The [dog] under our porch belongs to our neighbors.

1. on the beach blanket
2. along the edge
3. of Mexico
4. between the two tall buildings
5. for the delivery truck
6. beside the tape recorder
7. with six arms
8. under the hardwood floor
9. around John
10. down the road

ADVERB PHRASES

14c **An *adverb phrase* is a prepositional phrase that modifies a verb, an adjective, or an adverb.**

An adverb phrase tells *how, when, where, why,* or *to what extent* (such as *how long, how many,* or *how far*).

EXAMPLES   My mother looks **like my uncle**. [The phrase modifies the verb *looks*, telling *how* my mother looks.]
They found the note **in an old book**. [The phrase modifies the verb *found*, telling *where* they found the note.]
Later **in the afternoon**, the storm brought high winds and rain. [The phrase modifies the adverb *Later*, telling *to what extent* later.]
The same movie had been playing **for eight weeks.** [The phrase modifies the verb phrase *had been playing*, telling *how long* the movie had been playing.]

An adverb phrase may come before or after the word it modifies. More than one adverb phrase may modify the same word.

EXAMPLE   **In 1969**, American astronauts landed **on the moon**. [Both phrases modify the verb *landed*, the first phrase telling *when* the astronouts landed and the second phrase telling *where* .]

EXERCISE 6 Identifying Adverb Phrases and the Words They Modify

In each of the following sentences, underline the adverb phrase once, and draw an arrow to the word or words it modifies.

EX.   1. The hummingbird flew to the special feeder.

1. Scientists have studied hummingbirds for a long time.

2. Is any other bird faster in flight?

3. A hummingbird gets its food from flowers.

4. The hummingbird hovers above a flower.

5. From the flower's nectar, the hummingbird gets energy.

6. The tiny hummingbird finds food only in the daytime.

7. During the night, the hummingbird's energy rate drops.

8. During the day, the hummingbird uses energy at a very high rate.

9. Some hummingbirds migrate about two thousand miles.

10. They work long hours in the summer, gathering extra nectar.

EXERCISE 7   Using Adverb Phrases

Use each adverb phrase below in a sentence of your own. Use at least two adverb phrases to modify adjectives and two adverb phrases to modify other adverbs. Write the sentence on your own paper. Then underline each phrase once and the word or words it modifies twice.

EX. 1. after the party

   1. We cleaned the basement after the party.

1. against the fence
2. on Thanksgiving Day
3. beneath the queen's throne
4. into the dark woods
5. behind the stone statue
6. before the end
7. for a thousand years
8. beyond our wildest dreams
9. at Tao Ling's Chinese Restaurant
10. with the final decision
11. around the islands
12. underneath the treasure chest
13. in place of the teacher
14. out of silver and gold
15. across the gymnasium
16. without Mona
17. off the sofa
18. inside a submarine
19. since December
20. near the Pacific Ocean

REVIEW EXERCISE

A. Identifying Prepositional Phrases, Prepositions, and Objects

In the paragraph below, underline the twenty prepositional phrases. In each phrase, put brackets around the preposition, and draw a second line under the object of the preposition. [Note: A sentence may contain more than one prepositional phrase.]

EX. [1] [In] 1991, Bethany Flippin [from] Danbury, North Carolina, won a national art contest.

[1] The Space Science Student Involvement Program sponsors competitions for students across the country. [2] Some of these students will seek careers other than ones in the science field. [3] For the 1991 art contest, each participant illustrated a settlement on Mars. [4] According to the rules, the drawings showed some type of life-support system. [5] The drawings also provided details about recreation and transportation. [6] Bethany Flippin won the National Junior High Award for her drawing. [7] In her illustration, the Martian settlement is enclosed within clear domes. [8] The domes sit on the fiery red surface of Mars. [9] High above the settlement, a NASA space station floats. [10] This space station provides a communication link with earth. [11] Beneath the domes, Bethany shows plants thriving among the buildings. [12] Water is shown clinging to the domes where it becomes rain and falls to the ground.

B. Identifying and Classifying Prepositional Phrases

In the following sentences, underline each prepositional phrase. Tell whether the phrase is an adjective phrase or an adverb phrase by writing *adj.* or *adv.* on the line before the sentence. Then draw an arrow to the word or words the phrase modifies.

EX.   _adv._   1. Meteor Crater is located in Arizona.

——— 1. A meteor from space gouged a crater nearly 170 feet deep.

——— 2. Over time, many meteorites have hit the earth.

——— 3. Meteorites cool as they complete their flight through earth's atmosphere.

——— 4. Many meteorites are buried beneath the antarctic ice sheets.

——— 5. Some scientists believe that dinosaurs became extinct because one or more meteorites collided with the earth.

——— 6. On account of these impacts, a huge dust cloud may have blocked the sun's rays and cooled the earth's climate.

——— 7. The Leonid meteor shower in 1966 was an incredibly spectacular shower.

——— 8. Mrs. Hewlett Hodges of Sylacauga, Alabama, may be the only person in the United States whom a meteorite has ever hit.

——— 9. Away from city lights, the sky in the country appears clear and bright.

——— 10. In daylight hours, meteor trails cannot be seen.

C. Writing a Story Using Phrases

On your own paper, add adverb or adjective phrases to the sentences below. Use each kind of phrase at least twice. Underline and label each phrase you add. [Note: You may need to add other words also.]

EX.   1. The trip started out to be routine.
     1. The trip to Salt Lake City started out to be routine. (adj.)

1. The night sky was moonless.
2. The air was cold.
3. The plane's engine failed.
4. The plane crashed into the mountain forest.
5. The passengers all survived.
6. One boy hiked for many miles.
7. Eventually, he found our mountain cabin.
8. We called the park service.
9. A helicopter arrived.
10. The passengers were returned safely.

PARTICIPLES AND PARTICIPIAL PHRASES

14d A *participle* is a verbal, or verb form, that can be used as an adjective.

(1) *Present participles* end in *–ing*.

EXAMPLES The comedian was **amusing**. [*Amusing*, a form of the verb *amuse*, modifies the noun *comedian*.]
The **playing** boys did not hear their mother call. [*Playing*, a form of the verb *play*, modifies the noun *boys*.]

(2) *Past participles* usually end in *–d* or *–ed*. Others are irregularly formed. [See the list of irregular verbs on pages 183–184.]

EXAMPLES That **faded** rug belonged to my aunt. [*Faded*, a form of the verb *fade*, modifies the noun *rug*.]
Hopelessly **lost** and **worried**, the driver stopped and asked the police officer for directions. [*Lost*, a form of the verb *lose*, and *worried*, a form of the verb *worry*, modify the noun *driver*.]

14e A *participial phrase* consists of a participle and its modifiers and complements. A participial phrase is used as an adjective.

To avoid confusion, place the participial phase as close as possible to the word it modifies.

EXAMPLES **Imagining herself in space,** Jeanette dreamed she was an astronaut. [The participial phrase modifies the noun *Jeanette*. The pronoun *herself* is the direct object of the present participle *Imagining*. The adverb phrase *in space* modifies *Imagining*.]
She imagined a young woman **floating smoothly outside a space capsule**. [The participial phrase modifies the noun *woman*. The adverb *smoothly* and the adverb phrase *outside a space capsule* modify the present participle *floating*.]
Soon, **soothed by these pleasant thoughts,** she drifted off to sleep. [The participial phrase modifies the pronoun *she*. The adverb phrase *by these pleasant thoughts* modifies the past participle *soothed*.]

EXERCISE 8 Identifying Participles and the Nouns or Pronouns They Modify

Underline the participles used as adjectives in each of the following sentences. Then put brackets around the noun or the pronoun each participle modifies.

EX. 1. <u>Humming</u> softly, [Lynda] cheerfully cleaned her bicycle.

1. A loud clap of thunder woke the sleeping children from their nap.

2. Cleaned and polished, the old desk looked bright and shiny.

3. The driver accidentally backed his truck into the parked car.

4. The tired, sweating runners finished the race.

5. Janey sat on her porch, thinking about her problems.

6. Waiting by the entrance, the reporter yelled out a question.

7. Reilung and Clay, playing the Japanese game *Go*, forgot about the meeting.

8. Pun, did you go to the training class last week?

9. Watch out for the tangled ropes!

10. The stolen money was returned yesterday.

EXERCISE 9 Writing Sentences with Participial Phrases

On your own paper, use each of the following participial phrases in a sentence. Then underline the phrase, and draw an arrow to the word it modifies. Place each phrase as close as possible to the noun or the pronoun that it modifies.

EX. 1. waiting for the yellow school bus

1. <u>Waiting for the yellow school bus</u>, the children talked about their science projects.

1. thinking happily about the summer
2. finding himself alone in the house
3. frightened by the loud noise
4. seen by several people
5. standing near the water

6. receiving the award
7. included in the package
8. smiling at me
9. creeping along the dock
10. stranded on the beach

GERUNDS AND GERUND PHRASES

14f **A *gerund* is a verbal, or verb form, that ends in *–ing* and is used as a noun.**

SUBJECT	**Cooking** is an art for some people.
PREDICATE NOMINATIVE	His favorite pastime is **painting.**
OBJECT OF A PREPOSITION	The road is closed because of **flooding.**
DIRECT OBJECT	Has the camera crew finished **filming**?

Do not confuse a gerund with a present participle used as part of a verb phrase or as an adjective.

EXAMPLE   My brother **was packing** instead of **cleaning** his room.
[*Packing* is part of the verb phrase *was packing. Cleaning* is a gerund that serves as the object of the preposition *instead of.*]

14g **A *gerund phrase* consists of a gerund and its modifiers and complements. A gerund phrase is used as a noun.**

EXAMPLES   **Approaching the dog slowly** was the most sensible idea.
[The gerund phrase is the subject of the sentence. The noun *dog* is the direct object of the gerund *Approaching.* The adjective *the* modifies *dog.* The adverb *slowly* modifies the gerund *approaching.*]
The poem celebrated **the gentle blossoming of a rose.** [The gerund phrase is the direct object of the sentence. The adjectives *the* and *gentle* and the adjective phrase *of a rose* modify the gerund *blossoming.*]
By **moving through the crowded room,** the mayor was able to greet all his supporters. [The gerund phrase is the object of the preposition *By.* The adverb phrase *through the crowded room* modifies the gerund *moving.*]

 NOTE   When a noun or a pronoun comes immediately before a gerund, use the possessive form of the noun or pronoun.

EXAMPLE   **Tanya's** doodling decorates all her notebook pages.

EXERCISE 10   Identifying Gerunds

Underline the gerunds in the sentences below. Then, on the line before each sentence, identify the function of the gerund by writing *s.* for *subject*, *p.n.* for *predicate nominative*, *d.o.* for *direct object*, or *o.p.* for *object of a preposition*.

EX.   _s._   1. Swimming strengthened his arm and leg muscles.

_____ 1. He was awakened by the constant ringing of the telephone.

_____ 2. Amy Tan's writing reflects her Asian American heritage.

_____ 3. My brother practiced kicking the ball into the goal.

_____ 4. Wondering what to do with his gift money was Josh's biggest problem.

_____ 5. He could hear the banging of the drums in the distance.

_____ 6. Reading about Black Hawk, who once led the Sauk Indians, taught me many interesting facts about this man.

_____ 7. Marsha enjoys singing Mexican *corridos*, or ballads.

_____ 8. You gain nothing by giving up.

_____ 9. Would you mind showing me your paragraph?

_____ 10. Exercising can be difficult at times.

EXERCISE 11   Writing Sentences with Gerund Phrases

On your own paper, write sentences that use each of the following gerund phrases as a subject, a predicate nominative, a direct object, or an object of a preposition. Underline each gerund phrase, and identify it by writing *s.* for *subject*, *p.n.* for *predicate nominative*, *d.o.* for *direct object*, or *o.p.* for *object of a preposition*.

EX.   1. getting up early in the morning

       1. *s.*
       Getting up early in the morning allows me to see the sunrise.

1. listening carefully to the directions
2. wandering aimlessly around town
3. figuring out the secret message
4. the loud creaking of the garden gate
5. fingerprinting the suspect
6. celebrating our victory
7. boiling water for tea
8. washing the shirt
9. shopping in the mall
10. signaling the coach

APPOSITIVES AND APPOSITIVE PHRASES

14j An *appositive* **is a noun or a pronoun placed beside another noun or pronoun to identify or explain it.**

Appositives are often set off from the rest of the sentence by commas. However, when an appositive is necessary to the meaning of the sentence or is closely related to the word it refers to, no commas are necessary.

EXAMPLES   The writer **Toni Morrison** is a respected American novelist.
[The noun *Toni Morrison* identifies the noun *writer.*]
Bill Cosby, a **comedian** and an **actor,** has written several books.
[The nouns *comedian* and *actor* explain the noun *Bill Cosby.*]

14k   An *appositive phrase* **consists of an appositive and its modifiers.**

EXAMPLES   Miss Domingues, **a teacher at the Douglas School,** is my aunt. [The adjective phrase *at the Douglas School* and the article *a* modify the appositive *teacher.*]
Martin Luther King, Jr., **the well-known leader in the civil rights movement,** was also a minister. [The adjective *the,* the adjective *well-known,* and the adjective phrase *in the civil rights movement* modify the appositive *leader.*]

EXERCISE 14   Identifying Appositives and Appositive Phrases

Underline the appositive or appositive phrase in each of the following sentences. Then put brackets around the word or words the appositive or appositive phrase identifies or explains.

EX.   1. Those [balloons], the ones on the table, are mine.

1. Two boys, Marco and Joey, can carry this tray of food upstairs.

2. The sign, the one that says "Happy Birthday," goes on the basement wall.

3. Popcorn, carrot sticks, and apple slices, a few of Caroline's favorite foods, will be served.

4. My friend Caroline will enjoy the card.

5. The streamers, those red and blue strips of paper, can be hung from the ceiling.

6. Her brothers, members of a rock band, will provide the music.

7. I hope she likes my gift, two tickets to next week's ice show.

8. Caroline is arriving soon on the bus, the express from the city.

9. We will give a loud cheer, "Surprise!" when she gets here.

10. She will be excited to see the guests, all her school friends.

EXERCISE 15   Combining Sentences with Appositives

Use appositives to combine each group of sentences below into one sentence. Write each sentence on your own paper.

EX.   1. This color is midnight blue. Midnight blue is my favorite color.

   1. This color, midnight blue, is my favorite color.

1. Clementine Hunter was an American painter from Louisiana. She created paintings about the everyday lives of African Americans.

2. Grand Canyon National Park is a breathtaking sight in Arizona. The Colorado River flows through the park.

3. Miss Clariss Fava speaks fluent Chinese, Japanese, French, and German. She is a translator. She is also a government employee.

4. Somebody brought us a surprise. The surprise was a new puppy.

5. The puppy loved to play with our shoelaces. It was a terrier.

6. Ramiro and Joao Mendes are brothers. They have a recording studio.

7. They are from Cape Verde. Cape Verde is a group of islands off the coast of Senegal.

8. Until 1975, Cape Verde was a colony. It was a trading center.

9. Cape Verdean music combines music from Europe and West Africa. It uses electronic and traditional instruments.

10. The Mendes brothers have recorded seven albums. They started recording in 1991.

CHAPTER REVIEW

A. Identifying Parts of Prepositional Phrases

In each sentence below, underline the preposition once and the object of the preposition twice. Then draw an arrow from the preposition to the word or words modified by the prepositional phrase.

EX. 1. Thick fog rolled off the ocean and blanketed the island.

1. A bluebird sang outside my bedroom window.

2. Between the giraffe and the zebra stood a small monkey.

3. We have had many kinds of weather this winter.

4. Because of road construction, our trip included a six-mile detour.

5. The paper underneath that book is your missing homework assignment.

6. Vincent and I presented our argument against an extended school day.

7. They walked far beyond the city limits.

8. Every student except Estrella and Michael arrived early.

9. The team's star basketball player was injured during the first few minutes and could not finish the game.

10. That sweat shirt seems too big for you.

B. Writing Sentences with Prepositional Phrases

On the lines provided, use each of the following phrases in a sentence. Follow the directions in parentheses.

EX. 1. after the game (*use as an adverb phrase*) After the game, we gathered at Matt's house for a victory party.

1. above their heads (*use as an adverb phrase*) _____

_____

2. without a coat or hat (*use as an adjective phrase*) _____

_____

3. during the thunderstorm (*use as an adverb phrase*) _____

_____

4. by Kevin and his friend Sudi (*use as an adjective phrase*) _____

_____

5. among the remaining people (*use as an adverb phrase*) _____

_____

C. Identifying Verbals and Appositives

Underline all the verbals (infinitives, gerunds, participles) and appositives in the sentences in the paragraph below. In the space above each word, identify each by writing *app.* for *appositive, inf.* for *infinitive, ger.* for *gerund,* or *part.* for *participle.*

EX. [1] Rocks, <u>small and plentiful missiles on the dirt road</u>, flew up, *(app.)*

    <u>clanging</u> loudly against the car's metal frame. *(part.)*

[1] Driving recklessly, the guide promised to get us to the hotel,

Palm Tree Inn, by noon. [2] Mr. Santos, the hotel manager, had been

firm when he warned us about arriving late for the noon meal.

[3] Now, as the rattling of the car jarred the silence, I was certain we

would arrive late. [4] Tired and sweaty, I longed for a bath.

[5] Looking at Mom, I realized that nothing ever seemed to bother her.

[6] Assured that things would turn out fine, she was always calm.

[7] Hoping she was right, I closed my eyes and tried to stop the noise

and the weariness. [8] It seemed to work. [9] Exhausted, I must have

fallen asleep. [10] The next thing I knew, Mom was shaking me to tell

me we were at the hotel and on time for lunch.

INDEPENDENT AND SUBORDINATE CLAUSES

15a **A *clause* is a group of words that contains a verb and its subject.**

Every clause contains a subject and a verb. However, not all clauses express complete thoughts.

SENTENCE   David Wagoner is a poet and a teacher who lives in Ohio. [complete thought]

CLAUSE   **David Wagoner is** a poet and a teacher. [complete thought]

s   v

CLAUSE   **who lives** in Ohio [incomplete thought]

s   v

There are two kinds of clauses, *independent* and *subordinate*.

15b **An *independent* (or *main*) *clause* expresses a complete thought and can stand by itself as a sentence.**

EXAMPLES   **The poet received many awards.** [This entire sentence is an independent clause.]

s   v

Lucille Clifton wrote "Sisters," and Diana Chang wrote "Saying Yes." [This sentence contains two independent clauses.]

s   v   s   v

15c **A *subordinate* (or *dependent*) *clause* does not express a complete thought and cannot stand alone as a sentence.**

A word such as *that, since,* or *what* signals the beginning of a subordinate clause.

EXAMPLES   **that** I memorized

s   v

what she said

s   v

since many people enjoy poetry

s   v

The meaning of a subordinate clause is complete only when the clause is attached to an independent clause.

EXAMPLES   "Lineage," **which is a poem by Margaret Walker**, is about the author's ancestors.

When I read Américo Paredes' poem "Guitarreros," I really liked it.

143

EXERCISE 1   Identifying Independent Clauses and Subordinate Clauses

On the line before each sentence, write *indep.* if the italicized clause is an independent clause or *sub.* if it is a subordinate clause.

EX.   _sub._   1.   Ramona told me a joke *that I really enjoyed.*

_____   1.   Albert brought the sandwiches, and *May Ellen made the punch.*

_____   2.   *Since you've been away*, the neighborhood has really changed.

_____   3.   I don't remember *where I put my jacket.*

_____   4.   *Virgil planted the flowers* that are blooming in my garden.

_____   5.   The student *who sits behind me in science class* moved here from Mexico last month.

_____   6.   Monday or Tuesday, *whichever day you choose*, is fine.

_____   7.   *The bride and bridegroom wore the Hmong wedding costume* that they brought from Laos.

_____   8.   *After they left their native country*, they decided to live in Rome.

_____   9.   The bicycle lock, *which I just bought*, is broken.

_____   10.   Mrs. Vanderlin, *whose car is so old and noisy*, just drove up the hill.

EXERCISE 2   Writing Sentences with Clauses

On your own paper, write a complete sentence by adding an independent clause to each subordinate clause below. Underline the independent clauses in your completed sentences.

EX.   1.   what he said
       1.   I couldn't hear what he said.

1.   since I moved to Texas
2.   that I prefer
3.   after the basketball game was over
4.   when I answered the phone
5.   whatever the teacher said

THE ADJECTIVE CLAUSE

15d An *adjective clause* **is a subordinate clause that modifies a noun or a pronoun.**

Unlike an adjective or adjective phrase, an adjective clause contains a verb and its subject.

ADJECTIVE	a **brown** bear
ADJECTIVE PHRASE	a bear **with brown fur**
ADJECTIVE CLAUSE	a bear **that has brown fur**

An adjective clause usually follows the word it modifies and tells *which one* or *what kind*.

EXAMPLES Those **who are competing in the next race** should take their starting positions now. [The adjective clause modifies the pronoun *those,* telling *which* racers.]

I especially like stories **that contain suspense**. [The adjective clause modifies the noun *stories,* telling *what kind* of stories.]

An adjective clause is usually introduced by a *relative pronoun*.

Relative Pronouns
that   which   who   whom   whose

The relative pronoun relates the adjective clause to the word or words that the clause modifies.

EXAMPLES Have you met the man **who lives next door**? [The relative pronoun *who* begins the adjective clause. It relates the clause to the noun *man.*]

Science, **which is taught by Mrs. Rambini**, is my favorite class. [The relative pronoun *which* begins the adjective clause. It relates the clause to the noun *science.*]

Sometimes a relative pronoun is preceded by a preposition that is part of the adjective clause.

EXAMPLES The TV program **in which he starred** was shown last night.
The woman **for whom I work** does medical research.

EXERCISE 3   Identifying Adjective Clauses and Their Uses

In each of the sentences below, underline the adjective clause once and the relative pronoun twice. Then circle the noun or pronoun that the adjective clause modifies.

EX.   1.   Cecilia Bartoli is an opera (singer) who lives in Rome.

1. The article that I read about her appeared in *Newsweek*.

2. This great singer, whose parents also performed in operas, began to study singing as a teenager.

3. Bartoli, who has received many complimentary reviews from music critics, seems to be both modest and self-confident.

4. The company in which she made her American operatic debut is the Houston Grand Opera.

5. She is someone for whom I have great respect.

EXERCISE 4   Combining Sentences with Adjective Clauses

Combine each pair of sentences below by changing the italicized sentence into an adjective clause. Write your sentences on your own paper.

EX.   1.   Jerry is one of our best basketball players. *He is not very tall.*
     1.   Jerry, who is not very tall, is one of our best basketball players.

1. This movie is one of my favorites. *It was directed by Steven Spielberg.*
2. The book is due at the library on May 2. *I loaned the book to Mavis.*
3. The World Trade Center has two large towers. *The towers rise above New York City.*
4. The runner is a student at Wittenburg University. *The runner won the gold medal.*
5. The girl is my sister. *You gave your ticket to the girl.*
6. The trees are red maples. *The trees line the driveway.*
7. The roses have withered. *We gathered the roses yesterday.*
8. During the afternoon there was a storm. *No one expected the storm.*
9. I called Mara. *Mara knows all about computers.*
10. The poem has been published. *Brian wrote the poem.*

THE ADVERB CLAUSE

15e An *adverb clause* is a subordinate clause that modifies a verb, an adjective, or another adverb.

Unlike an adverb or an adverb phrase, an adverb clause contains a verb and its subject.

ADVERB	Please speak **softly**.
ADVERB PHRASE	Please speak **in a soft voice**.
ADVERB CLAUSE	Please speak **as softly as you can**.

An adverb clause tells *how, when, where, why, to what extent, how much, how long,* or *under what conditions.*

EXAMPLES   Nabil missed the game **because he overslept**. [The adverb clause modifies the verb *missed*. It tells *why* Nabil missed the game.]

                 If Kim Lee is late, he will be unhappy. [The adverb clause modifies the adjective *unhappy*. It tells *under what conditions* Kim Lee will be unhappy.]

Adverb clauses are introduced by *subordinating conjunctions*—words that show the relationship between the adverb clause and the word or words that the clause modifies.

Common Subordinating Conjunctions			
after	as though	since	when
although	because	so that	whenever
as	before	than	where
as if	how	though	wherever
as long as	if	unless	whether
as soon as	in order that	until	while

The words *after, as, before, since,* and *until* are also commonly used as prepositions.

SUBORDINATING CONJUNCTION	**Before** we played the game, we had a long practice.
PREPOSITION	**Before** the game, we had a long practice.

EXERCISE 5   Identifying Adverb Clauses and Their Uses

On the line after each sentence below, write the adverb clause. Underline the subject of the clause once. Underline the verb in the clause twice. Then circle the subordinating conjunction.

EX.   1. I will call you as soon as we arrive at the hotel.

(as soon as) we arrive at the hotel

1. Since you need a ride to the game, why don't you come with us?

2. When he travels, he sends postcards home to his parents.

3. Georgia will come to the game if she finishes her homework.

4. While the team was in the locker room, we watched the band perform.

5. He acted as if he had never seen a puppy before.

6. Geraldine can swim the butterfly much faster than Tamara can.

7. Because the bell rang, we couldn't finish our discussion.

8. Let's sit by the fountain while we wait for Earline.

9. I'll help you so that you can finish your project in time.

10. Until Maria arrived, no one knew the location of the party.

THE NOUN CLAUSE

15f A *noun clause* is a subordinate clause used as a noun.

A noun clause may be used as a subject, a complement, (predicate nominative, direct object, indirect object), or an object of a preposition.

SUBJECT	**That I love baseball** is a well-known fact. [The noun clause is the subject of the verb *is*.]
PREDICATE NOMINATIVE	Bread was **what Marie made for the picnic**. [The noun clause follows a linking verb and identifies the subject *bread*.]
DIRECT OBJECT	He knew **which bear was in the cave**. [The noun clause is the direct object of the verb *knew*. It tells *what* he knew.]
INDIRECT OBJECT	I will give **whoever wins the race** a trophy. [The noun clause is the indirect object of the verb *will give*. It tells *to whom* I will give a trophy.]
OBJECT OF A PREPOSITION	She is grateful for **whatever help she can get**. [The noun clause is the object of the preposition *for*.]

Common Introductory Words for Noun Clauses		
how	when	who
if	where	whoever
that	whether	whom
what	which	whomever
whatever	whichever	why

The word that introduces a noun clause often has another function within the clause.

EXAMPLES	She never studies, except **when she has a major test**. [The introductory word *when* modifies the verb *has*. The entire noun clause is the object of the preposition *except*.]
	She told him **whom he should invite to the party**. [The introductory word *whom* is the direct object of the verb *should invite*—he should invite whom. The entire noun clause is the direct object of the verb *told*.]

EXERCISE 6   Identifying and Classifying Noun Clauses

Underline the noun clauses in the sentences below. On the line before each sentence, tell how the noun clause is used. Write *s.* for subject, *p.n.* for predicate nominative, *d.o.* for direct object, *i.o.* for indirect object, and *o.p.* for object of a preposition.

EX.   <u>p.n.</u>   1. The outcome of the story was not <u>what I had hoped</u>.

_____   1. Bring an extra blanket for whoever may need one.

_____   2. Whichever color you prefer is fine with me.

_____   3. I will give whoever finds my lost dog a generous reward.

_____   4 Dr. DeVito called me from where she was staying.

_____   5. That Mary was late was a surprise to Roberto.

_____   6. After a hard week, a lazy, slow Saturday is what you need.

_____   7. He asked when he could buy a copy of the story.

_____   8. The principal announced who would represent the school at the music festival.

_____   9. Give whoever wants it this extra ticket to the football game.

_____   10. My good friend Julia always listens to what I say.

EXERCISE 7   Writing Sentences with Noun Clauses

On your own paper, write five sentences that contain noun clauses. In your sentences, use noun clauses in at least three of the following five ways: subject, predicate nominative, direct object, indirect object, or object of a preposition. Underline the noun clause in each of your sentences. Then identify how each clause is used.

EX.   1. A cold glass of juice is <u>what I want right now</u>. (predicate nominative)

CHAPTER REVIEW

A. Identifying Independent Clauses and Subordinate Clauses

Decide whether each of the italicized clauses below is independent or subordinate. On the line before the sentence, write *indep.* if the clause is independent and *sub.* if it is subordinate.

EX. <u>sub.</u>　1. We didn't know *what was bothering Jake.*

_____ 1. While Jake and I were mowing Mrs. Rocco's lawn, *Jake started yelling and jumping around.*

_____ 2. *That he was acting oddly* was very upsetting to me.

_____ 3. *Jake told me once* that he has terrible allergies.

_____ 4. He starts sneezing *whenever there is pollen in the air.*

_____ 5. However, *this time he wasn't sneezing.*

_____ 6. *I ran over to him* because I was frightened.

_____ 7. When I got to him, I saw *what was wrong.*

_____ 8. While he was mowing the grass, *poor Jake ran over a bees' nest and was stung eight times.*

_____ 9. Mrs. Rocco and I took Jake to the hospital, *where a doctor gave him a shot.*

_____ 10. I was relieved when the doctor said *that Jake would be okay.*

B. Identifying and Classifying Subordinate Clauses

Underline the subordinate clause in each of the following sentences. On the line before the sentence, write *adj.* for adjective clause, *adv.* for adverb clause, and *n.* for noun clause.

EX. <u>n.</u>　1. People around the world watch the sky closely for <u>whatever messages might be there.</u>

_____ 1. The winds that bring the weather also carve the earth's surface.

_____ 2. In one story, the god Aeolus, who kept the winds in a bag, gave them to Odysseus.

_____ 3. When the monsoons blow in India, they bring the rainy season.

_____ 4. The Norse people believed that a huge tree stretched to the sky and held the universe together.

_____ 5. After some Australians saw dust storms over the brickyards, they named the warm wind "brickfielder."

_____ 6. The chinook wind is named for the language of Native Americans who live in Oregon and Washington.

_____ 7. When travelers are lost, they can wait for a clear night and use the stars to find their way.

_____ 8. People have often wondered about the weather because their crops depended on it.

_____ 9. "Backbone of night" is the name that the San gave the Milky Way.

_____ 10. What we sometimes call the empty sky contains air weighing 5,000 trillion tons.

C. Writing a Report

As a space scientist, you are working on the Phoebus Project. You and your team have sent a space probe to another solar system. The probe has discovered a new planet, which you have named Planet 514X. Now the probe has sent back data on the planet. Your job is to write a report based on the data. The report will be published in a leading scientific journal. On your own paper, write at least five sentences that might appear in your report. In your sentences, underline and identify at least one noun clause, one adjective clause, and one adverb clause. Here is the data that you have received so far.

- Average surface temperature: 53.9°C

- Gases found in atmosphere: oxygen, nitrogen, argon

- Surface features: jagged rocks, large masses of water

- Life forms detected: giant creatures with hard front wings like beetles

- Weather elements noted: high winds, measured at 70 kilometers per hour

EX.   1. The creatures that the probe identified looked like giant beetles. (adjective clause)

SIMPLE AND COMPOUND SENTENCES

16a A *simple sentence* has one independent clause and no subordinate clauses.

EXAMPLES   For two years, **Marlene has worked** at the supermarket.
s   v

A simple sentence may have a compound subject, a compound verb, or both.

EXAMPLES   **Percy** and **Otis are** on the track team.[compound subject]

            Ramona ran to the phone and **answered** it.[compound verb]

            Yesterday, **Clay** and his **father bought** lumber and **built** a composting bin.[compound subject and compound verb]

☞   **REFERENCE NOTE:** For more information about clauses, see pages 143–149.

16b A *compound sentence* has two or more independent clauses but no subordinate clauses.

The independent clauses are usually joined by a comma and a coordinating conjunction: *and, but, for, nor, or, so,* or *yet.*

EXAMPLES   **Marianne loaned** me a pencil, but **I lost** it.[two independent clauses joined by the conjunction *but*]

            The **sky grew** dark, strong **winds blew,** and hard **rains pounded** the street.[three short, closely related independent clauses, the last two joined by the conjunction *and*]

The independent clauses in a compound sentence are joined by a semicolon when no comma and no conjunction are used.

EXAMPLE   The **storm was** terrible; its high **winds toppled** many trees.

NOTE   Do not confuse a compound sentence with a simple sentence that contains a compound subject, a compound verb, or both.

    SIMPLE   **Pauline** and **Janyce repaired** the fence and then
    SENTENCE   **painted** it.[compound subject and compound verb]

EXERCISE 1   **Identifying Subjects and Verbs in Simple Sentences**

In each sentence below, underline the subject once and the verb twice. [Note: A sentence may have a compound subject, a compound verb, or both.]

EX.   1.   <u>Venezuela</u> <u>lies</u> on the northern coast of South America.

1. Colombia and Brazil are Venezuela's neighbors.

2. Angel Falls, at a height of 979 meters, is the highest waterfall in the world.

3. Thick forests and valuable deposits of minerals enrich Venezuela and provide the country with its greatest resources.

4. Oil, gold, iron, and copper are among Venezuela's most important mineral resources.

5. The highest mountains begin south of Lake Maracaibo.

EXERCISE 2   **Identifying Subjects and Verbs in Compound Sentences**

In each sentence below, underline the subjects once and the verbs twice.

EX.   1.   <u>Duc Tran</u> <u>came</u> to the United States six months ago, so <u>he</u> <u>is</u> a newcomer to the country.

1. He lives with his uncle and cousins, but life is difficult for him in the United States.

2. He does not understand much English, nor does he understand the customs of this country.

3. Duc was a good student in his native country; he studied hard.

4. His cousin, Anh, just enrolled in an English language class, and Duc will take the class, too.

5. Duc works part time at a seafood restaurant, so he will get Anh a job there.

COMPLEX AND COMPOUND-COMPLEX SENTENCES

16c A *complex sentence* has one independent clause and at least one subordinate clause.

The subordinate clause or clauses can appear at the beginning, in the middle, or at the end of a complex sentence.

EXAMPLE   Many people who enjoy sports subscribe to this magazine.

> INDEPENDENT CLAUSE   Many **people subscribe** to this magazine
>
> SUBORDINATE CLAUSE   **who enjoy** sports

16d A *compound-complex sentence* has two or more independent clauses and at least one subordinate clause.

EXAMPLE   I was sitting in the back of the hall, so I did not hear what Dan said about today's meeting.

> INDEPENDENT CLAUSE   **I was sitting** in the back of the hall
>
> INDEPENDENT CLAUSE   **I did** not **hear**
>
> SUBORDINATE CLAUSE   what **Dan said** about today's meeting

EXERCISE 3   Identifying Clauses in Complex Sentences

In each of the following sentences, underline the independent clause once and the subordinate clause twice. [Note: A sentence may contain more than one subordinate clause.]

EX.   1. The people who bought the old house will turn it into an inn.

1. Now that my uncle is retired, he is writing a book.

2. Most of the books that I sold in our garage sale were bought within the first hour of the sale.

3. If you have already made your plans, tell me what they are.

4. The dogs made a mess that I must clean up.

5. Several years ago, the land on which those houses stand was a beautiful, wild meadow.

6. As soon as I finished my breakfast, Janis said that she had a surprise for me.

7. The radio announcer offered everyone who was listening two free tickets to the concert.

8. In the winter, the empty lot that lies across the street from my apartment building gets filled with piles of snow that the snow plows leave behind.

9. When you get a chance, please show me what you made in art class today.

10. As a young student, Georgio has already proved that he has great skills as a poet.

EXERCISE 4   Identifying Clauses in Compound-Complex Sentences

In the sentences below, underline each independent clause once. Underline each subordinate clause twice.

EX.   1.   When Hilary called, she gave me your message, and she told me that you needed a ride to the game.

1. I love bananas, but I don't like bananas that are not ripe.

2. After we saw the movie, we went to a restaurant, and then we came straight home.

3. Floyd visited us when he came back, but he didn't stay long.

4. I know what you mean, for I have had a similar experience.

5. Cecilia knows many people in the neighborhood, but her best friends are the twins who live in the white house on the corner.

6. Jim paused, and then he said that he had changed his mind.

7. The contest was open to anyone who could write a poem about spring, so I sat down and began writing.

8. Only dogs that are leash trained are allowed in the building, so Dad took Melon to a training school.

9. Although you may disagree with me, this is my decision, and I believe that it's right.

10. Not many people who visit San Juan know about this park, so I feel lucky.

CHAPTER REVIEW

A. Identifying the Four Kinds of Sentence Structure

On the line before each sentence below, identify the sentence type by writing *simp.* for *simple sentence,* *comp.* for *compound sentence,* *cx.* for *complex sentence,* and *cd.-cx.* for *compound-complex sentence.*

EX. _____cx._____ 1. Just before the movie started, we left the theater because John got a bad headache.

_____ 1. My aunt discovered a skunk under her porch and called the Humane Society for help in removing it.

_____ 2. Before I could stop the cat, it jumped on the table, grabbed your sandwich, and ran away with it.

_____ 3. I remember his name; do you remember it?

_____ 4. Because all of the clerks who work at the shop got raises, no one was upset.

_____ 5. Over the past several years, many people have come to our town and have built new homes.

_____ 6. I am sorry; I said something that has hurt your feelings.

_____ 7. People who own animals should look after them carefully.

_____ 8. Mother told me what she needed from the store, and I got it for her.

_____ 9. Joe was sure that he had driven on that road last summer.

_____ 10. Sometimes I go for a walk; other times I read a book.

_____ 11. At exactly the same moment, the dog barked, the baby cried, and the phone rang.

_____ 12. Three years ago, Teresa and her husband arrived in the United States from Brazil.

_____ 13. Saburu, a nurse's assistant, walks to work at a local hospital; his friend, who is a factory worker, commutes twenty miles to work.

_____ 14. We study during the day, so we can enjoy the evening together.

_____ 15. Fraser often writes letters to his aunt in Rio de Janiero and hopes to visit there someday.

B. Identifying Clauses and Classifying Sentences

In the sentences below, underline each independent clause once and each subordinate clause twice. On the line before each sentence, classify the sentence by writing *simp.* for *simple, comp.* for *compound, cx.* for *complex,* or *cd.-cx.* for *compound-complex.*

EX.   _____comp._____   1. I've read through all of my lines, but I haven't memorized them.

_____ 1. We are excited about the play that we will present.

_____ 2. Gina, who was on the committee, suggested that we present *A View from the Bridge.*

_____ 3. Many of us had read that play, and we felt that it was too upsetting.

_____ 4. Some committee members preferred either a musical comedy or a mystery.

_____ 5. Jerome and I voted for the musical comedy *Oklahoma!;* do you know that play?

_____ 6. My grandmother has the records from the original production.

_____ 7. The songs in that play are beautiful, and I'm sure that our audience would enjoy it.

_____ 8. Let me play you one of the records, then you can tell me what you think.

_____ 9. This song is called "Oh, What a Beautiful Mornin'," and it is sung by the leading actor.

_____ 10. Perhaps you'd like the title song, too; it's called "Oklahoma!"

C. Writing a Description of a Movie Set

You are the set designer for a movie that takes place in an old castle. The producer has asked you to write a brief description of your plans for the set. On your own paper, write fifteen sentences to describe what one room in the castle might look like and what furniture or other props might appear in it. Include at least two simple sentences, two compound sentences, two complex sentences, and two compound-complex sentences. After you complete each sentence, write a label to identify its structure.

EX.   1. The banquet hall is dark, with high ceilings that are covered with mysterious drawings. (complex)

AGREEMENT OF SUBJECT AND VERB

Number is the form of a word that indicates whether the word is singular or plural.

17a **When a noun or pronoun refers to one person, place, thing, or idea, it is *singular* in number. When a noun or pronoun refers to more than one, it is *plural* in number.**

SINGULAR	dog	child	box	I	she	one
PLURAL	dogs	children	boxes	we	they	some

17b **A verb agrees with its subject in number.**

(1) Singular subjects take singular verbs.

EXAMPLE   The apple grows on the tree. [The singular verb *grows* agrees with the singular subject *apple*.]

(2) Plural subjects take plural verbs.

EXAMPLE   Many **apples grow** on that tree. [The plural verb *grow* agrees with the plural subject *apples*.]

The first auxiliary (helping) verb in a verb phrase must agree with its subject.

EXAMPLES   **She is** making breakfast.
             We are making breakfast.

             Does anyone want orange juice?
             Do any **campers** want orange juice?

NOTE   The pronouns *I* and *you* take plural verbs.

> EXAMPLE   **I play** on the school soccer team.
> EXCEPTION   **I am playing** soccer today.

☞   **REFERENCE NOTE:** For guidelines on forming plurals, see pages 287–289.

EXERCISE 1 Classifying Nouns and Pronouns by Number

On the line before each word below, write *sing.* if the word is a singular noun or pronoun or write *pl.* if it is a plural noun or pronoun.

EX. _____*sing.*_____ 1. horse

_____ 1. I   _____ 3. mice   _____ 5. neighbors

_____ 2. captains   _____ 4. day

EXERCISE 2   Identifying Subjects and Verbs That Agree in Number

Circle the subject in each sentence below. Then underline the verb or verb phrase that agrees in number with the subject.

EX.   1.   Every morning, (Floyd) (*gets*, *get*) up at five o'clock.

1. Unlike most of the students in his class, he (*has*, *have*) a job before school.

2. He (*delivers*, *deliver*) the morning newspaper.

3. At 5:15, the district manager (*drops*, *drop*) two huge bundles of newspapers outside Floyd's apartment building.

4. In about an hour, Floyd (*has delivered*, *have delivered*) all the papers.

5. (*Do*, *Does*) you believe that Floyd still finds time for studying?

EXERCISE 3   Identifying Verbs That Agree in Number with Their Subjects

For each sentence below, underline the verb or verb phrase that agrees in number with the subject.

EX.   [1] Ella (*plays*, *play*) the trumpet in the community band.

[1] On our block, we (*has*, *have*) a large group of musicians. [2] For example, Ella's grandfather (*is*, *are*) a professional violin player.   [3] He (*plays*, *play*) with the Cleveland Symphony Orchestra. [4] Other neighborhood musicians (*includes*, *include*) Charley McAllister and Chris Lomax.   [5] They (*is giving*, *are giving*) a concert tonight. [6] With these adults, we students (*is forming*, *are forming*) a community band. [7] I (*is putting*, *am putting*) up posters in the lobbies of the apartment buildings. [8] So far, I (*has signed*, *have signed*) up twelve students and six adults. [9] (*Does*, *Do*) anyone know a trombone player? [10] We (*needs*, *need*) one to round out the brass section.

PREPOSITIONAL PHRASE INTERRUPTERS

> **17c** **The number of a subject is not changed by a prepositional phrase that modifies the subject.**
>
> NONSTANDARD Many students in my class is interested in world affairs.
> STANDARD Many **students** in my class **are** interested in world affairs.
>
> NONSTANDARD The stamps in the book on the shelf is valuable.
> STANDARD The **stamps** in the book on the shelf **are** valuable.
>
> **REFERENCE NOTE:** For a discussion of standard and nonstandard English, see page 221–222.

EXERCISE 4 Identifying Subjects and Verbs That Are Separated by Prepositional Phrases

In each of the following sentences, underline the subject once and the verb or verb phrase twice.

EX. 1. Orange slices for the soccer team (*is, are*) in the cooler.

1. Children from the kindergarten (*is having, are having*) a costume party.

2. Many restaurants along the highway (*stays, stay*) open all night.

3. The gift from your grandparents (*is, are*) in that big red box.

4. Workers in that factory (*gets, get*) two weeks off every year for vacation.

5. One of the students in my class (*does, do*) volunteer work.

6. The fields behind the school (*is, are*) used for soccer practice.

7. The owners of that house on the corner (*is, are*) away on vacation.

8. Each worker at the offices of Dane & Gray (*gets, get*) a free turkey at Thanksgiving.

9. An article about the life and accomplishments of Arthur Ashe (*appears, appear*) in this morning's newspaper.

10. The flowers in your grandmother's garden (*looks, look*) beautiful.

11. The parents in our neighborhood (*is, are*) forming a basketball league for their children.

12 Two rare white lions at Philadelphia's wildlife preserve (*attracts, attract*) many visitors.

13. My favorite collection of short stories (*is, are*) by Edgar Allan Poe.

14. My collection of programs from baseball games (*brings, bring*) back many memories of exciting games.

15. Pictures from my mother's childhood in Poland (*fills, fill*) this scrapbook.

EXERCISE 5   Using Prepositional Phrases and Verbs to Complete Sentences

Each of the items below is the subject for a sentence. Complete each sentence by adding a prepositional phrase and a verb after the subject. You may want to add other words as well to make your sentences more interesting.

EX.   1. The girl in the red dress is my sister. _____

1. Three dogs _____

_____

2. Many houses _____

_____

3. An elephant _____

_____

4. People _____

_____

5. These photographs _____

_____

SINGULAR AND PLURAL INDEFINITE PRONOUNS

A pronoun that does not refer to a definite person, place, thing, or idea is called an *indefinite pronoun*.

17d **The following indefinite pronouns are singular:** *anybody, anyone, each, either, everybody, everyone, neither, nobody, no one, one, somebody, someone.*

Pronouns like *each* and *one* are often followed by prepositional phrases. Remember that the verb agrees with the subject of the sentence, not with a word in a prepositional phrase.

EXAMPLES   **Every one of us is** going on the field trip.
                    Neither of my brothers **has** a car.
                    Does any one of you want another sandwich?

17e **The following indefinite pronouns are plural:** *both, few, many, several.*

EXAMPLES   **Both** of my brothers **collect** stamps.
                    How **many** of my friends **are going** to the concert?
                    A **few** of the senators **agree** with the decision.
                    Several of the invitations **have** already **been sent.**

EXERCISE 6   Identifying Subjects and Verbs That Agree in Number

For each of the following sentences, underline the subject once. Then underline the correct verb twice.

EX.   1. Everybody in the class (*has, have*) finished the assignment.

1. One of the girls on the team (*has, have*) left her shinguards on the bus.

2. Someone down the hall from us (*is, are*) calling your name.

3. (*Is, Are*) either of your parents coming to the play?

4. Each of the candidates (*wants, want*) to win.

5. No one in the stands (*was, were*) late for the start of the game.

6. Neither of the plants (*needs, need*) water right now.

7. (*Does, Do*) everyone have a ticket?

8. Somebody in the room next to ours (*has, have*) broken the mirror in the hall.

9. If anybody from either of those video stores (*calls, call*), please take a message for me.

10. Neither of these dresses (*fits, fit*) me well.

EXERCISE 7   Proofreading for Subject-Verb Agreement

If the verb in each of the sentences below is incorrect, write the correct verb form on the line before the sentence. If a sentence contains no errors, write C on the line.

EX. _____*is*_____ 1. Everyone at my little brother's birthday party are excited about seeing the clown.

_____ 1. Many of the wolves in that pack has died during the long, cold winter.

_____ 2. A few of the teachers at this school are taking a night course in African American history.

_____ 3. One of the most interesting women in recent history were Golda Meir, the prime minister of Israel from 1969 to 1974.

_____ 4. If anyone on the swim team find my missing goggles, please call me.

_____ 5. Have anyone tried these recipes before?

_____ 6. Each of the recipes for cooking fish are different.

_____ 7. One recipe use tomatoes and onions.

_____ 8. Several of them requires making a sauce.

_____ 9. A few recipes for broiled fish has lemon juice added.

_____ 10. Both of my sisters enjoys any kind of fish.

ALL, ANY, MOST, NONE, *AND* SOME

> **17f   The following indefinite pronouns may be either singular or plural:** *all, any, most, none, some.*
>
> The number of the subject *all, any, most, none,* or *some* is determined by examining the object of the prepositional phrase following or describing the subject. If the subject refers to a singular object, the subject is singular. If the subject refers to a plural object, the subject is plural.
>
> EXAMPLES   **All** of the milk **is** gone. [*All* refers to the singular object *milk.*]
> **All** of the children **are** thirsty. [*All* refers to the plural object *children.*]
> **Is any** of the bread stale? [*Any* refers to the singular object *bread.*]
> **Are any** of the cookies left? [*Any* refers to the plural object *cookies.*]
> **Most** of the wood **is** rotten. [*Most* refers to the singular object *wood.*]
> **Most** of the windows **are** broken. [*Most* refers to the plural object *windows.*]

EXERCISE 8   Identifying Subjects and Verbs That Agree in Number

On the line before each of the following sentences, write *sing.* if the indefinite pronoun and the object of the preposition are singular. Write *pl.* if the indefinite pronoun and the object of the preposition are plural. Underline the verb form that agrees in number with the subject.

EX.   ___pl.___   1.   None of the dogs (*has, have*) learned new tricks.

_____   1.   Some of my friends (*likes, like*) jazz.

_____   2.   Most of the water in the puddles (*has, have*) dried now.

_____   3.   All of the desserts (*tastes, taste*) delicious.

_____   4.   (*Was, Were*) any of the literature on our reading list written by Jack London?

_____   5.   None of the paint (*has, have*) been stirred yet.

_____   6.   Some of the perfumes (*smells, smell*) good.

_____ 7. Most of the company (*enjoys, enjoy*) long holiday weekends.

_____ 8. (*Does, Do*) any of the children need a ride home?

_____ 9. (*Was, Were*) all of the fruit washed?

_____ 10. None of the students (*is, are*) finished with the test.

EXERCISE 9   Proofreading Sentences for Errors in Subject-Verb Agreement

On the line before each sentence below, write the verb that agrees in number with the subject. If the sentence contains no errors, write *C* on the line.

EX.   ___*have*___   1. None of the contestants on the show has answered the question.

_____ 1. Some of the furniture are dusty.

_____ 2. A few of the boys in my class play lacrosse.

_____ 3. All of the money in her savings account have been spent.

_____ 4. Are any of the silverware dirty?

_____ 5. Do all of the representatives agree?

_____ 6. None of the juice have been poured yet.

_____ 7. All of the students is busy right now.

_____ 8. Most of the honey have been collected from the hives.

_____ 9. Some of our vacation were really fun.

_____ 10. All of the leftover soup is in the refrigerator.

_____ 11. Everyone in my family use safety belts when they drive.

_____ 12. We believe that both of our children is safer because of seat belts.

_____ 13. If anyone ask us, we'll give them other reasons.

_____ 14. Few of our friends disagrees with us.

_____ 15. Do both of your neighbors drive?

REVIEW EXERCISE 1

A. Identifying Subjects and Verbs That Agree in Number

In each of the following sentences, underline the verb form that agrees in number with the subject.

EX. 1. One of the most interesting cities in Ohio (*is, are*) Canton.

1. Canton, Ohio, (*was, were*) named after the estate of one of its early residents, Bezaleel Wells.

2. Many of its earliest settlers (*was, were*) Swiss and German immigrants.

3. Since its early days, Canton (*has, have*) grown into a major industrial center.

4. It (*remains, remain*) a city attractive to tourists.

5. Many of them (*visits, visit*) the Pro Football Hall of Fame.

6. This museum (*shows, show*) films of historic events in football.

7. Most of the history of the sport (*has, have*) been recorded on film.

8. Some of the exhibits in the museum (*includes, include*) items used by great players.

9. For example, one of the exhibits (*displays, display*) jerseys and helmets that many famous players wore.

10. Additionally, the Pro Football Hall of Fame's research library (*offers, offer*) visitors information on the history of football.

11. People in other countries (*thinks, think*) football is a sport played only in the United States.

12. Usually a football game (*lasts, last*) for sixty minutes.

13. One team (*has, have*) the football.

14. A player on that team (*takes, take*) the ball and (*runs, run*) down the field.

15. Members of the other team (*tries, try*) to tackle him.

16. When the ball goes over the goal line, the player (*scores, score*) a touchdown.

17. A touchdown (*counts, count*) for six points.

18. The fall and winter seasons (*is, are*) the best time for football games.

19. Many of the fans at the game (*wears, wear*) warm jackets and hats.

20. They (*enjoys, enjoy*) the action and excitement of the game.

B. Proofreading for Subject-Verb Agreement

In the paragraph below, draw a line through each verb or verb phrase that does not agree with its subject. Then write the correct form of the verb in the space above it.

EX. [1] Most of the cheese ~~have~~ *has* been grated for the pizza topping.

[1] Luigi's father owns a pizza restaurant down the street from our house. [2] Most of Luigi's older brothers and sisters works in the restaurant. [3] Sometimes Luigi help in the kitchen after soccer practice and on Saturdays. [4] All of the onions have to be peeled and chopped. [5] He also have to wash all the mushrooms and peppers. [6] Then all of the tomatoes has to be cooked and drained well. [7] At the end of the day, none of the leftover dough are saved. [8] Each morning, Luigi's dad makes fresh dough. [9] On Saturdays, Luigi sometimes mixes the dough or spread it in the pan. [10] Both of these jobs is really fun, as well as messy.

C. Using Correct Subject-Verb Agreement

You are a copywriter for the tourist bureau of your state. Create the copy for a tourist brochure that highlights your state's most interesting places to visit. Select five places that you feel visitors might enjoy visiting. Use encyclopedias and other reference materials to gather facts about each place. Then, on your own paper, write a one- to two-sentence informational blurb for each one. Check your sentences when you are finished to make sure that your subjects and verbs agree.

EX. 1. When you visit San Francisco, be sure to go to Fisherman's Wharf. While you look out at the water, you can eat fresh seafood.

COMPOUND SUBJECTS

17g   Subjects joined by *and* usually take a plural verb.

Most compound subjects joined by *and* name more than one person or thing. Therefore, they take plural verbs.

EXAMPLE   **Sylvia Plath** and **Anne Sexton were** famous poets. [Two persons were poets.]

A compound subject that names only one person or thing takes a singular verb.

EXAMPLE   The **producer and director** of the movie is Barbra Streisand. [One person is both the producer and the director.]

17h   Singular subjects joined by *or* or *nor* take singular verbs. Plural subjects joined by *or* or *nor* take plural verbs.

EXAMPLE   Either **Jerry** or **Julio is** going to lead the parade. [Either one will lead the parade.]

17i   When a singular subject and a plural subject are joined by *or* or *nor*, the verb agrees with the subject nearer the verb.

EXAMPLES   Neither the **coach nor** the **co-captains have** arrived yet. [The verb agrees with the subject nearer to it, *co-captains*.]
Neither the **co-captains nor** the **coach has** arrived yet. [The verb agrees with the subject nearer to it, *coach*.]

EXERCISE 10   Identifying Subjects and Verbs That Agree in Number

On the line before each of the following sentences, write *sing.* if the compound subject is singular. Write *pl.* if the compound subject is plural. Underline the verb that agrees with the subject.

EX.   _pl._   1.   The coach and the quarterback (*is*, *are*) discussing the next play.

_____   1.   Peanut butter and jelly (*is*, *are*) a favorite sandwich for many young people.

_____   2.   Henry Aaron and Babe Ruth (*is*, *are*) among the United States' greatest baseball players.

_____ 3. The leading singer and dancer in the movie (*was, were*) Ben Vereen.

_____ 4. Chalk and water (*is, are*) the main ingredients in whitewash paint.

_____ 5. Paul Simon and James Taylor (*has, have*) written most of the songs that they sing.

_____ 6. My science teacher and my baseball coach (*is, are*) Mr. Rodriguez.

_____ 7. Pittsburgh, Pennsylvania, and Wheeling, West Virginia, (*lies, lie*) in the Ohio River valley.

_____ 8. The capital of Texas and the home of the University of Texas (*is, are*) my hometown, Austin, Texas.

_____ 9. The costume designer and the set designer for our production (*has, have*) been Dante Conigliaro.

_____ 10. His chores and his homework (*takes, take*) a lot of time each day.

EXERCISE 11   Identifying Subjects and Verbs That Agree in Number

For each of the sentences below, underline the verb that agrees with the subject.

EX.   1. Neither Don nor Emilio (*runs, run*) as fast as Julio.

1. Either my sister or my brothers (*waits, wait*) for me after school.

2. Neither the television nor the radio (*works, work*) properly.

3. Judging by the menu, fresh vegetables and fresh fruits (*is, are*) available.

4. Either the hot-water faucet or the cold-water faucet (*leaks, leak*).

5. (*Does, Do*) Michelle Pfeiffer or Meryl Streep star in the movie?

6. According to the newspaper, neither juice nor apples (*is, are*) on sale at the supermarket.

7. Neither Ben Johnson nor Carl Lewis (*runs, run*) in today's race.

8. (*Is, Are*) rice or spaghetti your choice for dinner tonight?

9. Neither the prices nor the sizes (*has, have*) been printed on the tags.

10. The trapeze artist and the jugglers (*seems, seem*) ready for tonight's performance.

OTHER AGREEMENT PROBLEMS

17j   Collective nouns may be either singular or plural.

A *collective noun* is singular in form but names a group of persons, animals, things, or ideas.

Common Collective Nouns			
army	club	fleet	number
assembly	committee	flock	public
audience	crowd	fraction	swarm
band	dozen	group	team
class	family	herd	troop

A collective noun takes a singular verb when the noun refers to the group as a unit. A collective noun takes a plural verb when the noun refers to the individual parts or members of a group.

EXAMPLES   My **family is going** to Cleveland for vacation. [The family as a unit is going on vacation together. The verb is singular.]
My **family** always **tell** each other about the day's events. [The different members of the family tell about the day's events. The verb is plural.]

EXERCISE 12   Writing Sentences with Collective Nouns

From the list above, select five collective nouns. On your own paper, use each one as the subject of two sentences. In the first sentence, make the subject singular. In the second sentence, make the subject plural.

EX.   1.   a.   The team is on the bus.
            b.   The team are voting today for a new captain.

17k **When the subject follows the verb, find the subject and make sure that the verb agrees with it. The subject usually follows the verb in a sentence beginning with *here* or *there* and in a question.**

EXAMPLES   There **is** my **bike.**
                 There **are** our **bikes.**

                 Who **is** the **captain** of the team?
                 Who **are** the best **players** on the team?

Contractions such as *here's, there's, where's,* and *who's* contain the verb *is.* Therefore, they should be used only with singular subjects.

NONSTANDARD   There's the new students.
    STANDARD   There **are** the new **students.**

EXERCISE 13 Proofreading for Subject-Verb Agreement

On the line before each sentence below, write the correct form of any verbs that do not agree with their subjects. If the sentence contains no errors in subject-verb agreement, write *C* on the line.

EX.   *Have*   1. Has you seen the movie *Glory*?

_____ 1. There's several books and movies about the first African American Army regiment, the Massachusetts 54th.

_____ 2. Here's two videotapes of *Glory*, starring Matthew Broderick.

_____ 3. Does you know about the Massachusetts 54th?

_____ 4. There's a monument on the Boston Common to the members of the regiment who died during the U.S. Civil War.

_____ 5. The public is always welcome at the monument.

_____ 6. Where's the pictures of the men in the regiment?

_____ 7. Who were the president of the United States then?

_____ 8. Here's two interesting facts about that period.

_____ 9. For the first time in history, the troops of soldiers was photographed.

_____ 10. The Union army of volunteers number four million.

DON'T AND DOESN'T

---

171 **The contractions *don't* and *doesn't* must agree with their subjects.**

Use *don't* with plural subjects and with the pronouns *I* and *you*.

EXAMPLES   The **boys don't** have practice today. [plural subject]
             Don't you like rye bread? [the pronoun *you*]

EXERCISE 14   **Writing Sentences with *Don't* and *Doesn't***

Complete each of the sentences below by writing *don't* or *doesn't* and any other words to make the meaning of the sentence clear. Write the complete sentences on your own paper. Be sure to use the contraction that agrees with the subject.

EX.   1. The team
      1. The team doesn't play softball at this park anymore.

1. Although I like most foods, I

2. José and Kareem

3. Lawanda

4. You

5. Our city

6. The green truck

7. Jason's horse

8. Dominique

9. My house

10. Jasper, the sheep dog

11. The loud parakeet

12. The park rangers at the state park

13. My father's coffee cups

14. My pet rabbit

15. My sister

REVIEW EXERCISE 2

A. Proofreading for Subject-Verb Agreement

On the line before each sentence below, write the correct form of any verbs that do not agree with their subjects. If a sentence contains no errors in subject-verb agreement, write C on the line.

EX. _taste_ 1. Most of the crackers tastes stale.

_____ 1. These carrots doesn't look crisp.

_____ 2. Neither the actors nor the director seem ready for opening night.

_____ 3. Does Cheryl and Pete live on your street?

_____ 4. Nariz doesn't enjoy playing soccer, but I does.

_____ 5. Each of these artists have a studio in his or her home.

_____ 6. The players and the team mascot are in the locker room.

_____ 7. Hilda don't know the answer to the question.

_____ 8. Is either June or Ana on the cheerleading squad?

_____ 9. Doesn't you have an extra key to your locker?

_____ 10. Where's the refreshments for the team members?

B. Writing a Letter

Your grandparents are giving you a bike for your birthday. They want you to give them some information about which kind of bike they should buy. They also want to know the reasons for your choice. First, read newspaper ads or do some research to discover what kind of bike you want. Then, on your own paper, write five sentences, telling your grandparents your choice and your reasons for it. Be sure to use subject-verb agreement.

EX. Dear Grandma,
I would like a mountain bike because it can go anywhere.
I can ride it through fields and in the woods as well as on the road.

PRONOUN AGREEMENT

17m A pronoun agrees with its antecedent in number and gender.

When a pronoun refers to a noun or to another pronoun, that word is called the pronoun's *antecedent*.

Some singular personal pronouns have forms that indicate gender. *Masculine* pronouns (*he, him, his*) refer to males. *Feminine* pronouns (*she, her, hers*) refer to females. *Neuter* pronouns (*it, its*) refer to things (neither male nor female), ideas, and animals.

EXAMPLES   **Susan** hurt **her** leg in the race.
                Roberto finally found **his** lost dog.
                That **bicycle** is missing **its** seat.

The antecedent of a personal pronoun can be another kind of pronoun, such as *each, neither,* or *one*. To determine the gender of a personal pronoun that refers to one of these other pronouns, look in the phrase that follows the antecedent.

EXAMPLES   **One** of the **women** has left **her** briefcase in the conference room.
                Neither of the **men** has bought **his** ticket yet.

☞   **REFERENCE NOTE:** For more information about antecedents, see page 91.

(1) A singular pronoun is used to refer to *anyone, anybody, each, either, everybody, everyone, neither, nobody, one, no one, someone,* or *somebody*.

EXAMPLES   **Each** of the dogs has **its** own bed.
                Someone on the girls' track team has forgotten **her** cleats.

(2) A singular pronoun is used to refer to two or more singular antecedents joined by *or* or *nor*.

EXAMPLES   **Maria or Fern** will donate **her** time to the committee.
                Either **Justin or Andrew** will drive **his** car to the meeting.

NOTE   Sometimes the gender of the antecedent may be either masculine or feminine. To avoid using *his or her*, revise the sentence completely.

AWKWARD   Either **Ezra or Nicole** might bring **her** baseball.
CLEAR   **Ezra** might bring **his** baseball, and **Nicole** might bring **hers**.

(3) A plural pronoun is used to refer to two or more antecedents joined by *and*.

EXAMPLES   My **uncle and aunt** sold **their** house and moved back to Italy.
The **bluebird and** the **sparrow** have built **their** nests.

EXERCISE 15   Identifying Antecedents and Writing Pronouns That Agree with Them

Complete each of the sentences below by inserting a pronoun that agrees with its antecedent.

EX.   1.   Both of my brothers write down _____their_____ daily thoughts in a journal.

1.   Someone on the boys' basketball team has left _____ jersey on the bus.

2.   All of the students have learned _____ lines for the play.

3.   Polly or Beth will lead off the debate with _____ own opinion.

4.   Nina has completed her homework, and Marcelo has completed _____ .

5.   The elephants raised _____ trunks and called to each other.

6.   All of the people at the family reunion brought _____ cameras.

7.   Either of the girls will sign _____ name on your nomination papers.

8.   Neither the father nor the son had worn _____ watch.

9.   Aunt Beatrice and Uncle Lorenzo sent _____ best wishes to the bride and groom.

10.   Mrs. Leon put _____ baby in the car seat.

CHAPTER REVIEW

A. Correcting Errors in Subject-Verb Agreement

On the line before each sentence below, write the correct form of any verb or verb phrase that does not agree with its subject. If a sentence contains no errors in subject-verb agreement, write C on the line.

EX. __was__ 1. Leon were a witness to an accident.

_____ 1. Several players on the college all-star team is over seven feet tall.

_____ 2. Neither of these pianos sounds in tune.

_____ 3. Several of the people in the President's cabinet is women.

_____ 4. None of the students in home-economics class have ever eaten falafel, hummus, tabbouleh, or any other Middle Eastern foods.

_____ 5. The writer and director of *Sleepless in Seattle* were Nora Ephron.

_____ 6. Neither Paulo nor his brothers has ever been to Brazil.

_____ 7. The crowd always cheers when a player hits a home run.

_____ 8. Here's the directions for putting together the bicycle.

_____ 9. In the box near the bookcase is several new novels.

_____ 10. Many people enjoy flying, but I doesn't.

B. Correcting Errors in Pronoun-Antecedent Agreement

In each of the following sentences, underline the pronoun that does not agree with its antecedent. On the line before each sentence, write the correct form of the pronoun. If a sentence contains no errors, write C for correct.

EX. __C__ 1. Neither Ms. Fuller nor Ms. Sanchez could stop her car.

_____ 1. That bicycle needs to have her gears adjusted.

_____ 2. Each of the campers has their own tent and sleeping bag.

_____ 3. Neither Sue nor Sabrina has finished their book report.

_____ 4. One player on the boys' soccer team injured her leg during the game.

_____ 5. My grandmother and grandfather just sold their house in San Antonio.

_____ 6. The Salisbury Cathedral in England is famous for his 404-foot spire.

_____ 7. My Chinese cousin showed me an alphabet him uses that has five thousand characters.

_____ 8. Everyone in the neighborhood brought their lunch to the picnic.

_____ 9. One of my mother's friends, Mrs. Sperno, loaned its van.

_____ 10. The deer looked for his food at sundown.

C. Writing Questions and Answers for Television

You are one of the writers for a television quiz show. Your assignment for the next show is to create ten questions about the Alamo. Use reference books and encyclopedias to gather information. On your own paper, write your questions. Be sure to include answers so that the quiz-show host will have all the needed information. When you have completed your questions and answers, proofread them carefully. Make sure that they contain no errors in subject-verb agreement or in pronoun-antecedent agreement.

EX.   1. What are the names of two famous men who lost their lives during the battle at the Alamo?
       Answer: David Crockett and James Bowie

PRINCIPAL PARTS AND REGULAR VERBS

The four basic forms of a verb are called the *principal parts* of the verb.

18a   The principal parts of a verb are the *base form*, the *present participle*, the *past*, and the *past participle*.

Base Form	Present Participle	Past	Past Participle
walk	(is) walking	walked	(have) walked

Notice that the present participle and the past participle require helping verbs (forms of *be* and *have*).

EXERCISE 1   Identifying the Principal Parts of Verbs

Underline the verb or verb phrase in each sentence. On the line before the sentence, identify the verb's principal part. Write *base* for *base form*, *pres. part.* for *present participle*, *past* for *past*, or *past part.* for *past participle*.

EX.   _past_   1.   We <u>hiked</u> a long way yesterday.

_____   1.   Are they walking all the way to the summit?

_____   2.   Julio and Emilio discovered a new trail on the map.

_____   3.   The hikers have stopped for a short rest.

_____   4.   On our hikes we always use canteens for water.

_____   5.   Denise is climbing to the top of a huge rock.

_____   6.   After a few minutes, the other hikers waited for Denise on the trail.

_____   7.   Jill has definitely needed new boots for a long time.

_____   8.   Julio is drying his wet socks by the campfire.

_____   9.   Those horrible mosquitoes have attacked the group every night.

_____   10.   These mosquito bites are really itching.

179

18b   A *regular verb* forms its past and past participle by adding –*d* or –*ed* to the base form.

Base Form	Present Participle	Past	Past Participle
hope	(is) hoping	hoped	(have) hoped
answer	(is) answering	answered	(have) answered

EXERCISE 2   Writing the Forms of Regular Verbs

On your own paper, write the correct form of the verb given in italics. Use clues in the sentence to pick the form that expresses the correct time.

EX.   1.   Last night we *watch* the stars through a telescope.

    1. watched

1. We are *use* our new telescope.
2. Jim and I have *start* a star journal.
3. In the journal, we are *note* details about the constellations.
4. We have *fill* one notebook so far.
5. People in ancient Greece *name* many constellations.
6. Have you *look* at the notes about the constellation Cassiopeia?
7. Jim and I *discover* something interesting about Cassiopeia.
8. Five of its brightest stars *form* a crooked letter W.
9. Tomorrow we are *visit* the planetarium.
10. I am *try* to learn as much as possible about stars and constellations.
11. I have *read* the astrology report in the newspaper.
12. But today we *learn* that astrology is not a science.
13. No one has *prove* that the positions of the stars control human destiny.
14. Still, my friends and I have *enjoy* the astrology column.
15. When we were *discuss* my horoscope on my birthday, I *learn* something important.

IRREGULAR VERBS

18c An *irregular verb* forms its past and past participle in some other way than by adding *–d* or *–ed* to the infinitive form.

 NOTE   If you are not sure about the principal parts of a verb, look in a dictionary. An entry for an irregular verb lists the principal parts of the verb. If the principal parts are not given in the dictionary entry, the verb is a regular verb.

EXERCISE 3   Choosing Correct Irregular Verbs

On the line before each sentence below, write the correct past form of each verb.

EX.   _____chose_____   1. Chan-Shan (*choose, chose*) to build a frame house.

_____   1. She (*beginned, began*) by grading her lot.

_____   2. The contractor (*send, sent*) a bulldozer.

_____   3. They (*builded, built*) the basement floor.

_____   4. It (*costed, cost*) a lot for materials.

_____   5. Hammers (*rang, rung*) on nails.

_____   6. The nails (*sank, sunk*) into the wood.

_____   7. Dust (*fell, felt*) everywhere.

_____   8. A worker (*catched, caught*) her leg on a beam.

_____   9. She (*hurts, hurt*) herself.

_____   10. She (*rode, rid*) in an ambulance.

EXERCISE 4   Proofreading Sentences for Errors in Verb Forms

Each of the following sentences contains one incorrect verb form. Underline the errors that you find. Then, on the line before each sentence, write the correct form of each verb.

EX.   _____brought_____   1. Mario <u>brung</u> his drawings to the interview.

_____   1. Mario has got a job as an artist.

_____   2. He seen the ad in the newspaper for the job of editorial cartoonist.

_____ 3. He sended his résumé to the editor of the local newpaper.

_____ 4. Throughout high school, Mario drawed cartoons for the school newspaper.

_____ 5. He has took many art courses and is quite talented.

_____ 6. A few days after the editor received Mario's letter and résumé, she speaked to Mario on the telephone.

_____ 7. She maked an appointment for a personal interview.

_____ 8. Now Mario has went to the interview and is waiting to hear from the editor again.

_____ 9. When they meet, the editor was very complimentary about Mario's portfolio of cartoons.

_____ 10. The editor just called and give Mario the job.

EXERCISE 5   Using the Past and Past Participle Forms of Irregular Verbs

On the line in each of the following sentences, write the past or past participle forms of two of the verbs on the list. Use each verb at least once. Make sure that your finished sentences make sense.

begin	fall	lead	see
bring	get	meet	send
build	give	put	take
choose	go	read	tell
do	know	say	write

EX.   1. No one could imagine why he _____did; said_____ that.

1. I was amazed that you _____ that.

2. She has _____ the story.

3. Yesterday, he _____ me a package.

4. We have _____ the most beautiful pictures.

5. They _____ about their adventures.

6. We have _____ our leader.

7. What have you _____?

8. I have _____ some very interesting people.

9. She has _____ the dog to the veterinarian.

10. He was sorry that he _____ it.

COMMON IRREGULAR VERBS			
Base Form	Present Participle	Past	Past Participle
begin	(is) beginning	began	(have) begun
bite	(is) biting	bit	(have) bitten *or* bit
blow	(is) blowing	blew	(have) blown
break	(is) breaking	broke	(have) broken
bring	(is) bringing	brought	(have) brought
build	(is) building	built	(have) built
burst	(is) bursting	burst	(have) burst
catch	(is) catching	caught	(have) caught
choose	(is) choosing	chose	(have) chosen
come	(is) coming	came	(have) come
cost	(is) costing	cost	(have) cost
do	(is) doing	did	(have) done
draw	(is) drawing	drew	(have) drawn
drink	(is) drinking	drank	(have) drunk
drive	(is) driving	drove	(have) driven
eat	(is) eating	ate	(have) eaten
fall	(is) falling	fell	(have) fallen
feel	(is) feeling	felt	(have) felt
freeze	(is) freezing	froze	(have) frozen
get	(is) getting	got	(have) gotten *or* got
give	(is) giving	gave	(have) given
go	(is) going	went	(have) gone
grow	(is) growing	grew	(have) grown
hurt	(is) hurting	hurt	(have) hurt
know	(is) knowing	knew	(have) known

COMMON IRREGULAR VERBS

Base Form	Present Participle	Past	Past Participle
lead	(is) leading	led	(have) led
lend	(is) lending	lent	(have) lent
lose	(is) losing	lost	(have) lost
make	(is) making	made	(have) made
meet	(is) meeting	met	(have) met
put	(is) putting	put	(have) put
ride	(is) riding	rode	(have) ridden
ring	(is) ringing	rang	(have) rung
run	(is) running	ran	(have) run
say	(is) saying	said	(have) said
see	(is) seeing	saw	(have) seen
sell	(is) selling	sold	(have) sold
send	(is) sending	sent	(have) sent
shrink	(is) shrinking	shrank	(have) shrunk
sing	(is) singing	sang	(have) sung
sink	(is) sinking	sank	(have) sunk
speak	(is) speaking	spoke	(have) spoken
stand	(is) standing	stood	(have) stood
steal	(is) stealing	stole	(have) stolen
swim	(is) swimming	swam	(have) swum
swing	(is) swinging	swung	(have) swung
take	(is) taking	took	(have) taken
tell	(is) telling	told	(have) told
throw	(is) throwing	threw	(have) thrown
wear	(is) wearing	wore	(have) worn
win	(is) winning	won	(have) won
write	(is) writing	wrote	(have) written

VERB TENSE

18d The *tense* of a verb indicates the time of the action or state of being expressed by the verb.

Tense	Examples
Present	I see, you see, she sees
Past	I saw, we saw, they saw
Future	I will (shall) see, you will see, he will see
Present Perfect	I have seen, you have seen, he has seen
Past Perfect	I had seen, you had seen, he had seen
Future Perfect	I will (shall) have seen, she will have seen, he will have seen

This time line shows the relationship between the six tenses.

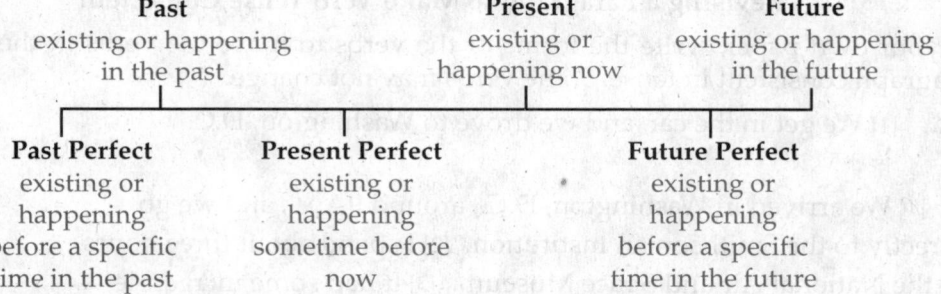

Past	Present	Future
existing or happening in the past	existing or happening now	existing or happening in the future

Past Perfect	Present Perfect	Future Perfect
existing or happening before a specific time in the past	existing or happening sometime before now	existing or happening before a specific time in the future

18e Do not change needlessly from one tense to another.

When writing about events that take place in the present, use verbs that are in the present tense. When writing about events that occurred in the past, use verbs that are in the past tense.

NONSTANDARD   When I went to the store, I see Melba. [*Went* is in the past tense, and *see* is in the present tense]

STANDARD   When I **went** to the store, I **saw** Melba. [Both *went* and *saw* are in the past tense.]

STANDARD   When I **go** to the store, I **see** Melba. [Both *go* and *see* are in the present tense.]

EXERCISE 6   Revising Sentences for Correct Verb Tense

In each of the sentences below, draw a line through the incorrect form of the verb, and write the correct form above it.

EX.   1. If the rain ~~stopped~~ *stops*, the track meet will continue.

1. We used to lived in Chicago.

2. Our school is visit the Art Institute.

3. If you took the train, get off at Jackson.

4. We will be have lunch in Grant Park.

5. Last year we swum in Lake Michigan.

6. The Cubs losed again.

7. Have you ever had a stuffed pizza?

8. The chicken wings be so spicy they burn my lips.

9. Don't sent me out in this cold, please!

10. They meaned the Sears Building to be the tallest in the world.

EXERCISE 7   Revising a Paragraph to Make Verb Tense Consistent

On your own paper, write the forms of the verbs to make the verbs in the paragraph consistent in tense. Some verbs may not change.

EX.   [1] We get in the car, and we drove to Washington, D.C.
       1. got

[1] We arrived in Washington, D.C., around 9 A.M., and we go directly to the Smithsonian Institution. [2] I spend about three hours in the National Air and Space Museum. [3] It had some incredible displays, like Charles Lindbergh's plane, the *Spirit of St. Louis*, and one of the Gemini space capsules. [4] From the exhibit area, I walked into the theater and see a film. [5] The film makes me feel as if I were soaring above the earth in a sailplane. [6] The photography was beautiful, but sometimes it makes me feel dizzy, almost seasick. [7] After the film, I walk to the lobby and meet Bobby Ray and Samantha. [8] We stroll out onto the mall by the Washington Monument and found a great spot for a picnic. [9] After lunch, we visit the Vietnam Veterans Memorial. [10] Then we got in the car and drive to my favorite Washington landmark, the Jefferson Memorial.

SIT *AND* SET *AND* RISE *AND* RAISE

SIT AND SET

18f **The verb *sit* means "to rest in an upright, seated position." *Sit* seldom takes an object. The verb *set* means "to place" or "to put (something)." *Set* usually takes an object. Unlike *sit*, *set* has the same form for the base form, past, and past participle.**

Base Form	Present Participle	Past	Past Participle
sit	(is) sitting	sat	(have) sat
set	(is) setting	set	(have) set

EXAMPLES   I'll **sit** in the front row. [*Sit* takes no object.]
I'll **set** your papers here. [Set what? *Papers* is the object.]

EXERCISE 8   Using Forms of *Sit* and *Set*

Write the correct form of *sit* or *set* on the line or lines in each sentence below. If the verb that you use is a form of *set*, underline its object.

EX.   1. Wanda had____*set*____ the <u>vase</u> in her grandmother's room.

1. Please _____ next to me at the movies.

2. Liona can't remember where she _____ her purse.

3. After our hike, we _____ by the fire and talked.

4. Let's _____ down while Earline _____ the table.

5. The team manager will _____ the equipment on the bench.

6. The woman _____ down and _____ the food on the tray.

7. Were you _____ in this chair?

8. They had _____ in the waiting room for an hour before the train finally arrived.

9. When you are _____ new, young plants into the soil, be sure to give them plenty of water.

10. _____ the packages near the front door so that you won't forget to take them to the post office in the morning.

187

RISE AND RAISE

18g **The verb *rise* means "to go up," or "to get up." *Rise* rarely takes an object. The verb *raise* means "to lift up" or "to cause (something) to rise." *Raise* usually takes an object.**

Base Form	Present Participle	Past	Past Participle
rise	(is) rising	rose	(have) risen
raise	(is) raising	raised	(have) raised

EXAMPLES   Please **rise** from your seat to greet our guest. [*Rise* takes no object.]
Please **raise** your hand if you have a question. [Raise what? *Hand* is the object.]

EXERCISE 9   Identifying the Correct Forms of *Rise* and *Raise*

Underline the correct form of *rise* or *raise* to complete each sentence below. If the verb you choose is a form of *raise*, underline its object.

EX.   1.   Most car manufacturers have (*risen, raised*) their prices.

1.   The fans will (*rise, raise*) their banners and cheer when the team runs onto the field.

2.   We are (*rising, raising*) funds for a celebration rally on International Women's Day, which is March 8.

3.   Did the price of fresh vegetables (*rise, raise*)?

4.   About ten days after Isabel planted the seeds, little shoots (*rose, raised*) from the ground.

5.   Simon, you have (*risen, raised*) a very interesting question about how sushi is made.

6.   The young girl (*rose, raised*) from her seat to speak.

7.   Has the sun (*risen, raised*) yet?

8.   Three people (*rose, raised*) the question.

9.   Who (*rose, raised*) the flag for Cinco de Mayo?

10.   The river has been (*raising, rising*) since last night.

LIE *AND* LAY

18h **The verb *lie* means "to rest," "to recline," or "to be in place." *Lie* never takes an object. The verb *lay* means "to put (something) in a place." *Lay* usually takes an object.**

Base Form	Present Participle	Past	Past Participle
lie	(is) lying	lay	(have) lain
lay	(is) laying	laid	(have) laid

EXAMPLES   Dad **is lying** in the hammock. [*Is lying* takes no object.]
The waiter **is laying** a fresh tablecloth on the table. [Laying what? *Tablecloth* is the object.]
The dog **lay** asleep all afternoon. [*Lay* takes no object.]
Last night, we **laid** our blankets on the floor and pretended that we were camping out. [Laid what? *Blankets* is the object.]

EXERCISE 10   Identifying the Correct Forms of *Lie* and *Lay*

Underline the correct form of *lie* or *lay* to complete each of the following sentences. If the verb that you choose is a form of *lay*, underline its object.

EX.   1. (*Lie*, *Lay*) down your rake, and rest for a while.

1. The Connecticut River (*lies*, *lays*) on the border between New Hampshire and Vermont.

2. She can't come to the phone because she is (*lying*, *laying*) down and taking a nap.

3. Workers have (*lain*, *laid*) a new carpet in the auditorium.

4. The trash barrels have (*lain*, *laid*) by the side of the road all day.

5. My kickstand broke, so I must (*lie*, *lay*) my bike on its side.

6. Yesterday I (*lay*, *laid*) down for a nap.

7. My new bracelet is (*lying*, *laying*) on the table.

8. Please (*lie*, *lay*) the atlas on my desk.

9. After studying for the geography test, Sharon (*lay, laid*) down for a rest.

10. When the time is up, please (*lie, lay*) down your pencils.

11. Helga has (*laid, lain*) your study notes on your chair.

12. In Chile, where do the Andes Mountains (*lie, lay*)?

13. Rich deposits of copper have (*lain, laid*) in the foothills of the Andes for thousands of years.

14. The teacher (*lay, laid*) down the rules.

15. Sonja (*lay, laid*) too long under the sunlamp.

EXERCISE 11   Proofreading for the Correct Use of *Lie* and *Lay*

In the sentences below, draw a line under each error in the use of *lie* or *lay*. On the line before each sentence, write the correct form of *lie* or *lay*. If a sentence contains no errors, write C on the line.

EX.   _____laid_____   1. Aunt Phoebe's chickens have <u>lain</u> brown eggs.

_____   1. Some people say that when cows are laying down in a meadow, rain is on the way.

_____   2. Fran lay the spare key to her greenhouse under a rock in the garden.

_____   3. The children have laid down for a nap.

_____   4. Bernadette is laying the tickets on the counter.

_____   5. Bags of paper for recycling laid in the garage.

_____   6. I found it where she had lain it.

_____   7. He lie there wondering how he had made such a mess.

_____   8. She stared at the broken bat, which lay in pieces about her.

_____   9. It had laid there for so long it was now moldy.

_____ 10. But it was just laying there.

CHAPTER REVIEW

A. Proofreading a Paragraph for Correct Verb Forms

If a sentence in the paragraph below contains the wrong form of a verb, draw a line through the verb. Write the correct form above it.

EX.   [1] George A. Reisner ~~lead~~ *led* the archaeological expedition to Africa.

[1] Various sites in Nubia, one of Africa's ancient civilizations, have gave evidence of being complex and artistic. [2] Nubia laid along the Nile River, south of Egypt. [3] Historians have wrote that many Nubians lived to the age of 120. [4] The Nubian people built large temples out of stone and maked beautiful statues and jewelry out of bronze and gold.

[5] Nubia's location is unusual for a major civilization, for the climate was extremely hot and dry. [6] Many years ago, the Egyptians create a dam on the Nile River, near the site of the ancient Nubian civilization. [7] Then, in 1906, the Egyptians rose the dam by 16.5 feet. [8] Before they done that, they invited an archaeologist named George A. Reisner to explore the area for ancient relics. [9] Deep in the sand, he and others finded many tombs of ancient Nubian rulers. [10] Thanks to archaeologists, modern people have began to understand the glory of that African civilization.

B. Identifying the Correct Forms of *Sit* and *Set*, *Rise* and *Raise*, and *Lie* and *Lay*

For each of the following sentences, underline the correct verb in parentheses.

EX.   1. Please (*sit*, *set*) the pot of soup on the stove.

1. Crossing the prairie, the covered wagons (*rose*, *raised*) a cloud of dust.

2. The frog (*sat*, *set*) on a lily pad in the shallow pond.

3. After listening for twenty minutes, the audience (*rose, raised*) to show respect for the speaker.

4. While I was (*lying, laying*) in bed last night, I was awakened by thunder and lightning.

5. We (*sat, set*) at our table for a long time.

6. The storm made the sea (*rise, raise*), and waves crashed onto the boardwalk.

7. Our school has (*set, sit*) the date for a multicultural festival.

8. Luanne (*lay, laid*) another log on the campfire.

9. Yukio had (*risen, raised*) at dawn in order to get to the railroad station on time.

10. Your wet boots are (*lying, laying*) on a sheet of newspaper in the back hall.

11. Don't just (*lay, lie*) there; (*set, sit*) up!

12. The preacher said, "All (*rise, raise*)!" and they (*raised, rose*).

13. They (*rose, raised*) their flags and waved them.

14. The whale (*rose, raised*) up quickly and spouted.

15. I saw you (*lie, lay*) it out on the table.

C.   Writing Notes for an Exhibit

For a science fair, you are presenting an exhibit that shows how a volcano works. Use encyclopedias and other reference works to learn about volcanoes. On your own paper, take notes during your research. Then turn your notes into ten complete sentences. In your sentences, explain what causes a volcano to erupt and what happens during the eruption. When you finish your sentences, proofread them carefully for the correct use of verbs. Underline the verbs you have used.

EX.   1. Some volcanic eruptions blow mountains apart.

CASES OF PRONOUNS

Case is the form of a noun or a pronoun that shows how it is used. There are three cases:

- *nominative*
- *objective*
- *possessive*

A noun uses the same form for both the nominative and the objective cases. For example, a noun used as a subject (nominative case) does not change form when used as an indirect object (objective case). A noun changes its form for the possessive case, usually by adding an apostrophe and an *s*.

NOMINATIVE CASE   The **doctor** is being interviewed. [subject]
OBJECTIVE CASE   Someone is interviewing the **doctor.** [direct object]
POSSESSIVE CASE   The **doctor's** waiting room was empty. [ownership]

☞ **REFERENCE NOTE:** For more information on nominative case pronouns, see page 195; for objective case pronouns, see pages 197 and 199; for possessive case pronouns, see pages 273 and 275.

Unlike nouns, most personal pronouns have different forms for all three cases.

PERSONAL PRONOUNS		
Singular		
Nominative Case	**Objective Case**	**Possessive Case**
I	me	my, mine
you	you	your, yours
he, she, it	him, her, it	his, her, hers, its
Plural		
Nominative Case	**Objective Case**	**Possessive Case**
we	us	our, ours
you	you	your, yours
they	them	their, theirs

NOTE   Some teachers prefer to call possessive pronouns, such as *my*, adjectives. Follow your teacher's directions in labeling possessive forms.

EXERCISE 1   Identifying Personal Pronouns and Their Cases

Identify the case of the italicized pronoun by writing *nom.* for *nominative,* *obj.* for *objective,* and *poss.* for *possessive* on the line before each sentence.

EX.   _obj._   1. James brought *her* flowers.

_____   1. A man named Frederick Douglass escaped slavery, and *he* later wrote about his experiences.

_____   2. *They* made a purple and white piñata for the party.

_____   3. Remember to return your violin to *its* case.

_____   4. The Algonquins made *their* wigwams of small sticks and bark.

_____   5. I visited New Mexico and bought beautiful pottery bowls for *you.*

_____   6. *My* father makes delicious mango ice cream.

_____   7. Yun showed *me* the correct way to hold chopsticks.

_____   8. *We* decided to organize a softball game.

_____   9. Reggie takes dancing lessons, and *he* will be in a show this weekend.

_____   10. Please tell *them* when the orchestra will be playing.

Mother Goose & Grimm reprinted by permission: Tribune Media Services.

NOMINATIVE CASE PRONOUNS

19a The subject of a verb is in the nominative case.

A *subject* tells *whom* or *what* the sentence is about.

EXAMPLE **I** play the guitar. [*I* is the subject of *play*.]
He and **I** formed a band. [*He* and *I* are the subjects of *formed*.]
We practice while **they** listen. [*We* is the subject of *practice*. *They* is the subject of *listen*.]

NOTE A pronoun is capitalized when it is the first word in a sentence. The pronoun *I* is always capitalized.

To choose the correct pronoun in a compound subject, try each form of the pronoun separately as the simple subject of the verb.

EXAMPLE Geraldo and (*him, he*) won first prize.
Him won first prize.
He won first prize.
ANSWER Geraldo and **he** won first prize.

19b A *predicate nominative* is in the nominative case.

A *predicate nominative* follows a linking verb and explains or identifies the subject of the verb. A personal pronoun used as a predicate nominative follows a form of the verb *be* (*am, is, are, was, were, be,* or *been*).

EXAMPLE The woman in the front row was **she**. [*She* follows the linking verb *was* and identifies the subject *woman*.]
The first speakers will be **he** and **I**. [*He* and *I* follows the linking verb *will be* and identifies the subject *speakers*.]

NOTE Expressions such as *It's me*, *That's her*, and *It was them* are accepted in everyday speaking. In writing, however, such expressions are generally considered nonstandard and should be avoided.

☞ **REFERENCE NOTE:** For more information about predicate nominatives, see page 119.

EXERCISE 2   Identifying Personal Pronouns Used as Subjects and Predicate Nominatives

On your own paper, rewrite each of the sentences below, using the correct pronoun in parentheses.

EX.   1. It might have been (*him, he*) in the background.

    1. It might have been he in the background.

1. One fan thought that the woman wearing glasses was (*her, she*).
2. Mr. Marcus thought that it was (*we, us*).
3. (*She, Her*) and (*I, me*) are both good tennis players.
4. If the teacher is not (*he, him*), I will not sign up for the class.
5. The best skateboarders are (*he, him*) and (*I, me*).
6. My brother and (*me, I*) are planning a carwash, but (*we, us*) need some help.
7. The woman who met (*we, us*) in Victoria Square was (*she, her*).
8. Will (*him, he*) take the dog for a walk?
9. Melvin and (*she, her*) are building a model of a water wheel.
10. (*We, Us*) thought it was (*she, her*) who sang that song.

EXERCISE 3   Proofreading for the Correct Use of Pronouns in the Nominative Case

In the paragraph below, draw a line through each pronoun that is used incorrectly, and write the correct pronoun in the space above it. Some sentences may contain no errors in pronoun format.

EX.   [1] Charlie and ~~me~~ are writing a report.

[1] Him and I both like playing games, so we are writing about them. [2] The person doing the research is me. [3] After school on Wednesday, him and me will meet with Mrs. Wu. [4] Her and her sister still play the old form of mahjong. [5] They learned the game when they were young girls in China. [6] My grandfather said that him and Grandma play mahjong, too. [7] They could have been our teachers, but Grandma and Grandpa play a newer form of the game. [8] Charlie and me wanted to learn the original game. [9] Even though we both play well, the better player is him. [10] Now in art class he is making a mahjong set for my grandparents and me.

PRONOUNS AS DIRECT OBJECTS

19c   A *direct object* is in the objective case.

A *direct object* follows an action verb and tells *whom* or *what* receives the action of the verb.

EXAMPLES   Niñita called **me** about the homework assignment. [*Me* tells *whom* Niñita called.]
The dog buried **them** under a bush. [*Them* tells *what* the dog buried.]

To choose the correct pronoun in a compound direct object, try each form of the pronoun separately in the sentence.

EXAMPLE   Mr. Benally invited Rose and (*I, me*) for a visit.
Mr. Benally invited *I* for a visit.
Mr. Benally invited *me* for a visit.
ANSWER   Mr. Benally invited Rose and **me** for a visit.

EXERCISE 4   Writing Pronouns Used as Direct Objects

Complete each of the following sentences by writing an appropriate pronoun on the line in the sentence. Use a variety of pronouns, but do not use *you* or *it*.

EX.   1.   The principal congratulated Toby and __her__ .

1.   One performer invited T. J. and _____ up on stage!

2.   A computer identified_____ and _____ from partial fingerprints.

3.   Do you want to call _____ now or later?

4.   Virginia photographed _____ and _____ in front of the Washington Monument.

5.   After putting up the rest of the posters, Leo will meet _____ and _____ .

6.   All night long, the bus carried_____ across the plain.

7.   Will we include _____ and _____ on our team?

8.   About an hour before the meeting, someone called _____ .

9. The waves tossed _____ and _____ around like corks.

10. I researched Dr. Martin Luther King, Jr., and _____ for my
    report.

EXERCISE 5 ' Choosing Correct Pronoun Forms

In each sentence below, underline the correct pronoun form from the pair in
parentheses.

EX.   [1] Lonnie called Theresa and (*I*, *me*) at home.

[1] Did you see (*us*, *we*) in the picture in the newspaper last week?

[2] On Tuesday night, a reporter called Theresa and (*me*, *I*) about a

feature story. [3] The reporter wanted (*she*, *her*) and me for a

photograph. [4] His story would feature (*she*, *her*) and me as

volunteers at the local hospital. [5] I thanked (*he*, *him*), but explained

that I am camera-shy. [6] But Theresa wanted (*we*, *us*) for the paper.

[7] The reporter told (*me*, *I*) that this story could help the community.

[8] Others might see Theresa and (*I*, *me*) helping and want to

volunteer. [9] They convinced (*me*, *I*) to pose. [10] Many people did

compliment (*we*, *us*) after they saw our picture and read the

reporter's story.

EXERCISE 6   Proofreading Sentences for Correct Pronoun Forms

If a sentence below has an incorrect pronoun, write the correct form on the
line before the sentence. If the sentence is correct, write C.

EX.   __C__ 1. Ellie served them last night.

_____ 1. They met my mother and I at the cafeteria.

_____ 2. During the last week of August, Juan invited us to his home
           in Mazatlán.

_____ 3. If this idea worries you or she, I'll change the plan.

_____ 4. The people at the last table called the girls and he.

_____ 5. It must have taken Luís and they several hours to decide.

OTHER OBJECTIVE CASE PRONOUN USES

19d   An *indirect object* is in the objective case.

An *indirect object* tells to *whom* (or to *what*) or for *whom* (or for *what*) after an action verb.

EXAMPLES   The runner handed **me** the torch. [*Me* tells *to whom* the runner handed the torch.]

Mrs. Rembert gave **us** a challenging assignment. [*Us* tells *to whom* Mrs. Rembert gave the assignment.]

To help you choose the correct pronoun in a compound indirect object, try each form of the pronoun separately in the sentence.

EXAMPLE   Lilia handed Lester and (*I, me*) five peaches.
Lilia handed *I* five peaches. [incorrect use of nominative case]
Lilia handed *me* five peaches. [correct use of objective case]
ANSWER   Lilia handed Lester and **me** five peaches.

EXERCISE 7   Writing Pronouns Used as Indirect Objects

Choose appropriate pronouns to write on the lines in the following sentences. Use a variety of pronouns, but do not use *you* or *it*.

EX.   1. Have you seen __them__ lately?

1. We gave Alan and _____ tickets to the dinosaur exhibit.

2. Did you make Berta and _____ paella for supper?

3. According to this brochure, we should write _____ a letter by Friday.

4. The man showed _____ two sand paintings.

5. Mr. Makek threw _____ a ball to play with.

6. Who taught _____ sign language during the summer?

7. Volunteer workers had built _____ a new home.

8. I was surprised that they presented _____ an award for speech.

9. Before Sergio can debate, someone will have to give _____ a little coaching.

10. The doctors showed _____ the X-rays.

19e   An *object of a preposition* is in the objective case.

A *prepositional phrase* is a group of words consisting of a preposition, a noun or pronoun that serves as the object of the preposition, and any modifiers of that object.

EXAMPLES   by the **sofa**   next to **them**   behind the **curtain**
           in front of **me**   after **Shani** and **him**   instead of **us**

☞ **REFERENCE NOTE:** For a list of prepositions, see page 109. For more information on prepositional phrases, see pages 125–129.

A pronoun used as the object of a preposition should always be in the objective case.

EXAMPLES   Everyone except **us** knew Valentina Tereshkova's name. [*Us* is the object of the preposition *except*.]
           Salvador smiled as the herd came toward **him**. [*Him* is the object of the preposition *toward*.]
           Suddenly the rainbows were visible to **them** and **me**. [*Them* and *me* are the compound object of the preposition *to*.]

EXERCISE 8   Choosing Correct Pronouns Used as Objects of Prepositions

For each sentence below, choose the correct pronoun form from the pair in parentheses. Underline the pronoun that you choose.

EX.   1. You may bring one guest in addition to (*her*, *she*).

1. Mr. Garabedian began band practice without (*me*, *I*).

2. The girl beside (*he*, *him*) plays the trumpet.

3. Usually, the trombone players march in front of (*they*, *them*).

4. According to (*her*, *she*), anyone can play the kazoo.

5. Who can sing in place of (*they*, *them*)?

6. The singer behind Ravi and (*me*, *I*) has a wonderful voice.

7. We played those marches for the director and (*they*, *them*).

8. Uncle Yanni sings in a chorus, and I joined the chorus because of (*him*, *he*).

9. Before we knew it, the performance was upon (*we*, *us*)!

10. My parents are in the last row, and yours are in the balcony above (*them*, *they*).

WHO *AND* WHOM

19f   The pronoun *who* has different forms in the nominative and objective cases. *Who* is the nominative form; *whom* is the objective form.

NOTE   In spoken English the use of *whom* is becoming less common. When you speak, you may correctly begin any sentence with *who*, regardless of the grammar of the sentence. In written English, however, you should distinguish between *who* and *whom*. *Who* is used as a subject or as a predicate nominative, and *whom* is used as an object.

To help you choose between *who* and *whom* in a clause, follow these steps:

Step 1:   Find the clause.

Step 2:   Decide how the pronoun is used—as subject, predicate nominative, object of the verb, or object of a preposition.

Step 3:   Determine the case of the pronoun according to the rules of standard English.

Step 4:   Select the correct form of the pronoun.

EXAMPLE   Can you guess (*who, whom*) they are?

Step 1:   The clause is (*who, whom*) *they are.*

Step 2:   In this case, the subject is *they*, the verb is *are*, and the pronoun is the predicate nominative: *they are* (*who, whom*).

Step 3:   A pronoun used as a predicate nominative should be in the nominative case.

Step 4:   The nominative case is *who.*

ANSWER   Can you guess **who** they are?

EXAMPLE   (*Who, Whom*) did you meet in Mexico?

Step 1:   The clause is (*Who, Whom*) *you did meet.*

Step 2:   In this case, the subject is *you*, the verb is *did meet*, and the pronoun is the direct object of the verb: *you did meet* (*Who, Whom*).

Step 3:   A pronoun used as a direct object should be in the objective case.

Step 4:   The objective case is *whom.*

ANSWER   **Whom** did you meet in Mexico?

EXERCISE 9   Using *Who* and *Whom* Correctly

In each sentence below, underline the correct pronoun form.

EX.   1. The singer (*who*, *whom*) you heard was Della Reese.

1. Rebecca, (*who*, *whom*) sits beside you in homeroom?

2. McPhee, to (*who*, *whom*) this pen once belonged, writes mainly nonfiction.

3. A biographer is a person (*who*, *whom*) writes the story of another person's life.

4. Yes, they are the ones (*who*, *whom*) we read about in the book *Kon-Tiki*.

5. (*Who*, *Whom*) did you invite to the book sale?

EXERCISE 10   Proofreading for the Correct Use of *Who* and *Whom*

Proofread the following paragraph for the correct use of pronouns in the nominative and objective cases. Draw a line through any pronoun that is used incorrectly, and write the correct pronoun in the space above it. Some sentences may contain no errors in pronoun forms.

EX.   [1] ~~Who~~ did you borrow the photograph album from?
(Whom written above)

[1] My mother, who worked on our album with me, identified a picture for me. [2] That photograph shows Uncle Mason, whom was really my great-uncle. [3] He is the person for who my little brother is named. [4] Uncle Mason was the only relative from my grandparents' generation who I remember clearly. [5] He was also the one who I liked the most. [6] He was a man who always found time to talk to me. [7] His sister, who I called Aunt Vi, knew a lot about Uncle Mason. [8] She always said that he was the relative who I most resembled. [9] Uncle Mason was a person who loved to laugh. [10] He was the one whom told me stories about Kweku Ananse, a character Uncle Mason also called *Spider*.

PRONOUN APPOSITIVES AND REFLEXIVE PRONOUNS

PRONOUNS AS APPOSITIVES

Sometimes a pronoun is followed directly by an *appositive*, a noun that identifies the pronoun.

19g   To choose which pronoun to use before an appositive, omit the appositive and try each form of the pronoun separately.

EXAMPLE   (*We, Us*) skaters have rehearsal.
          We have rehearsal.
          Us have rehearsal.
ANSWER   **We** skaters have rehearsal.

EXAMPLE   The mayor praised (*we, us*) lifeguards.
          The mayor praised *we*.
          The mayor praised *us*.
ANSWER   The mayor praised **us** lifeguards.

EXERCISE 11   Choosing Correct Pronouns

For each sentence below, underline the correct pronoun form in parentheses.

EX.   1. (<u>We</u>, *Us*) Robinsons will be traveling to Kansas.

1. My teacher told (*we, us*) history students about an interesting event.

2. Every July, (*we, us*) New Yorkers travel to Kansas.

3. The annual Emancipation-Homecoming Celebration draws (*we, us*) travelers.

4. Dad took a picture of (*we, us*) twins in front of Township Hall.

5. Did you know that (*we, us*) vacationers love this place?

REFLEXIVE PRONOUNS

A *reflexive pronoun* refers to the subject and directs the action of the verb back to the subject.

EXAMPLES   Bryce calls **himself** a terrific chef. [The reflexive pronoun *himself* refers to the subject *Bryce*.]
You should always ask **yourself** three questions. [The reflexive pronoun *yourself* refers to the subject *you*.]

19h The words *hisself*, *theirself*, and *theirselves* are nonstandard English. Do not use them in your writing. Instead, use *himself* or *themselves*.

EXAMPLES   Raúl congratulated **himself**. [not *hisself*]
Two of my friends offered **themselves** as baby sitters. [not *theirself* or *theirselves*]

Do not use a reflexive pronoun where a subject pronoun or an object pronoun belongs.

EXAMPLES   Dad and **I** love to eat *tortillas españolas*. [not *myself*]
Did the Lings meet Pam and **you** at the soccer game? [not *yourself*]

EXERCISE 12 Using Reflexive Pronouns Correctly

On the line before each sentence, write C if the reflexive pronoun is correct. If the pronoun is not correct, write the correct form.

EX.   _himself_ 1. Eric told hisself to calm down.

_____ 1. Did the Elliots go with Herb and yourself to Toronto?

_____ 2. Bring Malcolm and myself souvenirs from Guadalajara.

_____ 3. As he planned our day, my brother Emilio talked to hisself.

_____ 4. Why did your sisters excuse theirselves from the trip to the museum?

_____ 5. A local friend invited himself along as a guide.

CHAPTER REVIEW

A. Identifying Correct Forms of Pronouns

For each sentence below, underline the correct pronoun in parentheses. On the line after the sentence, tell how the pronoun is used. Write *s.* for *subject*, *p.n.* for *predicate nominative*, *d.o.* for *direct object*, *i.o.* for *indirect object*, or *o.p.* for *object of a preposition*.

EX. __d.o.__ 1. My father took (*I, me*) to an opera.

_____ 1. In the entire audience, the person who loves opera most was probably (*he, him*).

_____ 2. Someone once gave (*he, him*) tickets to a Marian Anderson concert.

_____ 3. Was your father as impressed by (*she, her*) as everyone else?

_____ 4. My mother and (*he, him*) loved Anderson's voice.

_____ 5. Did she ever hear (*they, them*) sing "Ave Maria"?

B. Correcting Errors in the Use of Pronouns

Each sentence below has a pronoun that has been used incorrectly. Draw a line through each incorrect pronoun. Write the correct pronoun on the line before the sentence.

EX. __us__ 1. Mr. Ramirez taught we students about Mexican customs.

_____ 1. Who did you learn about them from?

_____ 2. Claire and myself read a book about the Vikings.

_____ 3. Mario and Sabrina built the stage set theirselves.

_____ 4. Victor and me gave an oral report on the Everglades.

_____ 5. The sudden snowstorm surprised my parents and myself.

_____ 6. Sterling gave Christina and they a tour of the city.

_____ 7. The chef who makes the best guacamole is him.

_____ 8. Ms. Okada demonstrated a Japanese tea ceremony for we students.

_____ 9. Flora showed they slides of El Salvador, her home country.

_____ 10. Her and I jogged to the bus station.

C.   Writing a Postcard About Amelia Earhart

You have been given the opportunity to travel back in time. You used this chance to visit an airfield in 1932 to meet the great aviator Amelia Earhart. You were able to speak with her and to learn details about her life. Now that you are back home, you want to write a postcard about her to a friend.

1.   Use biographies, reference books, or encyclopedias to learn some details about Amelia Earhart. Note some of her experiences on the lines below.

2.   Choose one or two details that you find interesting. Include them on your postcard you write on your own paper. Correctly use at least five pronouns in your message. Underline the pronouns you use.

Early Life: _____

_____

Education: _____

_____

Accomplishments: _____

_____

EX.

> October 1, 1994
>
> Dear Jamie,
>
> Amelia Earhart agreed to meet with <u>me</u>. Did <u>you</u> know that <u>she</u> attended Columbia University? That fact certainly surprised <u>me</u>. <u>I</u> was also surprised to learn that <u>she</u> had once been...
>
> Jamie Rodriguez
>
> 11 Rust Street
>
> New York, NY 11968
>
> PLACE STAMP HERE

COMPARISON OF ADJECTIVES AND ADVERBS

20a **The three degrees of comparison of modifiers are** *positive*, *comparative*, **and** *superlative*.

ADJECTIVES   That snake is **long.** [positive—no comparison]
This snake is **longer** than that one. [comparative—one compared with another]
That snake is the **longest** of all the snakes in the story. [superlative—one compared with many others]

ADVERBS   I solved the first problem **quickly.** [positive–no comparison]
I solved the second problem **more quickly** than the first one. [comparative–one compared with another]
Of the three problems, I solved the third one **most quickly.** [superlative–one compared with two others]

(1) Most one-syllable modifiers form their comparative and superlative degrees by adding *–er* **and** *–est*.

Positive	Comparative	Superlative
fat	fatter	fattest
safe	safer	safest
shy	shier	shiest

(2) Some two-syllable modifiers form their comparative and superlative degrees by adding *–er* **and** *–est*. **Other two-syllable modifiers form their comparative and superlative degrees by using** *more* **and** *most*.

Positive	Comparative	Superlative
happy	happier	happiest
often	more often	most often
thankful	more thankful	most thankful

When you are unsure about which way a two-syllable modifier forms its degrees of comparison, look up the word in a dictionary.

(3) Modifiers that have three or more syllables form their comparative and superlative degrees by using *more* and *most*.

Positive	Comparative	Superlative
beautiful	more beautiful	most beautiful
eagerly	more eagerly	most eagerly
skillfully	more skillfully	most skillfully

(4) To show decreasing comparisons, all modifiers form their comparative and superlative degrees with *less* and *least*.

Positive	Comparative	Superlative
colorful	less colorful	least colorful
proud	less proud	least proud
smoothly	less smoothly	least smoothly

EXERCISE 1   Forming the Degrees of Comparison of Modifiers

On your own paper, write the forms for the comparative and superlative degrees of each of the following modifiers.

EX.   1. light
     1. lighter; lightest

1. big	6. cold	11. cheerful
2. heavy	7. silly	12. easily
3. furious	8. expensive	13. sad
4. carefully	9. important	14. interesting
5. bright	10. quickly	15. close

EXERCISE 2   Using Comparison of Adjectives and Adverbs

On your own paper, write five sentences comparing one of the following pairs. Use comparative forms of adjectives and adverbs in your sentences. Show at least one decreasing comparison.

EX.   1. Most dogs seem friendlier than most cats.

1. soccer and football   3. rock music and rap music

2. in-line skates and skateboards   4. cats and dogs

IRREGULAR COMPARISON

20b **Some modifiers do not form their comparative and superlative degrees by using the regular methods.**

Positive	Comparative	Superlative
bad	worse	worst
far	farther	farthest
many/much	more	most
well/good	better	best

EXERCISE 3   Writing Comparative and Superlative Forms of Modifiers

On the line in each of the sentences below, write the form of the italicized adjective or adverb that will correctly complete the sentence.

EX.   1. *bad*   Tyron's ankle sprain is ____worse____ than mine.

1. *well*   Are you feeling _____ than you felt yesterday?

2. *good*   Of all the cities in the United States, which is the
_____ to visit?

3. *well*   I do well in math, but my friend Leon does _____ .

4. *much*   This house has _____ closets than that one.

5. *far*   Who on the track and field team can throw the javelin
_____ ?

6. *bad*   These are the _____ photographs I have ever
taken.

7. *many*   Of the two cookbooks, this one has _____ recipes.

8. *good*   The _____ time to see the eclipse is at midnight.

9. *much*   Our garden produced _____ sweet corn this
summer than it did last summer.

10. *far*   Mr. Luongo said the bus stop is _____ from my
house than it is from yours.

REVIEW EXERCISE

A. Proofreading to Correct Errors in Forms of Modifiers

Revise each of the sentences below by drawing a line through any incorrect modifier. Write the correct form on the line.

EX. 1. Which of the two beaches do you like ~~best~~?

_____better_____

1. The sand on South Carolina beaches is more hard than the sand on New England beaches.

_____

2. Riding your bike along the water is easier in the hard sand, and I can't think of anything enjoyabler than a beach ride.

_____

3. Of all the coastlines in the United States, Maine's rocky coast has the better scenery I've seen.

_____

4. Even so, swimming is gooder at South Carolina beaches than at Maine beaches because the water is warmer.

_____

5. In fact, of my three favorite beaches, Old Orchard Beach in Maine has the chillier water.

_____

B. Writing Sentences With Correct Forms of Modifiers

You are a writer for your local newspaper. On your own paper, take notes about two special places that tourists might like to visit in your town. Write ten complete sentences. Use either the comparative or superlative form of modifiers in each sentence. Show at least one decreasing comparison.

EX. 1. The restored hotel on Main Street is less popular with tourists than the new motel by the mall is.

OTHER MODIFIER PROBLEMS

20c Use the comparative degree when comparing two things. Use the superlative degree when comparing more than two.

COMPARATIVE	This piece of wood is **lighter** than that one.
	Of a canary or a parakeet, which bird sings **more sweetly?**
	This jacket is **less expensive** than that one.
SUPERLATIVE	The North Star is the **brightest** star in the sky.
	Of the three actresses, Pilar was the **most talented.**
	Of all the baseball players on our team, Wade strikes out **least.**

Avoid the common mistake of using the superlative degree to compare two things.

NONSTANDARD	Of the two puppies, which is cutest?
STANDARD	Of the two puppies, which is **cuter?**

20d Include the word *other* or *else* when comparing a member of a group with the rest of the group.

NONSTANDARD	Ulani can sing better than any member of the chorus. [Ulani is a member of the chorus and cannot sing better than herself.]
STANDARD	Ulani can sing better than any **other** member of the chorus.

20e Avoid using double comparisons.

A *double comparison* is the use of both –er and *more (less)* or both –est and *most (least)* to form a degree of comparison. For each degree, comparisons should be formed in only one of these two ways, not both.

NONSTANDARD	Houston, Texas, is more larger than Dallas
STANDARD	Houston, Texas, is **larger** than Dallas.

20f Avoid using double negatives.

NONSTANDARD	I don't have no chores left to do.
STANDARD	I have **no** chores left to do.
STANDARD	I **don't** have any chores left to do.

EXERCISE 4   Proofreading for Correct Use of Comparative and Superlative Forms

For each sentence below, draw a line through the incorrect use of the comparative or the superlative form, and write the correct form above it.

EX.   [1] Alexandra Jorgensen has one of the *best* ~~most good~~ jobs you can have.

[1] Of the two articles about sign language interpreters, the one about Alexandra Jorgensen was best. [2] Jorgensen believes that one of the beautifulest languages in the world is sign language. [3] The work that made her happiest than any other work was interpreting conversations in operating rooms, police stations, and classrooms. [4] Her greater challenge is introducing children who are hearing-impaired to orchestra music.

EXERCISE 5   Proofreading for Correct Use of Modifiers

In each of the sentences below, draw a line through any errors in the use of modifiers. On the line after the sentence, write the correct form of the modifier. If a sentence is correct, write C.

EX.   1. Of my three brothers, Vernon is the ~~most tallest~~.   *tallest*

1. Onida is more better at telling jokes than I am. _____

2. Those roses smell stronger than any flowers in the garden. _____

3. There wasn't no one in the house. _____

4. Of the two movies, I can't decide which I like least. _____

5. Who will carry the heavier of the two grocery bags? _____

6. We don't never feed the wild animals. _____

7. Lisa runs faster than anyone on her track team. _____

8. This is the most cheapest necklace in the store. _____

9. Ansel didn't tell no one his idea. _____

10. Mariah has never tasted polenta. _____

PLACEMENT OF MODIFIERS

20g Place modifying phrases and clauses as close as possible to the words they modify.

Notice how the meaning of the following sentence changes when the position of the phrase *in outer space* changes.

EXAMPLES   The astronaut showed pictures of his last flight **in outer space.** [The phrase modifies *flight.*]

The astronaut **in outer space** showed pictures of his last flight. [The phrase modifies *astronaut.*]

The astronaut showed pictures **in outer space** of his last flight. [The phrase modifies *showed.*]

A *prepositional phrase* is a group of words consisting of a preposition, a noun or pronoun that serves as the object of the preposition, and any modifiers of that object. A prepositional phrase used as an adjective should be placed directly after the word it modifies.

MISPLACED   This article describes what kind of books the author liked to read as a child **by Laurence Yep.**

CLEAR   This article **by Laurence Yep** describes what kind of books the author liked to read as a child.

A prepositional phrase used as an adverb should be placed near the word it modifies.

MISPLACED   Archaeologists found the fossil of a dinosaur egg after digging for two years at the same site **in 1992.**

CLEAR   Archaeologists found the fossil of a dinosaur egg **in 1992** after digging for two years at the same site.

CLEAR   **In 1992,** archaeologists found the fossil of a dinosaur egg after digging for two years at the same site

Avoid placing a prepositional phrase in a position where it can modify either of two words. Place the phrase so that it clearly modifies the word you intend it to modify.

MISPLACED	Tony said **on the bus** he was going to Denver. [Does the phrase modify *said* or *was going?*]	
CLEAR	**On the bus,** Tony said he was going to Denver. [The phrase modifies *said.*]	
CLEAR	Tony said he was going to Denver **on the bus.** [The phrase modifies *was going.*]	

EXERCISE 6   Revising Sentences with Misplaced Prepositional Phrases

Find the misplaced prepositional phrases in the sentences below. Then, on your own paper, revise each sentence, and place the prepositional phrase as close as possible to the word or words it modifies.

EX.   1. Dad filmed the baby taking his first steps with his video camera.

    1. With his video camera, Dad filmed the baby taking his first steps.

1. I heard that snow is expected on this morning's weather report.

2. That woman was chasing her dog in a robe and slippers.

3. We stopped to buy sandwiches for lunch along Highway 37.

4. The Kathakali dancers perform tales from Hindu literature in their elaborate costumes.

5. When the hot lava flows down the mountain and into the ocean from the volcano, you can hear a hissing sound.

6. I bought a book about King Arthur in the airport.

7. There is a car in our driveway with no bumper.

8. Juan rescued the frightened cat from the roof with great courage.

9. Our teacher said in 1861 the Civil War began.

10. Sue ordered the skirt from the catalog with big pockets.

PLACEMENT OF PARTICIPIAL PHRASES

A *participial phrase* consists of a verb form—either a present participle or a past participle—and its related words. A participial phrase modifies a noun or a pronoun.

20h **A misplaced participial phrase is a phrase that sounds awkward because it modifies the wrong word.**

Like a prepositional phrase, a participial phrase should be placed as close as possible to the word it modifies.

MISPLACED	Selena waved to the people on the porch **riding her bike.**
CLEAR	**Riding her bike,** Selena waved to the people on the porch.
MISPLACED	**Made with fresh tomatoes and green chiles**, Pedro stirs the tortilla soup.
CLEAR	Pedro stirs the tortilla soup **made with fresh tomatoes and green chiles.**

20i **A participial phrase that does not clearly and sensibly modify any word in the sentence is a *dangling participial phrase.***

To correct a dangling phrase, supply a word that the phrase can modify or change the phrase to a clause.

DANGLING	**Dancing all night at the party,** my feet were sore.
CLEAR	**Dancing all night at the party,** I got sore feet.
CLEAR	My feet were sore **because I danced all night at the party**.

EXERCISE 7 Revising Sentences with Misplaced and Dangling Participles

Each of the sentences below contains a misplaced or dangling participial phrase. On your own paper, revise each sentence. [Hint: You will need to add, delete, or rearrange some words.]

EX. 1. We saw hundreds of snail shells walking along the beach.
　1. Walking along the beach, we saw hundreds of snail shells.

1. Bending down to get a closer look, one of the shells crawled away.
2. Hidden inside the shell, my friend Lori saw a crab.
3. Touching one of its claws, the tiny crab withdrew.
4. The crabs live alone inside empty shells called "hermit crabs."
5. Outgrowing its shell, a new and bigger shell must be found.

EXERCISE 8   Proofreading for Misplaced and Dangling Participles

Revise each sentence below to eliminate dangling or misplaced modifiers.

EX.   1. The toad had gleaming, bronze-colored bands around its eyes that
          we found under a pine log.
          The toad that we found under a pine log had gleaming, bronze-
          colored bands around its eyes.

1. The flamenco dancer wore a red dress whom Susana liked most.

    _____

2. You can substitute scallions for red onions in a pinch. _____

    _____

3. Speaking so softly no one could hear her, we asked Andrea to

    repeat what she said. _____

    _____

4. My dog chased the school bus, barking and growling. _____

    _____

5. Hoping to find a good price, the bookstore in the mall was our

    first stop. _____

    _____

6. The basketball team received a standing ovation at the banquet

    whose playing had improved so much. _____

    _____

7. Tied tightly to buoys, the sailors saw that the boats had survived

    the storm. _____

    _____

8. Tisa and Jahi peeked at the crowd over the low wall. _____

    _____

9. The pushcarts held hundreds of spring flowers that stood on the

    sidewalk near the museum. _____

    _____

10. Raining for a week, the campers finally decided to end their trip early.

    _____

PLACEMENT OF ADJECTIVE CLAUSES

An *adjective clause* modifies a noun or a pronoun. Most adjective clauses begin with a relative pronoun—*that, which, who, whom,* or *whose.*

☞ **REFERENCE NOTE:** For more information about adjective clauses, see page 145.

20j   Like an adjective phrase, an adjective clause should be placed directly after the word it modifies.

MISPLACED   A girl sat beside me on the bus **that looks like my cousin**.
   [Does the bus look like my cousin?]
CLEAR   A girl **that looks like my cousin** sat beside me on the bus.

MISPLACED   Children's Day is on May 5, **which is a national holiday in Japan**. [Is May 5 a national holiday?]
CLEAR   Children's Day, **which is a national holiday in Japan**, is on May 5.

EXERCISE 9   **Revising Sentences with Misplaced Clause Modifiers**

In the following sentences, underline the misplaced adjective clauses. Then, on the line after each sentence, revise the sentence by placing the adjective clause near the word it modifies.

EX.   1.   The article is about pollution that I read.

   The article that I read is about pollution.

1.   The dog belongs to our neighbor that has such an annoying bark. _____

_____

2.   Luisa put her car in the garage which has no headlights. _____

_____

3.   My father's hardware store is closed for July, which is on Mystic

   Avenue. _____

_____

4. Plants usually live in swampy areas that eat insects. _____

_____

5. Naomi Shihab Nye gets some ideas for poems from neighbors and

friends who wrote "The Rider." _____

_____

6. Jazz became popular in the 1920s, which has its roots in the songs

of African Americans. _____

_____

7. The skirt belongs to my sister Jane that has a broken zipper. _____

_____

8. The ancient people remain a puzzle whose statues stand on Easter

Island. _____

_____

9. The lifeguard at Long Beach saved a tired swimmer whom we

want to reward. _____

_____

10. Van speaks French like a native, who has been to Paris many

times. _____

_____

EXERCISE 10   Writing a Letter

Your neighbor just had a block party to celebrate the Fourth of July. On your
own paper, write a letter about the party to a friend who used to live next
door to you. Describe the music, the events, the food, the guests. In your
letter, use at least five adjective clauses. Be sure to place each clause directly
after the word it modifies. Underline the adjective clauses that you use.

EX.   *Dear Scott,*
      You would've had so much fun at the block party, which lasted past
      midnight.

CHAPTER REVIEW

A. Identifying and Correcting Errors in the Use of Modifiers

In the sentences below, underline each error in the use of modifiers. Then revise each sentence by writing the correct form of the modifier on the line provided.

EX. 1. The crossword puzzle in today's paper was <u>difficulter</u> than yesterday's puzzle.

more difficult

1. Of all the humor writers for the newspaper, I think Dave Barry is the funnier.

2. The travel section of the newspaper is more interesting to me than any section.

3. Which sports writer do you like most, Dan Shaughnessy or Larry Whiteside?

4. According to an article on the front page, the governor hasn't done nothing to cut taxes.

5. *Calvin and Hobbes* is more better than any other comic strip.

B. Correcting Misplaced Modifiers

Each of the following sentences contains a misplaced or dangling modifier in italics. On the lines provided, revise each sentence so that it is clear and correct.

EX. 1. *Growing up in a woody area of New Jersey,* nature was something that Susan Jeffers learned to appreciate when she was young.

Growing up in a woody area of New Jersey, Susan Jeffers learned to appreciate nature when she was young.

1. *Wanting to be an artist,* The Pratt Institute of Art in New York City was where Susan Jeffers went to college. _____
   _____

2. Ms. Jeffers designed book covers and did page layouts for several different publishing companies *after graduation.* _____
   _____

3. Her first book of illustrations was written by Joseph Jacobs, *which was The Buried Moon.* _____
   _____

4. *To illustrate a new book,* doodling little sketches is her first step.
   _____

C. Writing a Letter

You have just come from an auto show where you saw an amazing experimental car. On your own paper, write a letter to a friend telling about the car's interesting and unique details. Use at least two prepositional phrases, one adjective clause, and one participial phrase. Underline and label the modifying phrases and clauses that you use.

EX. Dear Jan,
                                          adj. clause
       I have just seen a car that you will not believe.

ACCEPT / BAD, BADLY

This chapter contains an alphabetical list of common problems in English usage. Throughout the chapter, examples are labeled *standard* or *nonstandard*. **Standard English** is the most widely accepted form of English. **Nonstandard English** is language that does not follow the rules and guidelines of standard English.

accept, except   *Accept* is a verb that means "to receive." *Except* may be either a verb or a preposition. As a verb, *except* means "to leave out" or "to exclude"; as a preposition, *except* means "other than" or "excluding."

EXAMPLES   Please **accept** this gift.
Please do not **except** Paul from your guest list. [verb]
My mom works every day **except** Sunday. [preposition]

affect, effect   *Affect* is a verb meaning "to influence." *Effect* used as a verb means "to bring about." Used as a noun, *effect* means "the result of some action."

EXAMPLES   The lack of rain **affected** crop growth.
The new principal **effected** many changes in the school.
Scolding has no **effect** on that child.

all ready, already   *All ready* means "completely prepared." *Already* means "previously"or "even now."

EXAMPLES   The packages are **all ready** for shipment.
When we arrived, the play had **already** begun.

all right   Used as an adjective, *all right* means "unhurt" or "satisfactory." Used as an adverb, *all right* means "well enough." *All right* should always be written as two words.

EXAMPLES   The doctor says I am **all right**. [adjective]
The toaster was working **all right**. [adverb]

a lot   *A lot*, meaning "a great number or amount," should always be written as two words.

EXAMPLE   We spent **a lot** of time working on the experiment.

among   See **between, among**.

as   See **like, as**.

> **bad, badly**   *Bad* is an adjective. *Badly* is an adverb.
>
> EXAMPLES   My uncle's temper is **bad**.
> The young pianist played **badly**.

EXERCISE 1   Correcting Errors in Usage

For each of the sentences below, find the error in usage, and rewrite it correctly on your own paper. If a sentence is correct, write C.

EX.   1.   Her answers on the test were allright.
     1. all right

1.   The effects of the tornado were visible for months.
2.   No one accept Wanda knew how to write a computer program.
3.   His suits were already to be sent to the cleaners.
4.   Certificates of merit were given to a lot of the seniors.
5.   Because she hurt her ankle, the athlete played bad.
6.   In 1964, Martin Luther King, Jr., excepted the Nobel Peace Prize for his civil rights work.
7.   The photographs of starving children effected everyone.
8.   Those who passed the test were accepted from homework.
9.   The new boy from Brazil all ready knew how to play soccer.
10. I had a difficult time hearing him, for the telephone connection was bad.

EXERCISE 2   Using Words Correctly in Sentences

On your own paper, write a sentence that shows the correct use of each of the words below.

EX.   1.   badly
     1. I really played badly Saturday.

1.   already
2.   except
3.   badly
4.   a lot
5.   affect
6.   accept
7.   all ready
8.   bad
9.   effect
10. all right

BECAUSE / HARDLY, SCARCELY

because See **reason . . . is because.**

between, among Use *between* when referring to two things at a time, even though they may be part of a group containing more than two. Use *among* when referring to three or more in a group rather than to separate individuals.

EXAMPLES   The agreement is **between** Vince and Nora.
Some students like to read **between** classes. [Although the students have more than two classes, they may read between any two classes.]
We divided the fruit **among** the four of us. [As a group, the four divided the fruit.]

bring, take *Bring* shows action directed *toward* the speaker or writer. *Take* shows action directed *away from* the speaker or writer. Think of *bring* as being related to *come* and of *take* as being related to *go*.

EXAMPLES   Please **bring** your books when you come to class.
Take these old clothes to the recycling center when you go.

could of Do not use *of* with the helping verb *could*. Use *could have*. Also avoid using *ought to of, had of, should of, would of, might of*, and *must of*.

EXAMPLES   Miguel **could have** identified those stars. [not *could of*]
If I **had** found it, I **would have** given it to you. [not *had of* or *would of*]

effect See **affect, effect.**

except See **accept, except.**

fewer, less *Fewer* is used with plural words. *Less* is used with singular words. *Fewer* tells "how many"; *less* tells "how much."

EXAMPLES   Because of the drought, the trees produced **fewer** apples.
Use **less** salt on the salad.

good, well *Good* is always an adjective. Never use *good* as an adverb. Instead, use *well*.

NONSTANDARD   Angelo pitched good during the first few innings.
STANDARD   Angelo pitched **well** during the first few innings.

hardly, scarcely   The words *hardly* and *scarcely* have negative meanings. They should never be used with another negative word.

EXAMPLES   Binti **could hardly** stay awake. [not *couldn't*]
We **scarcely had** time to eat. [not *hadn't*]

EXERCISE 3   Identifying Correct Usage

In each sentence below, underline the correct usage in parentheses.

EX.   1. She worked (*good, well*) with the other crew members.

1. Sally Ride felt (*good, well*) when she was chosen to be the first American woman in space.

2. She (*could hardly, couldn't hardly*) imagine a more exciting assignment.

3. Ms. Ride was (*among, between*) a group of over eight thousand applicants.

4. She was a good athlete and (*could of, could have*) become a professional tennis player.

5. There are (*less, fewer*) women astronauts than men astronauts.

EXERCISE 4   Correcting Errors in Usage

In each sentence below, draw a line through each error in usage, and write the correct form above it.

EX.   1. Be sure to ~~take~~ *bring* your camera along when you come to see us.

1. The students couldn't hardly wait to go whale watching.

2. The guide pointed out differences among the markings on the whales.

3. There are less whales to watch now because so many have migrated to warmer waters.

4. The whale population also could of been effected by pollution.

5. The guide did good when he tried to imitate the whale's song.

HISSELF / TRY AND

hisself   *Hisself* is nonstandard English. Use *himself*.

EXAMPLE   Mark gave **himself** a haircut. [not *hisself*]

its, it's   *Its* is a personal possessive pronoun. *It's* is a contraction of *it is* or *it has*.

EXAMPLES   The seal tossed **its** ball into the air. [possessive pronoun]
It's now raining. [contraction of *it is*]
It's been an interesting year. [contraction of *it has*]

kind, sort, type   The words *this, that, these,* and *those* should agree in number with the words *kind, sort,* and *type.*

EXAMPLES   Most viewers enjoy **this sort** of program. [*This* and *sort* are both singular.]
These kinds of trips are exhausting. [*These* and *kinds* are both plural.]

learn, teach   *Learn* means "to acquire knowledge." *Teach* means "to instruct" or "to show how."

EXAMPLES   Nathalie is **learning** how to ski.
Her mother is **teaching** her how to ski.

less   See **fewer, less**.

like, as if, as though   In informal situations, the preposition *like* is often used in place of the compound conjunctions *as if* or *as though.* In formal situations, however, *as if* or *as though* is preferred.

EXAMPLES   They acted **as if** nothing had happened. [not *like*]
She looked **as though** she had lost her best friend. [not *like*]

might of, must of   See **could of**.

reason . . . is because   In informal situations, *reason . . . is because* is often used instead of *reason . . . is that.* In formal situations, use *reason . . . is that* or revise your sentence.

INFORMAL   The reason he plays the oboe well is because he practices.
FORMAL   The **reason** he plays the oboe well **is that** he practices.
or
He plays the oboe well **because** he practices.

scarcely See **hardly, scarcely**.

some, somewhat Do not use *some* instead of *somewhat*, the adverb.

NONSTANDARD   Your handwriting has improved some.
  STANDARD   Your handwriting has improved **somewhat**.

take See **bring, take**.

this here, that there The words *here* and *there* are unnecessary after *this* and *that*.

EXAMPLE   Do you want **this** book or **that** one? [not *this here* or *that there*]

try and In informal situations, *try and* is often used instead of *try to*. In formal situations, *try to* should be used.

INFORMAL   Try and complete your homework on time.
  FORMAL   **Try to** complete your homework on time.

EXERCISE 5 Correcting Errors in Usage

In the sentences below, find the errors in usage, and correct them on your own paper. If a sentence is correct, write C.

EX.   1. People enjoy hearing these kind of story.
      1. this kind

1. Try and imagine the young Patrick Henry.
2. This here boy was just an ordinary fellow.
3. It looked as if Patrick would not amount to much.
4. The lad amused hisself by fishing, playing his fiddle, and wandering through the woods of Virginia.
5. After failing as a farmer, Patrick wanted to be learned a new trade.
6. One reason he was such a good speaker was because he had a great speaking voice.
7. He must of realized he could be a successful lawyer.
8. As good as he was, he improved somewhat over the years.
9. Its the speech he made in 1775 that made him famous.
10. That there speech will be long remembered.

well See **good, well**.

when, where Do not use *when* or *where* incorrectly when writing a definition.

NONSTANDARD   A miser is when a person hoards money.
    STANDARD   A miser is a person who hoards money.

where Do not use *where* for *that*.

EXAMPLE   I read **that** the climate is changing. [not *where*]

who, which, that The relative pronoun *who* refers to people only. *Which* refers to things only. *That* refers to either people or things.

EXAMPLES   Clyde is the one **who** sent the flowers. [person]
      The computer, **which** has a color monitor, is mine. [thing]
      She is the one **that** raises money for the homeless. [person]
      This is the novel **that** I wanted to read. [thing]

who's, whose *Who's* is the contraction of *who is* or *who has*. *Whose* is the possessive form of *who*.

EXAMPLES   **Who's** baking bread? [Who is]
      Who's been taking care of the goldfish? [Who has]
      Whose dictionary is this?

without, unless Do not use the preposition *without* in place of the conjunction *unless*.

EXAMPLE   I can't take sailing lessons **unless** I can pass a swimming test.
      [not *without*]

would of See **could of**.

your, you're *Your* is the possessive form of *you*. *You're* is the contraction of *you are*.

EXAMPLES   **Your** duffle bag is in the locker.
      You're one of the best athletes in school.

227

EXERCISE 6   Identifying Correct Usage

Underline the correct word or expression in parentheses in each sentence below.

EX.   1. This is the artist (*which*, <u>*that*</u>) painted my favorite painting.

1. *Stump Speaking* is the title of (*who's*, *whose*) painting?

2. George Caleb Bingham is the artist (*who*, *which*) created it.

3. *Stump speaking* is (*when a politician travels around a district to make speeches*, *traveling around a district to make speeches*).

4. (*Your*, *You're*) aunt has a print of the painting in her study.

5. I read in an art book (*where*, *that*) the artist enjoyed painting scenes from everyday life.

EXERCISE 7   Identifying Errors in Usage

For each pair of sentences below, circle the letter of the sentence that contains an error in usage.

EX.   1. a. My aunt, who's a good tennis player, won the tournament.
           b. I read where the team lost again.

1. a. We read that the game had been postponed.
    b. Your supposed to take this toaster to the repair shop.

2. a. We will go unless it rains.
    b. The brakes won't work without you fix them.

3. a. Whose going on the field trip?
    b. Ms. Sánchez really played that song well.

4. a. A donor is when a person gives away something.
    b. Who's been taking care of your dog?

5. a. He made a good taco out of clay.
    b. She used the electric saw, which was heavy, very good.

6. a. Don't drive without a license.
    b. It's illegal to drive without you have a license.

7. a. They all wondered who's jacket it was.
    b. The jacket that was his was the blue one.

8. a. When you whisper, I can't hear you.
    b. That boy, who's name is Markus, lived in Switzerland.

9. a. "You're a wonderful guest," she said.
    b. Always do you're best.

10. a. I would of been there, but I was ill.
     b. A good learner is someone who listens well.

CHAPTER REVIEW

A. Identifying Correct Usage

Underline the correct expression in parentheses in each sentence below.

EX.   1. What have (*your, you're*) teachers (*learned, taught*) you today?

1. You may have read (*where, that*) the Vikings were fierce warriors.

2. (*Between, Among*) A.D. 790 and 1100, they set sail in their long ships to raid other lands and explore the world.

3. The sight of a Viking fleet sailing up a river toward the village (*must have, must of*) been terrifying.

4. (*Try and, Try to*) imagine the reaction of the villagers.

5. There (*was scarcely, wasn't scarcely*) any warning.

6. It seemed (*like, as though*) no one was safe from attack.

7. By 860 A.D., the Vikings had (*already, all ready*) established (*alot, a lot*) of settlements throughout France and Germany.

8. (*Except, Accept*) for the courage of one ruler, the Vikings (*might of, might have*) overrun all of England.

9. The reason they did not succeed was (*because, that*) King Alfred the Great stopped them.

10. He took back (*alot, a lot*) of English territory by forcing the Vikings to pull back to the eastern third of the country.

B. Identifying Errors in Usage

For each of the following pairs of sentences, circle the letter of the sentence that contains an error in usage.

EX.   1. (a.) He did it hisself.
　　　　b. He taught it to the class.

1. a. Come over here, and take those messy boots with you.
    b. Accept only your best from yourself.

2. a. His vocabulary is good, and he spells very well.
    b. How many less almonds is that tree producing?

3. a. She was uneffected by his begging.
    b. We had a lot of leftover potatoes.

4. a. They were already for the weekend trip.
    b. Those sorts of buildings use varied materials.

5. a. You might've told me before!
    b. Act like you belong there.

C. Correcting Errors in Usage

If any of the following sentences contain an error in usage, draw a line through the error and write the correct form above it. If a sentence is correct, write C on the line before the sentence.

EX. _____ 1. What ~~affect~~ *effect* does Mexico's climate have on ~~it's~~ *its* crops?

_____ 1. The reason Mexico grows a lot of different food crops is because it has a varied landscape and climate.

_____ 2. Between the Atlantic and Pacific coasts lies a plateau.

_____ 3. A plateau is when the land is high and level.

_____ 4. Two huge mountain ranges who run down each side of the country separate the plateau from low-lying coastal regions.

_____ 5. Corn is one of the main crops of this here country.

_____ 6. Its the vegetable from which tortillas are made.

_____ 7. Mildred won't scarcely eat a meal without this round, flat bread is served with it.

_____ 8. Would you have guessed that beans are also an important part of the Mexican diet?

_____ 9. Avocados grow good in Mexico because of it's climate.

_____ 10. Less people nibble on chilies, because the burning sensation these peppers cause can last for days.

D. Writing a Letter

The year is 2315. You are a crew member on an outer-space research laboratory. You can send letters home only once a month. On your own paper, write a letter to a friend, describing what you see and how you feel. In your letter, use five of the words or expressions covered in this chapter. Underline the words and expressions you use.

EX.   June 22, 2315

    Dear Melba,
        This mission has <u>hardly</u> begun, and <u>already</u> I have noticed several changes <u>because</u> of the effects of gravity.

THE PRONOUN I AND PROPER NOUNS

22a Capitalize the pronoun *I*.

EXAMPLE   Sabrina and **I** learned how to water-ski last summer.

22b Capitalize proper nouns.

A *common noun* names a group of persons, places, things, or ideas. A *proper noun* names a particular person, place, thing, or idea.

Common Nouns	Proper Nouns
athlete	Dawn Fraser
river	Amazon
month	November
team	Cincinnati Reds

Some proper nouns consist of more than one word. In these names, short prepositions (those of fewer than five letters) and articles (*a, an,* and *the*) are not capitalized.

EXAMPLES   the Great Wall **of** China   Ludwig **van** Beethoven
            Peter **the** Great   Joan **of** Arc

    REFERENCE NOTE: For more about common and proper nouns, see page 89.

EXERCISE 1   Using Capital Letters Correctly

In the word groups below, draw a line through each error in capitalization. Write the correction above the error.

EX.   1. in south dakota

1. tim raines, the white Sox player
2. early january
3. my sister and i
4. the ohio river
5. the delaware memorial bridge
6. abraham lincoln
7. the treaty of paris
8. lieutenant franklin
9. bloomfield, connecticut
10. the catskill mountains

11. a Vacation in france
12. the old highway 80
13. lake erie
14. the minnesota vikings
15. ming vase from China

16. My Mother and i
17. Katherine anne Porter
18. Poi from hawaii
19. new Delhi, india
20. the fourth of July

EXERCISE 2 Proofreading for Correct Capitalization

In the paragraph below, correct the errors in capitalization by drawing a line through each error and writing the correction above it.

EX.   [1] When we were ten years old, my best friend ~~kyoko~~ *Kyoko* and I
       started a tradition.

[1] Almost every saturday Kyoko and I go roller-skating. [2] Last week we rented skates from city sports for the first time. [3] We walked to the charles river before we put on our skates. [4] There is blacktop, which is ideal for skating, behind the museum of science. [5] We skated along cambridge parkway for over Two Hours. [6] Later, over lunch, Kyoko invited me to the bon festival at the northeast buddhist center next saturday. [7] I asked Kyoko, "what is the bon festival?"

[8] "The bon festival is the japanese celebration of lanterns," she said. [9] "We dance, sing, and have a picnic with traditional japanese food. And to honor our ancestors, we light lanterns that float on water."

[10] I love to skate, but I'm really looking forward to celebrating the bon festival with kyoko next Saturday.

PLACES AND PEOPLE

22c **Capitalize geographical names.**

Type of Name	Examples
towns, cities	Charleston, Bangor, Toronto, St. Louis
counties, states	Cook County, Orange County, Texas, New Mexico
countries	Sri Lanka, Argentina, Vietnam, New Zealand
islands	Long Island, Madagascar, Muskeget Island, Tonga
bodies of water	Lake Huron, Hudson Bay, Red Sea, Ohio River
forests, parks	Sherwood Forest, Robinson State Park, Glacier National Park, Central Park
streets, highways	Park Avenue, Ninth Street, Rue Lobau, Route 66
mountains	Mount Etna, Rocky Mountains
continents	Asia, Africa, South America, Antarctica
regions	South Pacific, New England, the West, the South

NOTE In a hyphenated street number, the second part of the number is not capitalized.

EXAMPLE   East Forty-second Street

NOTE Words such as *east, west, north,* and *south* are not capitalized when they indicate direction.

EXAMPLES   heading north along the coast, southwest of Houston

22d **Capitalize the names of planets, stars, and other heavenly bodies.**

EXAMPLES   Pluto, Mars, Andromeda, Sirius, the Little Dipper

NOTE The word *earth* is not capitalized unless it is used along with the names of other heavenly bodies. Do not capitalize *sun* and *moon.*

EXAMPLE   The Earth is larger than Mercury.

233

22e   Capitalize the names of persons.

EXAMPLES   Mr. Akmajian, Connie Chung, María López

EXERCISE 3   Correcting Errors in Capitalization

Correct each expression below by drawing a line through the error in capitalization and writing the correct form above it.

EX.   1. the *S* spring *F* fling dance

1. the state of north Carolina
2. the works of pablo picasso
3. the milky way, venus, jupiter, and the pole star
4. mount st. helens, mount hood
5. 29 east seventy-third street
6. doctor martin luther king, jr.
7. the colorado river
8. former governor ella grasso
9. kabuki theater
10. the bering sea
11. the american southwest, the grand canyon
12. the australian continent
13. chicago's south side
14. the globe theater in london
15. mongolian barbeque

EXERCISE 4   Proofreading a Paragraph for Errors in Capitalization

Correct the errors in capitalization in the paragraph below by drawing a line through each error and writing the correct form above it.

EX.   1. My parents and I enjoy traveling through southwestern ~~colorado~~. *Colorado*

[1] Last summer we visited mesa verde national park. [2] We climbed up the trail and explored the ruins of a city built by the anasazi people. [3] The dwellings in the ruins are arranged in levels and are connected by a system of ladders and handholds. [4] Our guide, a ranger from the national park service, pointed out that the anasazi had a long history of living in extended family groups. [5] The buildings at mesa verde show that these native americans had been living there for nearly one thousand years.

GROUPS, ORGANIZATIONS, AND RELIGIONS

22f Capitalize the names of teams, organizations, businesses, institutions, and government bodies.

Type of Name	Examples
teams	Dallas Cowboys, Seattle Seahawks, New England Patriots
organizations	Department of African Studies, Future Farmers of America
businesses	Eastman Kodak Co., Wordworks Publishing Services
institutions	Bloomington North High School, Howard University
government bodies	U.S. Coast Guard, U.S. Department of Transportation

22g Capitalize the names of nationalities, races, and peoples.

EXAMPLES   African American, Asian, Caucasian, Hispanic, Lakota Sioux, Vietnamese

NOTE   The words *black* and *white* may or may not be capitalized when they refer to races of people.

> EXAMPLE   Charles Drew, a famous black [or Black] physician, designed the Red Cross blood banking system.
> John Wesley Powell was the first white [or White] man to explore the Grand Canyon by boat.

22h Capitalize the names of religions and their followers, holy days, sacred writings, and specific deities.

Type of Name	Examples
religions and followers	Christianity, Muslims, Amish
holy days	Easter, Ramadan, Passover
holy books	Torah, Koran, Rig Veda
specific deities	God, Allah, Great Spirit

NOTE The word *god* is not capitalized when it refers to a god of ancient mythology. However, the names of specific gods, such as *Apollo* or *Juno*, are capitalized.

EXERCISE 5   Identifying Correct Capitalization

In the word groups below, identify the errors in capitalization. Draw a line through the error, and write the correct form above it.

EX.   1. The ᴹminnesota Twins

1. a mexican dance

2. federal Bureau of Investigation

3. Midland senior high school

4. Athena, Greek Goddess of Wisdom

5. christmas day

6. A and R copy service

7. jesuit Priest

8. the ambassador from Samoa

9. Oglala lakota college

10. feast of lights

11. saint Patrick's day

12. los angeles lakers

13. Junior achievement

14. Nez perce people

15. England's house of lords

16. a workshop on buddhism

17. west side laundry

18. state employment commission

19. continental congress

20. Grambling state university

OBJECTS, EVENTS, STRUCTURES, AND AWARDS

22i **Capitalize the brand names of business products.**

EXAMPLES   Honda Civic, Puma shoes, Wrangler jeans, Nikon camera

22j **Capitalize the names of historical events and periods, special events, and calendar items.**

Type of Name	Examples
historical events	Revolutionary War, Crusades, Battle of Gettysburg, Korean War
historical periods	Great Depression, Jurassic Period, Dark Ages, Renaissance
special events	Oscars, Kansas State Fair, Olympic Games, Parents' Day
calendar items	Monday, Cinco de Mayo, August, Thanksgiving Day, Valentine's Day

 NOTE   The name of a season is not capitalized unless it is part of a proper name.

EXAMPLES   the first day of spring   the Fall Foliage Festival

22k **Capitalize the names of trains, ships, airplanes, and spacecraft.**

Type of Name	Examples
trains	*Silver Meteor, Orient Express*
ships	*Mayflower, Old Ironsides*
airplanes	*Spirit of St. Louis, Flyer I*
spacecraft	*Apollo 11, SS United States*

22l **Capitalize the names of buildings and other structures.**

EXAMPLES   Sears Tower, Brooklyn Bridge, Arie Crown Theater, Plaza Hotel, Taj Mahal

22m **Capitalize the names of monuments and awards.**

EXAMPLES   Washington Monument, Lincoln Memorial, Pushcart Prize

EXERCISE 6   Proofreading Sentences for Correct Capitalization

For each sentence below, correct the errors in capitalization. Draw a line through each error, and write the correct form above it.

EX.   1.   My favorite ~~Summer~~ month is ~~july~~.
         summer   *July*

1. Someday i'd like to win an academy award or an emmy.

2. My older Brother works part time at mac's hardware.

3. Do you know when the revolutionary war in america occurred?

4. After we saw the model of the space shuttle *challenger,* we visited grant's tomb.

5. Several years ago, the golden gate bridge was badly damaged during an earthquake.

6. My favorite building in New York City is the chrysler building.

7. I hope to see the marvelous Ruins of angkor wat someday.

8. Many famous paintings hang in the louvre in Paris, France.

9. Although she died in 1963, Sylvia Plath was not awarded a pulitzer prize until 1982.

10. In our country, the congressional medal of honor is the highest award a soldier can be given.

© Randy Glasbergen

GLASBERGEN

"It's a new concept in teaching machines. You get 50 points for every grammatical error you blast away!"

TITLES

22n   Capitalize titles.

(1) Capitalize the title of a person when the title comes before the name.

EXAMPLE   **Governor** Clinton became **President** Clinton in 1993.

(2) Capitalize a title used alone or following a person's name only when you want to emphasize the position of someone holding a high office.

EXAMPLES   The **Secretary** of **Defense** spoke to reporters about the attack.
The secretary of the student council took notes at the meeting.
Did you want to see me, **Doctor?**

(3) Capitalize the first and last words and all important words in titles of books, magazines, newspapers, poems, short stories, historical documents, movies, television programs, and works of art and music.

Unimportant words in titles include articles (*a, an, the*), coordinating conjunctions (*and, but, for, nor, or, so, yet*), or prepositions of fewer than five letters (*at, for, from, with*).

NOTE   The article *the* before a title is not capitalized unless it is the first word of the title.

Type of Name	Examples
books	*The Pearl, The World Almanac*
newspapers	*Louisville Courier-Journal, Boston Globe*
magazines	*Sports Illustrated, Ebony*
poems	"In Cold Storm Light", "Trades"
short stories	"Three Wise Guys", "Two Kinds"
historical documents	the Geneva Convention, Treaty of Versailles
movies	*The Wizard of Oz, Casablanca, Rocky*
television programs	*Nova, 48 Hours, A Different World*
works of art	*Girl Before a Mirror, The Morning Walk*

> **(4) Capitalize a word showing a family relationship when the word is used before or in place of a person's name.**
>
> Do not capitalize a word showing a family relationship when a possessive comes before the word.
>
> EXAMPLES   Both **A**unt Leah and **M**om collect antiques.
> Yolanda's **m**other and my **a**unt Chandra teach a yoga class.

EXERCISE 7   Using Capital Letters in Titles

For each sentence below, correct the errors in capitalization by drawing a line through each error and writing the correct form above it.

EX.   1.   My brother and ~~i~~ could watch ~~star wars~~ *Star Wars* for days at a time.

1. Laura Ingalls Wilder is best known for her *little house on the prairie* book series, which describes her life in the midwest.

2. I sent uncle Bill and aunt mary the Disney video *cinderella* for their anniversary.

3. Alex Haley's book *roots* was made into a mini-series.

4. Has President clinton ever met The reverend billy graham?

5. On weekends, dad reads his favorite magazine, *popular mechanics.*

6. Rico decided to call his painting *still life with eggplant.*

7. James Weldon Johnson's poem "the creation" is quite inspiring.

8. One of the most popular of all news programs is *60 minutes.*

9. Paulo read an article about hiking in a magazine called *backpacker.*

10. *The growing pains of adrian mole* is a novel by Sue Townsend.

11. Our Aunt Betsy lives near Tulsa.

12. Government officials signed the Chamizal convention in 1963.

13. In what year was John Adams elected president?

14. Please tell me, doctor, when I should come back.

15. The *americas review* publishes works by many Chicano authors.

SCHOOL SUBJECTS, FIRST WORDS, PROPER ADJECTIVES

22o Do *not* capitalize the names of school subjects, except languages and course names followed by a number.

EXAMPLES I'm taking Spanish, physical education, social studies, and Algebra I.

Last semester I took biology, English, and Geometry II.

22p Capitalize the first word in every sentence.

EXAMPLE An osprey is a bird of prey. It likes to build its nest in high places.

The first word of a sentence that is a direct quotation is capitalized even if the quotation begins within a sentence.

EXAMPLE "Who's out there?" I muttered.

My sister's voice rang out, "It's just me, silly."

Traditionally, the first word in a line of poetry is capitalized.

EXAMPLE Adventuring you and I did go,
On an unmarked road we did not know.
The challenges there were many and vast,
But we rose to them all and won at last.

☞ **REFERENCE NOTE:** For more about using capital letters in quotations, see page 269.

22q Capitalize proper adjectives. A *proper adjective* is formed from a proper noun and is almost always capitalized.

Proper Nouns	Proper Adjectives
Vietnam	Vietnamese culture
Samuel F. B. Morse	Morse code
Thailand	Thai food
Queen Victoria	Victorian dress

EXERCISE 8 Using Capital Letters Correctly

In the paragraph below, draw a line through each error in capitalization, and write the correct form above it.

EX.   [1] In ~~english~~ class we read a short short story, "~~the captive,~~" by the ~~argentinian~~ writer Jorge ~~luis~~ Borges.

(corrections above: English; The Captive; Argentinian; Luis)

[1] The story is part of a collection in a book called *a personal anthology*. [2] i was startled when I recognized this small part of a tale as the basis for a movie called *the emerald forest*. [3] Borges wrote only in spanish for most of his life. [4] one of his first short stories published in the united states is a translation of the mystery "The Garden of forking Paths," which originally appeared in *Ellery Queen's mystery magazine*. [5] After reading this story, I wrote a poem that begins

the night was dark and the water still.

fear gripped my heart with an iron will.

EXERCISE 9 Identifying and Correcting Errors in Capitalization

In the sentences below, underline each error in capitalization, and write the correct form above it.

EX.   1. Jan asked, "<u>oh</u>! <u>did</u> you read about the attack llamas?"

(corrections above: Oh Did)

1. "yes," said Naoshi. "the llamas belong to George and Peggy Bird."

2. Jan said, "the Birds live in the allegheny mountain area."

3. Naoshi asked, "how can llamas help these virginian farmers protect their sheep?"

4. "their llamas are Count Dondi and Smokey," said Jan. "they sound the alarm when a coyote comes near the flock."

5. Naoshi said, "that's right. the llamas then chase away coyotes."

CHAPTER REVIEW

A. Correcting Errors in Capitalization

Each sentence below contains errors in capitalization. Write your corrections on the lines provided, and separate your answers with a semicolon.

EX. 1. our School basketball team is known as the tigers.

Our; school; Tigers

1. sally Ride was the first woman Astronaut to be assigned a spaceflight by NASA.

_____

2. "that book belongs to ken," I said. "i can't lend it to you."

_____

3. I studied Chemistry, Art I, and biology II last semester.

_____

4. i like dancing to hip-hop, but my Cousin Keesha prefers pop.

_____

5. Jonathan Gave the notes for Algebra and french to Michael.

_____

6. The General led the army towards the eiffel tower.

_____

7. Students at emory university in atlanta began their semester yesterday.

_____

8. the nike shoe factory is closed for easter.

_____

9. I wonder what the london newspaper *the times* is saying about prince Charles.

_____

10. Cocheta and her parents moved to philadelphia, which is on the schuylkill river.

_____

B. Proofreading for Correct Capitalization

In the paragraph below, correct the fifteen errors in capitalization. Draw a line through each error, and write the correct form above it.

EX. 1 I usually exercise on ~~saturday~~ *Saturday* and ~~sunday~~ *Sunday*.

1   I had always hated Gym class until ms. Johnson decided that

2   we should try something she called funky Aerobics. i never

3   expected that I would like working up a sweat, but the Routines

4   she taught us this year are more like Dance than like Exercise. She

5   asked us for suggestions for Songs, and we gave her Titles from

6   Artists like Kris Kross and Hammer. i've never in my life worked

7   as hard as I do keeping up with the Aerobic routines she worked

8   out for us. Not only is gym class more Fun, but most of us are

9   getting some Great moves ready for the october homecoming

10 dance.

C. It's Your Turn

The Chamber of Commerce for your town needs a tourist brochure and a visitors' guide for your hometown or neighborhood. You'll need to select five of the categories below and describe two attractions for each category. Give the name of each place and two features that might be important to visitors. Be sure to include directions to the location. Write your answers on your own paper.

theaters	shopping
cultural sites	museums
entertainment areas	historical sites
special events	good places to eat
sports	recreational sites
scenic areas	

EX.   **Gino's Cafe.** Enjoy the show, and eat a great Italian meal at Gino's. On the menu you'll find pasta, salads, delicious desserts, and over fifty combinations for the vegetable pizza of your dreams. Gino's is just four blocks from the Milltown High Auditorium at 201 Main Street.

END MARKS AND ABBREVIATIONS

An *end mark* is a mark of punctuation placed at the end of a sentence. The three kinds of end marks are the *period*, the *question mark*, and the *exclamation point*.

23a   Use a period at the end of a statement.

EXAMPLE   Tryouts for the play will be held after school on Tuesday.

23b   Use a question mark at the end of a question.

EXAMPLE   Does anyone know how to operate this old movie projector?

23c   Use an exclamation point at the end of an exclamation.

EXAMPLES   What a spectacular race that was! Yikes! That was scary!

23d   Use either a period or an exclamation point at the end of a request or a command.

EXAMPLES   Please come in the house now. [a request]
Come in the house now! [a command]

EXERCISE 1   Adding End Marks to Sentences

Add the correct end mark to each sentence below.

EX.   1. Watch out for that car!

1. The students in the band held a carwash on Saturday and Sunday to earn money for new uniforms

2. Take out the trash after supper, please

3. How thrilling it was to shake hands with the President

4. What are the requirements for being accepted at the City School for the Performing Arts

5. Bring me that fire extinguisher quickly

6. How were we to know

7. She asked if we wanted a snack

8. Ask them not to play near the garbage cans

9. If they wanted us there at 7:00, why didn't they say so

10. What a horrible mess

23e Use a period after most abbreviations.

Abbreviations with Periods	
Personal Names	Nelson R. Mandela, J. D. Michaels
Titles Used with Names	Mr., Mrs., Ms., Dr., Jr., Sr.
States	Mass., Ky., Fla., Calif., N.J.
Organizations and Companies	Co., Inc., Corp., Assn.
Addresses	St., Rd., Ave., P.O. Box, Blvd.
Times	A.M., P.M., A.D., B.C.
Abbreviations Without Periods	
Government Agencies	IRS, FBI, CIA, OSHA, USDA
State Abbreviations Followed by a ZIP Code	Batavia, OH 45103 Charlotte, NC 28204
Units of Measure	cm, kg, ml, pt, gal, lb

 NOTE *Inch(es)* is abbreviated *in.* to avoid confusing it with *in,* the preposition. If you are not sure whether to use a period with an abbreviation, look in a dictionary.

EXERCISE 2   Punctuating Abbreviations

Add the correct punctuation to the abbreviations below.

EX.   1. Mrs. R. S. Lum

1. Lucas Arts Entertainment Co
2. the evening news at 6:00 PM
3. an 8 lb 6 oz baby girl
4. Dr Lenora M Belindo
5. Mr Jonah Nathan, Sr
6. Compugram, Inc
7. in P O Box 678
8. 4 yd 6 in

9. 40 Le Juene Rd, Miami, FL 33126
10. Nashville, Tenn
11. PTA meeting at 11:00 AM
12. 6 mi to the IRS headquarters
13. .394 in = 1 cm
14. Ms Paula S Cortez
15. Trenton, NJ

COMMAS IN A SERIES

A *comma* separates words or groups of words to help make the meaning of a sentence clear.

23f   Use commas to separate items in a series.

Commas separate words, phrases, and clauses in a series to show where one item in the series ends and the next begins.

Words in a Series
Naturalist George B. Schaller has studied and photographed gorillas, tigers, jaguars, and pandas. [nouns] Each athlete bikes, swims, and runs during the fifty-mile race. [verbs] The crowd that assembled outside the arena was large, noisy, and impatient. [adjectives]

Phrases in a Series
Walking to the podium, checking her notes one last time, and taking a deep breath, Reiko was ready to give her speech. [participial phrases] I left my purple jacket at school, on the bus, or at Franco's house. [prepositional phrases] Getting a part-time job, reading a book a week, and learning to water-ski are my goals for this summer. [gerund phrases]

Clauses in a Series
In her letter she explained where they had gone, what they had seen, and why they were returning home later than planned. [subordinate clauses] Thunder clapped, lightning flashed, and the dog barked. [short independent clauses]

When the last adjective in a series is part of a compound noun, the comma before the adjective is omitted.

EXAMPLE   I like cool, refreshing orange juice.

EXERCISE 3   Proofreading Sentences for the Correct Use of Commas

Add commas where they belong in the sentences below.

EX.   1.   Her hat, coat, gloves, and boots are in the front hall closet.

1.   Mom is shopping for a used car that is reliable roomy and economical.

2.   The photographer roamed the harsh desolate landscape of Tibet's northern plain to follow the trail of a herd of antelope.

3.   The police detective surveyed the crime scene looked for clues and talked to witnesses before writing his report.

4.   Listening to the radio humming his favorite tunes and tapping his foot to the rhythm of the Latin music, Kenneth washed and dried the dinner dishes.

5.   Joe the iceman Morris the ragman and Don the milkman are characters in *Sadie, Remember*, a book by Carol Kline.

6.   We liked watching *The Tall Blond Man With One Shoe Benji* and *Casper*.

7.   I put on my hat shorts and sandals and headed to the beach.

8.   Before dinner, we always wash our hands wash our faces change our shirts if they're dirty and set the table.

9.   Lee steered Vanya pushed on the left and Jewel pushed on the right, but the car was stuck.

10.   I like my salad with lots of vegetables a ranch dressing and croutons.

11.   Turn right at the corner go past the church and look for our house on the left.

12.   That ripe shiny red apple looks delicious!

13.   She put on her helmet adjusted her goggles and waited for the race to begin.

14.   Recycling conserving energy and planting trees help preserve our environment.

15.   Add the salt the pepper the chives and the cilantro before serving the soup.

COMMAS WITH COMPOUND SENTENCES

23g Use a comma before *and, but, or, nor, for, so,* and *yet* when they join independent clauses. However, when the independent clauses are very short, the commas before *and, but*, and *or* may be omitted. A comma is always used before *nor, for, so,* and *yet* when they join independent clauses.

EXAMPLES   Han-Ling played the piano**, *and*** her friend Jeannie played the flute.

The wind soon died down**, *but*** the rain continued for several more hours.

Mary laughed and Hal giggled.

He did not come to the party**, *nor*** did he answer my call.

Everyone had finished eating**, *so*** we cleaned off the table.

NOTE   Don't be misled by a simple sentence with a compound verb. A simple sentence has only one independent clause.

SIMPLE SENTENCE WITH COMPOUND VERB   **Anita runs** five miles every day and **lifts** weights three times a week.

COMPOUND SENTENCE   **Anita runs** five miles every day**, *and* she lifts** weights three times a week. [two independent clauses]

EXERCISE 4 Correcting Compound Sentences by Adding Commas

Add commas where they belong in the following compound sentences. If a sentence is correct, write *C* on the line before it.

EX. _____ 1. It's important to plan for the future**,** yet many people don't.

_____ 1. Colleen loves everything about the movies so she did her research paper on the history of filmmaking.

_____ 2. Her description of the painting contained many specific details yet I still could not picture it clearly.

_____ 3. My mother has never ridden on a roller coaster nor does she plan to ever ride on one.

_____ 4. In Japan, people use a detergent made from bacteria but this detergent is not available in the United States.

_____ 5. Rabbits have short ears and hares have long ears.

_____ 6. We had different opinions about how to do our science project but we still managed to finish it.

_____ 7. We will be discussing folk tales from different countries and the first tale is about an Inuit hunter.

_____ 8. You can come with Dad and me to the museum or go hiking with your brothers.

_____ 9. In the 1800s, the United States government offered free land in the West to settlers but thousands of American Indians were already living there.

_____ 10. Henri Matisse used bold, vivid colors in his paintings and he became a leader in the style known as fauvism.

EXERCISE 5   Using Commas in Compound Sentences

Make each pair of sentences below a compound sentence by adding a comma and a coordinating conjunction (*and, but, or, for, nor,* or *yet*). Write your sentences on your own paper. Use a variety of conjunctions.

EX.   1. I didn't go to the concert. I did go to the game.
    1. I didn't go to the concert, but I did go to the game.

1. The telephone rang. I didn't want to answer it.
2. Roscoe pulled into the driveway. It was time to call it a day.
3. We didn't win the first game. We didn't win the second game.
4. There is orange juice in the refrigerator. Perhaps you would prefer to have milk.
5. The cat perked up its ears. It went back to sleep.
6. I made extra enchiladas. Everyone can have two servings.
7. The apple looks sweet. It tastes sour.
8. You can mow the lawn early this morning. You can wait until this evening.
9. Tara's birthday is Friday. Let's take her to the movies.
10. Carlos practiced the song all morning. He still wasn't satisfied.

COMMAS WITH INTERRUPTERS

23h Use commas to set off a nonessential participial phrase or a nonessential subordinate clause.

A *nonessential* (or *nonrestrictive*) phrase or clause adds information that isn't necessary to the meaning of a sentence. Such a phrase or clause can be omitted without changing the main idea of the sentence.

NONESSENTIAL PHRASES	A rainbow, **shimmering in the sky,** suddenly appeared on the horizon.
	The schoolhouse, **built in 1905,** had only one room.
NONESSENTIAL CLAUSES	Loretta, **who is captain of the soccer team,** is also president of the math club.
	In the 1870s, many farmers joined the National Grange, **which helped them to gain political and economic strength**.

Do not set off an *essential* (or *restrictive*) phrase or clause. Since such a phrase or clause tells *which one(s)*, it cannot be omitted without changing the meaning of the sentence.

ESSENTIAL PHRASES	The students **trying out for the team** assembled in the gym. [*Which* students?]
	The announcement **made by the president** startled everyone. [*Which* announcement?]
ESSENTIAL CLAUSES	The dancer **who won the award** was not there to accept her prize. [*Which* dancer?]
	Mrs. Malatesta pointed to the map **that showed the movements of the early peoples from Asia to the Americas**. [*Which* map?]

NOTE An adjective clause beginning with *that* is usually essential.

REFERENCE NOTE: For more information about phrases, see pages 125–139. For more information about clauses, see pages 143–149.

EXERCISE 6 Using Commas in Sentences with Nonessential Phrases or Clauses

In the sentences below, add commas where needed to set off nonessential phrases or clauses. If a sentence is correct, write C on the line before it.

EX. _____ 1. Flora, who reads fast, enjoyed that short story by Toni Cade Bambara.

_____ 1. The story that Flora read was titled "Blues Ain't No Mockin Bird."

_____ 2. That story is from Bambara's first short-story collection which is called *Gorilla, My Love*.

_____ 3. The story's narrator who is both humorous and knowledgeable is similar to other characters created by Bambara.

_____ 4. Toni Cade Bambara raised in Harlem, Brooklyn, and Jersey City graduated from Queens College in New York City.

_____ 5. Bambara having studied the performing arts in Italy and France came back to New York and worked in city hospitals and community centers.

_____ 6. She became a teacher and taught at Spelman College which is in Atlanta, Georgia.

_____ 7. The writer whose last name is the name of a native people in northwest Africa has said that she likes writing happy, upbeat stories.

_____ 8. Her stories are filled with energy and optimism which she wants her readers to feel.

_____ 9. She models some of the characters in her stories after people in stories that she read and heard about as a child.

_____ 10. These people who were Bambara's childhood champions included Harriet Tubman, Paul Robeson, and her own grandmother.

OTHER USES OF COMMAS

23i Use commas to set off an appositive or an appositive phrase that is nonessential.

An *appositive* is a noun or pronoun used to explain or identify another noun or pronoun. An *appositive phrase* is made up of the appositive and its modifiers.

EXAMPLES   Does your science teacher, **Mr. Jee,** live in your building?
That dress is Mom's favorite color, **emerald green**.
Ansel Adams, **one of America's most famous nature photographers,** was an active conservationist.

Do not set off an appositive that tells *which one*(s) about the word it identifies. Such an appositive is essential to the meaning of the sentence.

EXAMPLE   Leonardo da Vinci's painting **the *Mona Lisa*** hangs in the French museum **the Louvre**. [*Which* painting? *Which* museum?]

23j Use commas to set off words used in direct address.

EXAMPLES   **Tyrone,** it's your turn to dry the dishes.
Please, **Veronica,** will you help me practice my lines?

23k Use commas to set off a parenthetical expression.

A *parenthetical expression* is a side remark that adds information or relates ideas. Some common parenthetical expressions include *by the way, for example, however, I think,* and *to tell the truth.*

EXAMPLES   Randy explained, **of course,** why he was so late.
On the other hand, do you ever want to go to the movie?

EXERCISE 7 Correcting Sentences by Adding Commas

In each of the following sentences, underline the appositive or appositive phrase, the words used in direct address, or the parenthetical expression. Add commas where needed.

EX.   1. Chico Mendes, a rubber tapper in Brazil, was known for his opposition to the destruction of the Amazon.

1. Do you know Todd what Chico Mendes did for Brazil's rain forest?

2. He proposed that land be set aside by the government for the rubber tappers' use I believe.

3. Originally, rubber tappers inhabitants of the rain forest for generations were being forced to leave their homes.

4. In my opinion Chico Mendes is a hero in the fight to preserve the rain forest.

5. Maria do you agree with my opinion?

6. Rubber trees the source of income for the rubber tappers were being cut down as land was cleared.

7. Chico Mendes of course did not sit quietly while this clearing was happening.

8. Over a period of years, he organized more than forty peaceful blockades lines of hundreds of people to stop the bulldozers from clearing the forest.

9. He asked the government to protect areas of the forest so that people who lived there could continue to collect latex the juice of the rubber tree.

10. He must have saved thousands of acres of rain forest I suppose.

EXERCISE 8 Using Commas in Sentences

You attended an International Food Banquet, and you want to describe your experience to a friend. On your own paper, write ten sentences, using the groups of words below as appositives or appositive phrases. Be sure that you insert commas where they are needed.

EX. 1. jicama and papaya
     1. Two of the foods, jicama and papaya, were new to me.

1. turmeric and fenugreek	6. the cayenne and the jalapeño
2. guava and mangoes	7. our home economics teacher
3. my favorite beverage	8. an unusual mixture
4. the main speaker	9. a delicious vegetable
5. a community-wide project	10. a great success

INTRODUCTORY WORDS, PHRASES, AND CLAUSES

23l Use a comma after *yes, no,* or any mild exclamation such as *well* or *why* at the beginning of a sentence.

EXAMPLES   Yes, I would like another piece of pizza.
Well, there may be a simpler solution to this problem.

23m Use a comma after an introductory phrase or clause.

(1) A comma is used after an introductory prepositional phrase if the phrase is long or if two or more phrases appear together. If the introductory prepositional phrase is short, a comma may or may not be used.

EXAMPLES   **Behind an elaborately carved door,** the king met secretly with his advisers.
From our window on the second floor, we watched the Thanksgiving Day parade.
At night, [or **At night**] the sound of crickets fills the air.

(2) A comma is used after a participial phrase or an infinitive phrase that introduces a sentence.

PARTICIPIAL PHRASE   **Thinking about her plans for the summer,** Lani became eager for school to end.

INFINITIVE PHRASE   **To avoid the traffic on the freeway,** the taxi driver took back roads to the airport.

(3) An adverb clause may be used at various places in a sentence. At the beginning of a sentence, the adverb clause is followed by a comma.

EXAMPLE   **When the concert is over,** please return the sound equipment to the music room.

    REFERENCE NOTE: For more about prepositional phrases, see page 125. For more about verbal phrases, see page 133. For more about adverb clauses, see page 147.

EXERCISE 9 Using Commas in Sentences with Introductory Words, Phrases, and Clauses

On the line before each sentence below, write the word that should be followed by a comma, and add the missing comma. Write C if the sentence is correct.

EX. _____ No, ____ 1. No I have never seen the work of artist Diego Rivera.

_____ 1. Because I have been reading about him would you like for me to tell you about Diego Rivera and his work?

_____ 2. Why I believe I know something about his life.

_____ 3. Reading about Rivera in this book on art history I learned that Rivera is one of Mexico's most famous painters.

_____ 4. For dramatic effect Rivera often painted huge murals or frescoes.

_____ 5. Partly because his murals decorated public buildings Rivera's painting became well known.

_____ 6. Born in the late 1800s the artist focused his work on the lives of Mexican peasants.

_____ 7. According to this book Rivera also produced paintings about the effects of industry on the United States.

_____ 8. Concerned with the well-being of the lower classes Rivera advocated social change with his pictures.

_____ 9. Feeling offended by the figure of Lenin in one fresco many people picketed and wrote angry letters.

_____ 10. In the earlier part of his career Rivera's painting was less focused on social issues.

_____ 11. When I visited a museum in San Francisco I saw Rivera's painting *Two Mexican Women and Child.*

_____ 12. In the painting a woman holding a small child is facing another woman.

_____ 13. Well what did you think about it?

_____ 14. As I studied the painting a feeling of calmness came over me.

_____ 15. To achieve that effect Rivera used muted colors and slow, softly rounded curves.

DATES, ADDRESSES, AND FRIENDLY LETTERS

23n Use commas to separate items in dates and addresses.

EXAMPLES   When Neil Armstrong stepped onto the moon on July 20,
1969, workers at the National Aeronautics and Space
Administration offices in Houston, Texas, cheered.
The 1992 Summer Olympic games took place in Barcelona,
Spain, at the same time that Expo '92 was being held
in Seville.
On Friday, August 26, I will celebrate my birthday.
My aunt Meredith lives at 122 East Fourth Avenue,
Altoona, Pennsylvania 16602.

Notice that in a date or an address, a comma separates the last item from
the words that follow it. However, a comma does *not* separate a month
and a day (*August 26*), a house number and a street name (*122 East Fourth
Avenue*), or a state name or abbreviation and a ZIP Code (*Pennsylvania
16602* or *PA 16602*). A comma also does not separate a month and a year
if no day is given (*February 1993*).

NOTE   If a preposition is used between items of an address, a comma is
not necessary before the preposition.

EXAMPLE   She works at 42 Belfast Place in Parkersburg, West
Virginia.

**23o Use a comma after the salutation of a friendly letter and after the
closing of any letter.**

EXAMPLES   Dear Uncle Guido,   Sincerely yours,   Yours truly,

EXERCISE 10   Adding Commas to Dates, Addresses, and Parts of a Letter

Add commas where they belong in the following items.

EX.   1. 1600 Pennsylvania Avenue, Washington, D.C.

1. Dear Fernando

2. May 10 1869 at Promontory Point Utah

3. at 612 First Avenue Seattle Washington 98104 on Sunday March 20

4. from November 9 1992 to October 24 1993

5. 2100 Charleston Road La Crosse Wisconsin 54602

6. Sincerely yours

7. September 11 1992 in Honolulu Hawaii

8. Dear Mrs. Nabiyev

9. High Street at Schoolhouse Road in West Hempstead New York

10. Yours truly

11. 124 Michigan Ave. Suite 1422

12. Chicago IL 60656

13. My dear Morgan

14. International Computers in Geneva Switzerland and New Delhi India

15. Yours hopefully

16. Rural Route 1 Box 12

17. downtown Cincinnati Ohio

18. until September 5 1994

19. in the Jefferson School at 110 Main Street Ames Iowa

20. Saturday May 15 through Sunday May 23

EXERCISE 11   Proofreading Sentences for the Correct Use of Commas

Add commas where they belong in the sentences below.

EX. 1. We cycled from Aztec ,New Mexico ,to Durango ,Colorado.

1. On March 4 1995 Ani will be fifteen years old.

2. Does the bus still stop in Aurora West Virginia and in Oakland Maryland?

3. Victor's new address is 1909 Cypress Point Austin Texas 78746.

4. Selise arrived in Columbus Ohio just as her sister was leaving Columbus to go to Bozeman Montana.

5. How exciting it was to drive across the Golden Gate Bridge into San Francisco California!

REVIEW EXERCISE

A. Proofreading Sentences for the Correct Use of End Marks and Commas

In the sentences below, insert end marks and commas where they are needed.

EX. 1. We walked ,we talked ,and we enjoyed ourselves .

1. Did you find the article Marshall about tigers that live in the forests of India

2. Yes it was in the March 1990 issue of the magazine

3. Khana National Park which became a tiger preserve in 1973 is in central India

4. The author a writer from the United States went to India to see the tigers

5. She also saw chital deer swamp deer and langur monkeys

6. The noisy playful monkeys chased each other through the trees

7. After standing with her guide on a hidden platform for a long time the author finally spotted a tiger

8. The guide who told Kristina to be extremely quiet knew a great deal about wild tigers

9. Chital deer warn other deer in the herd that a tiger is near by stomping their hooves making barking sounds and lifting their tails into the air

10. The monkeys ran up a tree but the tiger was not interested in chasing them

B. Proofreading a Paragraph for the Correct Use of Commas

In the following paragraph, insert commas where they are needed.

EX. [1] Sitting on top of the high cliff, the researchers used telescopes to spot grizzly bears.

[1] Steve and Marilynn French amateur naturalists like studying nature. [2] Observing studying and filming in Yellowstone National Park the couple research the behavior of the grizzly bears. [3] Being independent of any government agency they are free to conduct their

research as they please. [4] Their work however helps park officials to track the bears and to understand the bears' daily habits. [5] Steve French a doctor in Evanston Wyoming became interested in bears after operating on people who had been attacked by them. [6] When the couple began their research they learned that Yellowstone's bears had become used to human food. [7] To return the bears to a more natural diet and way of life the National Park Service took action. [8] It closed the park's dumps where the grizzlies were getting fat on human food. [9] Because some people felt this action was too sudden a bitter argument started. [10] People who wanted to phase out the dumps gradually argued protested and wrote articles about this situation.

C.   Writing Questions and Answers About Animals

You are a writer for a television game show in which contestants answer questions from a variety of categories. Your assignment for the next show is to write the questions for an animal category. You can do research about animals in an encyclopedia, science book, nature magazine, or any other reference source that provides accurate information. Then, on your own paper, write ten questions and answers related to animals. Include questions or answers that reflect five comma rules from this chapter.

EX.   QUESTION: Why does a camel have a hump?

ANSWER: When camels travel across the desert, they need to store nutrients and fat in their humps.

23p Use a semicolon instead of a comma between independent clauses that are not joined by *and, but, or, nor, for, so,* or *yet.*

EXAMPLES   After dinner, Marika wanted to go to the movies; Carrie planned to watch the basketball game on television.

The game was not exciting enough for me; I got bored and fell asleep.

 NOTE   Use a semicolon rather than a period between independent clauses only when the ideas in the clauses are closely related.

EXAMPLE   Carrie enjoys watching basketball. Mai would rather play.

Carrie enjoys watching basketball; Mai would rather play.

23q Use a semicolon between independent clauses joined by a conjunctive adverb or a transitional expression.

Conjunctive adverbs and *transitional expressions* show the relationship between the independent clauses that they join.

EXAMPLES   There was no proof that Mike's dog had trampled Mrs. Lavitka's flower garden; *nevertheless,* Mike offered to help repair the damage.

The phone rang repeatedly during dinner; *as a result,* my food was cold by the time I got to eat.

Commonly Used Conjunctive Adverbs			
accordingly	furthermore	instead	nevertheless
besides	however	meanwhile	otherwise
consequently	indeed	moreover	therefore
Commonly Used Transitional Expressions			
as a result	for example	for instance	that is
in addition	in spite of	in conclusion	in fact

23r   Use a semicolon rather than a comma before a coordinating conjunction to join independent clauses that contain commas.

EXAMPLES   A large, green frog leaped across the wet grass; and the frisky, playful kitten chased after it.

There will be no school the last Friday in November, the second week in January, and the third week in April; and on the first Thursday of each month, we will have a half day.

EXERCISE 12   Using Semicolons Correctly

Add semicolons where they belong in the sentences below.

EX.   1. The classroom was quiet; the students were reading silently.

1. Read about the history of the Incan treasure it's extremely fascinating.

2. Some people believe that the Incas hid treasure in the Llanganates Mountains as a result, many groups have traveled there.

3. Thick, dark clouds dot gray, threatening skies a damp, depressing mist surrounds the mysterious mountain range where the treasure is hidden.

4. The Incas supposedly hid several hundred tons of gold and silver objects in the Llanganates Mountains these objects included statues and other religious items.

5. In the 1500s, Francisco Pizarro and his followers came to Peru from Spain they were in search of gold and silver.

6. To the Incas, gold and silver objects were not valuable because of their monetary worth on the contrary, they were valued as religious symbols.

7. The Incas had been involved in a long civil war before Pizzaro arrived otherwise, Pizarro would not have been able to so easily capture their newly appointed king, Atahualpa.

8. Pizarro tricked Atahualpa into giving him gold and silver from some of the Incas' temples he promised to set Atahualpa free if Atahualpa would give him the gold and silver.

9. After getting the gold and silver, Pizzaro did not release Atahualpa instead, Pizarro killed him and went in search of more treasure.

10. One of Atahualpa's men, who was transporting tons of gold and silver, heard about Atahualpa's death he hid the treasure in the Llanganates Mountains, where it is still hidden.

COLONS

23s **Use a colon before a list of items, especially after expressions like** *as follows* **or** *the following items.*

EXAMPLES   Besides the ordinary luncheon items, the cafeteria offered
several unusual dishes: gazpacho, eggplant enchiladas,
pickled cauliflower, Sicilian swordfish, and spinach soufflé.
Computer equipment today includes the following hardware:
hard drives, monitors, laser printers, modems, CD/ROM
players, and speakers.

23t **Use a colon before a statement that explains or clarifies a preceding statement.**

When a list of words, phrases, or subordinate clauses follows a colon, the
first word of the list is lowercase. When an independent clause follows a
colon, the first word of the clause begins with a capital letter.

EXAMPLES   I had three things to do after dinner: take out the trash, do
my homework, and straighten my closet.
I recalled my grandfather's parting words clearly: "Work
hard, play harder, and remember to write home once
a week."

23u **Use a colon between the hour and the minute.**

EXAMPLES   6:00 P.M.   10:45 A.M.

23v **Use a colon after the salutation of a business letter.**

EXAMPLES   Dr. Stamos: Dear Sir or Madam: To Whom It May Concern:

23w **Use a colon between chapter and verse in referring to passages from the Bible.**

EXAMPLES   Joshua 7:6   Mark 8:27–30

EXERCISE 13   Using Colons Correctly

Change each word group below into a complete sentence by adding the information suggested in brackets. Insert colons and commas where they are needed.

EX.   1. Our plane leaves at [*time*]. _____
          Our plane leaves at 4:45 P.M. _____

1. Here is a list of ingredients that we need to make supper [*list*]. _____

    _____

2. Miss Garabedian will begin her science lecture promptly at [*time*]. _____

    _____

3. My father's favorite saying is as follows [*independent clause*]. _____

    _____

4. The first-aid kit contained the following items [*list*]. _____

    _____

5. The minister based his sermon on [*Bible chapter and verse*]. _____

    _____

6. Necessary ingredients are as follows [*list*]. _____

    _____

7. They couldn't buy her everything she needed before school

    started [*independent clause*]. _____

    _____

8. The train arrives around [*time*]. _____

    _____

9. Our family went to two movies this weekend [*list*]. _____

    _____

10. Vote for me for class president [*independent clause*]. _____

    _____

CHAPTER REVIEW

A.   Proofreading Sentences for the Correct Use of Commas

Add commas where needed in the sentences below.

EX.   1.   Tammy, let's watch the special on the Pecos River.

1.   This show was originally broadcast on January 20 1993.

2.   The Pecos River flows through three towns in New Mexico: Sena Villanueva and Colonias.

3.   Beginning north of Santa Fe the river travels from New Mexico to the Rio Grande River on the border of Texas and Mexico.

4.   The river which starts out as a clear mountain stream is muddied by runoff from the land.

5.   Some of the people who live along the river do not have electricity running water or any other modern conveniences in their homes.

6.   We Vida and I saw a show about the Mekong River.

7.   The Mekong River begins in the T'ang-ku-la Mountains and flows through Laos Cambodia and Vietnam.

8.   **The Mekong River which has a narrow width is approximately 2,600 miles long.**

9.   Ranging from 74° F to 89° F the temperature in the Mekong River basin is generally warm.

10.   Almost all of the people who live along the Mekong River are involved in agriculture producing mainly rice.

B.   Using End Marks, Commas, Semicolons, and Colons Correctly in a Paragraph

The sentences in the following paragraph need end marks, commas, semicolons, or colons. Add the missing punctuation.

1   Staring at the drawing on the page I thought about the artist

2   who had drawn it Käthe Kollwitz who lived in Germany during

3   World War II may have been the most famous artist of her time

4   Her drawings condemned by the Nazis were not cheerful or

5   uplifting instead many of them portrayed women and children in

6 misery poverty and despair Why did this artist who was the first
7 woman to be admitted to the Academy of Berlin dare to anger the
8 Nazis Considered dangerous by them she was dismissed from the
9 academy in addition her art could not be exhibited The Nazis
10 however could not punish threaten or scare her into giving up her
11 artwork She had a message to deliver Poor children and their
12 mothers are important we must never forget about them In April
13 1945 Käthe Kollwitz died at a friend's house in the German
14 countryside the place to which she had fled to escape the deadly
15 destructive bombing of Berlin.

C. Proofreading a Letter for Correct Use of End Marks, Commas, Semicolons, and Colons

Some parts of the letter below need end marks, commas, semicolons, or colons. Add the missing punctuation marks.

1   14 Drake Road
2   Colorado Springs Colorado 80915
3   September 15 1994

4   Maria Ortiz
5   16532 Ramona Drive
6   Ann Arbor Michigan 48106
7   Dear Miss Ortiz
8   My school Dale Junior High has an environmental awareness
9   program planned for two days this fall The dates for this program
10 are October 17 1994, and October 18, 1994 Topics for the program
11 are as follows the destruction of the world's rain forests
12 endangered species and the threats to the Florida Everglades
13   Several nights ago I was watching the national evening news
14 and I saw an interview with you about the disappearing
15 Everglades. Your dedication your enthusiasm and your proposals
16 to solve this problem inspired me they would inspire anyone
17 Therefore I hope you will accept this invitation to attend our
18 program Miss Ortiz you may select either date to attend but I
19 would appreciate a response before September 30 1994.
20   Sincerely
21   Howard Nichols

UNDERLINING (ITALICS)

Italics are printed letters that lean to the right, such as *the letters in these words*. In your handwritten or typewritten work, indicate italics by underlining.

24a **Use underlining (italics) for titles of books, plays, periodicals, works of art, films, television programs, recordings, musical works, trains, ships, aircraft, and spacecraft.**

Type of Title	Examples	
Books	*The Last of the Mohicans*	*Roots*
Plays	*Our Town*	*Romeo and Juliet*
Periodicals	*Sports Illustrated*	*Seventeen*
Works of Art	*The Music Lesson*	*Lovers Lane*
Films	*A Few Good Men*	*Jurassic Park*
Television Programs	*Nova*	*Evening Shade*
Recordings	*Texas Flood*	*Sweet Baby James*
Musical Works	*New World Symphony*	*Carmen*
Trains	*Twentieth Century*	*Santa Fe Chief*
Ships	*Titanic*	*Queen Mary*
Aircraft	*Flyer*	*Spirit of St. Louis*
Spacecraft	*Mercury 7*	*Sputnik I*

NOTE The article *the* is often written before a title but is not capitalized unless it is part of the official title. The official title of a newspaper or periodical is found on the masthead, which usually appears on the editorial page.

EXAMPLE   I like to read *The Boston Globe*.

24b   Use underlining (italics) for words, letters, and figures referred to as such.

EXAMPLES   Drop the final *e* before adding the suffix *–ed* to the word *hope*.
The last numeral in my ZIP Code is *8*.
The symbol *$* can be drawn with one or two vertical lines.

EXERCISE 1   Using Underlining (Italics) in Sentences

For each of the sentences below, underline the word or words that should be in italics.

EX.   1.   The musical drama Evita is based on the life of Eva Perón.

1. Mark W. Davis's column has appeared in Newsweek.

2. The March 1990 issue of National Geographic magazine has an interesting article about Siberia.

3. Two of my favorite recordings are the Gipsy Kings' Mosaique and Celia Cruz's Azucar Negra.

4. John Glenn was the astronaut who piloted the space capsule Friendship 7.

5. A rock opera, The Who's Tommy, opened in New York City on April 22, 1993.

6. Peter Ilich Tchaikovsky, a nineteenth-century Russian composer, wrote the opera Eugene Onegin.

7. The name Tchaikovsky is difficult to spell because the T is almost silent.

8. Viktor Petrenko, the 1992 gold medalist in Olympic figure skating, performed in the show called Skates of Gold.

9. Pequod was the ship in Herman Melville's novel Moby-Dick.

10. A film critic of the Toronto Sun used the word rare to describe the movie The Secret Garden.

QUOTATION MARKS

24c Use quotation marks to enclose a *direct quotation*—a person's exact words.

EXAMPLE   "Do you have an extra concert ticket?" Miguel asked.

24d A direct quotation begins with a capital letter.

EXAMPLE   Sylvia whispered, "Let's hide the clue under that big stone."

24e When the expression identifying the speaker interrupts a quoted sentence, the second part of the quotation begins with a small letter.

EXAMPLES   "I'm not sure," Dave admitted, "that I'm ready for the test." [A comma, not a period, follows the interrupting expression.] "Do you want to know a secret?" Fran asked. "My friend Rudolph is a magician!" [The first part of this quotation is a complete sentence. Because the second part begins a new sentence, it begins with a capital letter.]

24f A direct quotation is set off from the rest of the sentence by a question mark, a comma, or an exclamation point, but not by a period.

EXAMPLES   "Where did you go on your trip?" Lyndon asked.
"We flew over the Grand Canyon," I said.
"What a fantastic trip that must have been!" Lyndon said.

24g A period or a comma is always placed inside the closing quotation marks.

EXAMPLE   "Yes," said Sven, "she does sing beautifully."

24h A question mark or an exclamation point is placed inside the closing quotation marks when the quotation itself is a question or an exclamation. Otherwise, it is placed outside.

EXAMPLES   "Who brought the refreshments?" George asked. [The quotation is a question.]
What was the meaning of your message "Hope is on the way"? [The sentence, not the quotation, is a question.]

When both the sentence and the quotation at the end of the sentence are questions (or exclamations), only one question mark (or exclamation point) is used. It is placed inside the closing quotation marks.

EXAMPLE   Doesn't a song from the musical *Oliver* ask, **"Where is love?"**

EXERCISE 2   Correcting Sentences by Adding Capital Letters and Punctuation

For each sentence below, add capital letters and punctuation as needed.

EX.   1. "Yes, Jim said, my part in the school play has been announced.
   1. "Yes," Jim said, "my part in the school play has been announced."

1. Wow she exclaimed our seats are in the front row
2. Wasn't it Greta Garbo who said I want to be alone
3. Have you ever heard the song that asks, what kind of fool am I
4 Tonight Dad said we're going to have a special treat in downtown Philadelphia
5. Jim said Dad can we stay to hear the Pointer Sisters sing
6. When does their part of the program begin Dad asked
7. I checked the newspaper and then said they're singing on the steps of the art museum at nine o'clock
8. Great said Dad before the concert, we can see the African jewelry at the museum
9. The newspaper says dont miss this display of gold
10. Will there be any gold masks asked Jim
11. Mom said if you had said I'm going to need a ride you wouldn't have had to walk home
12. Did Johanna hear me say please bring your parents
13. Helena asked what are the pampas
14. Ramon Dolores asked did you see the schedule
15. Mrs. Boyd explained put a cover sheet on your essay

24i **When you write dialogue (conversation), begin a new paragraph each time you change speakers.**

EXAMPLE   "What food should we take to the International Picnic?" Nina asked. "Last year, we took guacamole."
     "Let's make burritos," I suggested. "Your burritos are fantastic, and I'll be happy to help you make them."
     "That's a great idea!" Nina replied.

24j **When a quotation consists of several sentences, place quotation marks at the beginning and at the end of the whole quotation.**

EXAMPLE   "All contestants for the race should report to the registration desk now. You will be given your number for the race. Please pin it to the front of your shirt. Then all runners should report to the starting line," the race official announced.

24k **Use quotation marks to enclose titles of short works such as short stories, poems, articles, songs, episodes of television programs, and chapters and other parts of books.**

Type of Title	Examples	
Short Stories	"The Waltz"	"The Rocking-Horse Winner"
Poems	"Mending Wall"	"Fall Wind"
Articles	"The Face of the Future"	"Highways to Heaven"
Songs	"America the Beautiful"	"Fire and Rain"
Episodes of Television Programs	"Spell of the Greasepaint"	"Knots on a Counting Rope"
Chapters and Other Parts of Books	"Punctuation"	"Comparison Shopping"

24l **Use single quotation marks to enclose a quotation within a quotation and to punctuate the title of a short work used within a quotation.**

EXAMPLES   "Which Robert Frost poem contains the line 'Good fences make good neighbors'?" Kayla asked.
     "I'll repeat the directions," Georgio said. "I said, 'Take Rand Street for two blocks, and then make a left turn.'"
     Mara asked, "Have you ever read the poem 'Calling in the Cat'?"

EXERCISE 3   Correcting Sentences by Adding Quotation Marks

On your own paper, rewrite each of the following sentences, adding quotation marks as needed.

EX.   1. Henri asked, Who wrote the poem about grandmothers?

　　　1. Henri asked, "Who wrote the poem about grandmothers?"

1. Sheila answered, That was the poet Margaret Walker.
2. The title of that poem is Lineage, she added.
3. The first chapter in the book *Heading Home* is called Discovery.
4. Who said, I have a dream that one day this nation will rise up? asked Leilani.
5. I read an article, Earthquake—Prelude to the Big One?, in the May 1990 issue of *National Geographic,* said Bly.

EXERCISE 4   Proofreading Dialogue for Errors in Punctuation

On your own paper, rewrite the following passage, adding paragraph breaks and quotation marks as needed.

EX.   Rudy said, Let's look through this carton of old records. Maybe we'll find some interesting music.

　　　Rudy said, "Let's look through this carton of old records. Maybe we'll find some interesting music."

1　　The first thing Rudy came across at Mrs. Fiorella's garage sale was
2　　a large box of old records. Flipping through them, he said to Maraya,
3　　Look at this one! It's an album by Sergio Mendes, *Brasil '66*! Do you
4　　like Brazilian music? Maraya asked. Well, Rudy answered, to tell you
5　　the truth, I don't know much about it. But my dad has Sergio
6　　Mendes's 1992 CD, *Brasiliero,* and he plays it all the time. My favorite
7　　song on that CD is called What Is This? Carmen Alice sings it. Why
8　　don't you buy that *Brasil '66* record for your dad? Maraya asked. I bet
9　　he'll love it. That's a great idea! exclaimed Rudy. His birthday is next
10　　week. I can give it to him then.

The *possessive case* of a noun or a pronoun shows ownership or relationship. An *apostrophe* is used to form the possessive case of nouns and some pronouns.

Ownership	Relationship
Julia's book the **teachers'** desks **our** house	a **day's** work **Ramon's** sister **everybody's**

24m To form the possessive case of a singular noun, add an apostrophe and an *s*.

EXAMPLES   the cat**'s** toy   an hour**'s** wait
                Thomas**'s** bike   the box**'s** lid

NOTE A proper noun ending in *s* may take only an apostrophe to form the possessive case if the addition of *'s* would make the name awkward to pronounce.

      EXAMPLES Mount Parnassus**'** elevation   Pocahontas**'** birthplace

24n To form the possessive case of a plural noun ending in *s*, add only an apostrophe.

EXAMPLES   the birds**'** nests   the Reilleys**'** dog   three dollars**'** worth

24o To form the possessive case of a plural noun that does not end in *s*, add an apostrophe and an *s*.

EXAMPLES   the children**'s** games the mice**'s** footprints the men**'s** chorus

NOTE Do not use an apostrophe to form the plural of a noun.

      INCORRECT   The kitten's have soft coats.
        CORRECT   The **kittens** have soft coats. [plural]
        CORRECT   The **kittens'** coats are soft. [plural possessive]

24p Do not use an apostrophe with possessive personal pronouns.

EXAMPLE   **His** painting is finished, but **hers** is not.

24q Use an apostrophe and an *s* to form the plurals of letters and numerals and of words referred to as words.

EXAMPLES   three *d*'**s**   your 2'**s**   her *and*'**s**

EXERCISE 5 Supplying Apostrophes

On the line before each of the following sentences, write the noun or nouns that should appear in the possessive case. Add the apostrophe in the correct place.

EX.   _____Nabil's_____   1. The committee members approved of Nabils plan.

_____   1. George Washingtons home is called Mount Vernon.

_____   2. I haven't had a minutes rest since I started washing the dishes.

_____   3. Marjorie Kinnan Rawlings book *The Yearling* is exciting and thought-provoking.

_____   4. The original Shetland ponies home was on the Shetland Islands, off the coast of Scotland.

_____   5. The geeses nest is under the bushes near the edge of the pond.

_____   6. The childrens first day back to school will be next Thursday.

_____   7. Each childs desk and books are ready.

_____   8. To answer questions about the school year, there will be a parents meeting in the library.

_____   9. My fathers friend forgot his keys.

_____   10. Everyone in the seventh-grade class hopes to get all As and Bs this year.

EXERCISE 6 Writing Possessives

On your own paper, rewrite each of the expressions below, adding an apostrophe to create the correct possessive form.

EX.   1. the films of Gary Cooper
       1. Gary Cooper's films

1. the paychecks of the workers
2. the feet of the horse
3. the time of a minute
4. the squeaks of the mice
5. the car of the O'Haras

6. the blankets of the babies
7. the advice of my mother
8. the house of Louis
9. the award of the champion
10. the help of Dee

CONTRACTIONS

A *contraction* is a shortened form of a word, a figure, or a group of words.

24r **To form a contraction, use an apostrophe to show where letters or numerals have been left out.**

Common Contractions			
I am	I'm	they had	they'd
1993	'93	where is	where's
let us	let's	we are	we're
of the clock	o'clock	he is	he's
she would	she'd	you will	you'll

The word *not* can be shortened to *n't* and added to a verb, usually without changing the spelling of the verb.

EXAMPLES			
is not	isn't	has not	hasn't
are not	aren't	have not	haven't
does not	doesn't	had not	hadn't
do not	don't	should not	shouldn't
was not	wasn't	would not	wouldn't

EXCEPTIONS			
will not	**won't**	cannot	**can't**

Do not confuse contractions with possessive pronouns.

Contractions	Possessive Pronouns
It's a great idea. [*It is*] **It's** been an interesting meeting. [*It has*]	The dog lost **its** collar.
Who's running for class president? [*Who is*] **Who's** left a message for me? [*Who has*]	**Whose** boots are those?
You're going to miss the bus. [*You are*]	**Your** painting is beautiful.
They're going to the movies. [*They are*]	**Their** mother is a doctor.
There's a bus stop on the corner. [*There is*] **There's** been a terrible storm. [*There has*]	The cat is **theirs**.

EXERCISE 7   Writing Contractions

Rewrite each of the phrases below as a contraction. Be sure to add an apostrophe in the correct place.

EX.   1. you would   _____you'd_____

1. could not _____   6. where is   _____

2. we are   _____   7. I am   _____

3. he would _____   8. they are   _____

4. they will _____   9. would not   _____

5. will not _____   10. let us   _____

EXERCISE 8   Punctuating Contractions

The sentences below contain words that need apostrophes. On the line before each sentence, write the contraction correctly.

EX.   _____They're_____   1. Theyre going to polish its fenders with wax.

_____   1. Roberto and Nasser cant come to your game today.

_____   2. Its an exciting day for them and for their father.

_____   3. At seven oclock, his old car will be delivered.

_____   4. Its been at a refinishing shop near your old neighborhood.

_____   5. Youll really see a difference when you see its new paint job.

_____   6. If your mom says that it is OK, lets go over there after the game.

_____   7. Hes bought a new engine for the car, too.

_____   8. Its exciting to see the car looking new again!

_____   9. Look at this present that Ive bought for the car's rearview mirror.

_____ 10. Theyre big dice, just like the ones he probably wouldve had on that car when it was new.

CHAPTER REVIEW

A. Revising Sentences for the Correct Use of Punctuation

On your own paper, rewrite each of the following sentences so that underlining, quotation marks, and apostrophes are used correctly. [Note: A sentence may contain more than one error.]

EX. 1. Dont the words accept and except sometimes cause confusion?
   1. Don't the words <u>accept</u> and <u>except</u> sometimes cause confusion?

1. I havent finished reading Hemingways book A Farewell to Arms.

2. Ive never been to one of Linda Ronstadts concerts, but Id love to see her perform that song called Desperado.

3. Of all the poems in the book Adventures in Appreciation, the two boys favorite is Dreams, by Langston Hughes.

4. Gina asked, Didnt Paul Simon write the lyrics to the song I Am a Rock?

5. I love the way Aretha Franklin sings the word respect in that song! Alice said.

6. The writing team of Holland, Dozier, and Holland wrote the song Baby Love, which became one of the Supremes greatest hits.

7. Unfortunately, the popularity of the Supremes faded after Diana Rosss departure from the group.

8. Critics have used the word satin to describe her voice.

9. I just happen to have two tickets to Dianas concert, my friend said. Wouldnt you like to go with me?

10. Ive heard the concert reviewed on a radio broadcast of Music America.

11. Dont forget to put i before e except after c.

12. Mr. Gilbert asked, Have you read the chapter called Where is Poetry?

13. The Browns horse jumped over the fence.

14. Before you may eat, youll have to wait until everyone else sits down.

15. My mother entered the race, said Toshi, and shes one of seven women running today.

B. Proofreading a Paragraph for Correct Punctuation

The following paragraph needs underlining, quotation marks, and apostrophes. On your own paper, rewrite the paragraph to correct all errors. Be sure to start a new paragraph each time the speaker changes.

EX.   Perhaps I was once Cleopatra, the woman said softly.
       "Perhaps I was once Cleopatra," the woman said softly.

1   Arlo and I were studying for our math test. It was hard, and
2   my mind was wandering. All the 3s started looking like 8s, and
3   the 1s started looking like 7s. Suddenly, I said, Arlo, guess what I
4   saw on television last night! It was an episode called This Is Your
5   Lives. It was all about people who believe that they have lived
6   other lives. I dont understand, Arlo said. what do you mean by
7   the word other. How can someone have another life? I said, They
8   think that they lived in another time. One woman believed that
9   she was once a soldier in the Roman army. Isnt that incredible?
10   Yes, it is, Arlo said. Lets stop doing math. Were going to imagine
11   that we had former lives. Who do you think you were? I dont
12   know, I said. But Id like to imagine that I was better at math,
13   whoever I was.

C. Writing Interview Notes

You and a partner are visiting Argentina. You are reporters for the *New York Times*. Your assignment is to write an article about the ranch hands, called *gauchos,* that work on the Argentine ranches. On your own paper, write ten interview questions that you might ask a gaucho you meet. You should include possible responses. Use encyclopedias or reference books for information on gauchos. Be sure to use quotation marks correctly.

EX.   1. What do you wear to protect yourself from the cold?
           Amado replied, "I wear a brightly colored cape called a poncho."

THE DICTIONARY

When you are not sure about the spelling of a word, look in a dictionary. A dictionary entry can also give you much useful information about a word. Here is a sample entry.

---

sim•ple (sim′ pəl) **–pler, –plest** [Latin *simplus* < Indo-European *sem–*(one) + *–plos*(fold)] *adj.* **1.** having or consisting of only one part or feature; not complex [a *simple* sentence]. **2.** having few parts; not complicated [a *simple* answer]. **3.** easy to do, solve, or understand [a *simple* task]. **4.** plain; not ornate, fancy, or highly decorated [a *simple* dress]. **5.** Zoology: not divided or made up of parts; not compounded [a *simple* eye]. **—sim′ple•ness,** *n.* **—sim•plic′i•ty,** *n.*

SYN. **easy, smooth.** *ANT.* **complicated, complex, difficult, hard**

---

1. **Entry word.** The entry word shows the correct spelling of a word and how it is divided into syllables. The entry word also may tell whether the word is capitalized and may provide alternate spellings.

2. **Pronunciation.** The pronunciation of a word is shown by the use of accent marks and either phonetic symbols or *diacritical marks*, special symbols placed above the letters. Refer to a pronunciation key for the meanings and the sounds that diacritical marks and phonetic respellings use.

3. **Other forms.** These forms include spellings of plural forms of nouns, tenses of verbs, and the comparative forms of adjectives and adverbs.

4. **Etymology.** The *etymology* is the origin and history of a word. It tells how the word (or its parts) entered the English language.

5. **Part-of-speech labels.** These labels, which are usually abbreviated, indicate how the entry word should be used in a sentence. Some words may be used as more than one part of speech.

6. **Definitions.** If a word has more than one definition, meanings are numbered or lettered.

7. **Examples.** Phrases or sentences may show how the word is used.

8. **Special usage labels.** These labels identify words that have special meanings or are used in special ways in certain situations.

9. **Related word forms.** These are alternate forms of the entry word, usually created by adding suffixes or prefixes.

10. **Synonyms and antonyms.** Sometimes synonyms or antonyms are listed at the end of a word entry.

EXERCISE 1   Using a Dictionary

Use a dictionary to answer the questions below. Then write your answers on the lines after the questions.

EX.   1.   Give two meanings for the word *incandescent.*
glowing with intense heat; very bright or gleaming

1.   How is *histrionic* divided into syllables? _____

2.   What are two possible spellings for the plural form of *concerto*?

_____

3.   Show phonetically how *frenzy* is pronounced. _____

4.   Give two definitions for *bureau*. _____

_____

5.   List two synonyms for *decline*. _____

EXERCISE 2   Finding Alternate Spellings for Words

Write the alternate spelling on the line after each of the following words.

EX.   1.   enthrall _____enthral_____

1.   dialog _____   4. purée   _____

2.   valor _____   5. traveler _____

3.   omelet _____

SPELLING RULES

---

ie and *ei*

25a Except after *c*, write *ie* when the sound is long *e*.

LONG E	achieve	believe	chief	field	medieval	piece
AFTER C	ceiling	conceit	deceit	deceive	receipt	receive

EXCEPTIONS   either   leisure   seize   weird

25b Write *ei* when the sound is not long *e*.

EXAMPLES	beige	forfeit	freight	height	heir
	neighbor	reign	their	veil	weigh

EXCEPTIONS   ancient   conscience   friend   mischief

—cede, —ceed, and *—sede*

25c The only word ending in *—sede* is *supersede*. The only words ending in *—ceed* are *exceed, proceed,* and *succeed*. All other words with this sound end in *—cede*.

EXAMPLES   concede   intercede   precede   recede   secede

EXERCISE 3   Spelling Words with *ie* and *ei*

On the lines in the following sentences, add the letters *ie* or *ei* to complete each word correctly.

EX.   1.   Yesterday I rec___*ei*___ved a letter from Meredith.

1. Please cut the pizza into _____ ght slices.

2. My fr_____ nd Salim was born in Somalia.

3. The members of both soccer teams met in the middle of the

    f_____ ld to shake hands after the game.

4. Our for_____ gn exchange student this year will be Suki
    Terasawa, from Tokyo, Japan.

5. The beads were strung on a p_____ ce of copper wire.

6. Ships from all over the world load cargo at the p_____ rs in the
    busy port of Singapore.

7. By reading stone carvings, archaeologists are trying to reconstruct the bel _____ fs of the Mayans.

8. N _____ ther Rachel nor Amanda was able to attend the meeting.

9. Nubia was an anc _____ nt civilization along the Nile River.

10. Meat, fish, and soybeans are rich in prot _____ n.

EXERCISE 4   Proofreading a Paragraph for Spelling Errors

In the paragraph below, underline the ten misspelled words. Write the correct spelling above each word.

EX.   [1] The singing of the national anthem will *precede* preceed the game.

[1] The baseball team at Central High School has exceded everyone's expectations. [2] The team has acheived a season record of ten wins and no losses. [3] Central High even beat nieghboring Lincoln High School, which often leads the league. [4] Although the credit goes to all team members, certain players have proceded to stand out as stars. [5] For example, shortstop Abdul Ramini has succeded in attaining a .342 season batting average. [6] Next week, pitcher Lee Chung will take to the feild for Michigan's High School All-Star Game. [7] He won his spot in the All-Star bullpen by pitching two no-hitters during the hieght of the season. [8] Niether Ramini nor Chung will be playing here next year. [9] They hope to make thier way onto college teams. [10] Our coach conceeds that the team will have a hard time replacing these fine players.

PREFIXES AND SUFFIXES

A *prefix* is a letter or group of letters added to the beginning of a word to change the word's meaning.

EXAMPLES   re + turn = **re**turn   pre + view = **pre**view
                un + seen = **un**seen   dis + honor = **dis**honor

25d   **When adding a prefix to a word, do not change the spelling of the word itself.**

EXAMPLES   mis + giving = **mis**giving   un + noticed = **un**noticed
                re + arrange = **re**arrange   im + possible = **im**possible

A *suffix* is a letter or group of letters added to the end of a word to change its meaning.

EXAMPLES   hope + ful = hope**ful**   talk + ed = talk**ed**
                sing + ing = sing**ing**   care + less = care**less**

25e   **When adding the suffix** *–ly* **or** *–ness* **to a word, do not change the spelling of the word itself.**

EXAMPLES   quick + ly = quick**ly**   light + ness = light**ness**
                real + ly = real**ly**   open + ness = open**ness**

EXCEPTIONS   For words that end in *y* and have more than one syllable, change the *y* to *i* before adding *–ly* or *–ness*.

                easy + ly = eas**ily**   happy + ness = happ**iness**

EXERCISE 5   Spelling Words with Prefixes and Suffixes

On the lines below, write each of the following words, adding the given prefix or suffix.

EX.   1. hour + ly   _____hourly_____

1. a + bound   _____   6. local + ly   _____

2. slow + ly   _____   7. empty + ness   _____

3. mis + spell _____   8. im + mature   _____

4. re + view   _____   9. lazy + ly   _____

5. dark + ness _____   10. un + important _____

25f   Drop the final silent *e* before a suffix beginning with a vowel.

EXAMPLES   change + ed = chang**ed**   sense + ible = sens**ible**
devote + ion = devot**ion**   vote + er = vot**er**

EXCEPTIONS   Keep the final silent *e* in a word ending in *ce* or *ge* before a suffix beginning with *a* or *o*.

EXAMPLES   advantage + ous = advantag**eous**
peace + able = peac**eable**

25g   Keep the final silent e before a suffix beginning with a consonant.

EXAMPLES   care + less = care**less**   live + ly = live**ly**
close + ness = close**ness**   replace + ment = replace**ment**

EXCEPTIONS   argue + ment = argu**ment**   nine + th = nin**th**
awe + ful = aw**ful**   true + ly = tru**ly**
judge + ment = judg**ment**   whole + ly = whol**ly**

EXERCISE 6   Spelling Words with Suffixes

On the lines below, write each of the following words, adding the given suffix.

EX.   1. state + ment ____statement____

1. engage + ing _____   11. knowledge +able _____
2. peace + ful _____   12. strange + ness _____
3. courage + ous _____   13. impose + ing _____
4. emote + ion _____   14. outrage + ous _____
5. forgive + ness _____   15. guide + ed _____
6. awe + some _____   16. dedicate + ion _____
7. remote + ly _____   17. pride + ful _____
8. like + able _____   18. peddle + er _____
9. hope + less _____   19. time + ly _____
10. skate + er _____   20. blue + ish _____

25h   For words ending in *y* preceded by a consonant, change the *y* to *i* before any suffix that does not begin with *i*.

EXAMPLES   dry + ed = dr**ied**   beauty + fy = beaut**ify**
busy + ly = bus**ily**   try + ing = try**ing**

25i   For words ending in *y* preceded by a vowel, keep the *y* when adding a suffix.

EXAMPLES   obey + ing = obey**ing**   play + ful = play**ful**
boy + ish = boy**ish**   display + ed = display**ed**

EXCEPTIONS   day + ly = da**ily**   lay + ed = la**id**   pay + ed = pa**id**

25j   Double the final consonant before a suffix beginning with a vowel if the word

(1) has only one syllable or has the accent on the last syllable *and*
(2) ends in a single consonant preceded by a single vowel.

EXAMPLES   hit + ing = hi**tting**   prefer + ed = prefer**red**
sit + er = si**tter**   commit + ee = commi**ttee**
dip + ed = di**pped**   occur + ence = occur**rence**

The final consonant is usually not doubled before a suffix beginning with a vowel.

EXAMPLES   speak + er = speak**er**   twirl + ing = twirl**ing**
deep + est = deep**est**   local + ity = local**ity**

EXERCISE 7   Spelling Words with Suffixes

On the lines below, write each of the following words, adding the given suffix.

EX.   1. herd + ed   ___herded___

1. shop + er   _____   6. cry + ed   _____

2. bury + ed   _____   7. fry + ing   _____

3. heat + ing   _____   8. joy + ful   _____

4. ship + ed   _____   9. hot + est   _____

5. pray + ing   _____   10. permit + ing _____

EXERCISE 8   Proofreading a Paragraph for Misspelled Words

The following paragraph contains twenty spelling errors. Underline each misspelled word, and write the correct spelling above it.

EX.   [1] The museum <u>commitee</u> bought a painting by José Clemente Orozco.

committee

1   Students siting in the Baker Library at Dartmouth College can

2   see a dramatic paintting by Mexican artist José Clemente Orozco.

3   It does not go unoticed, for it is probably the bigest painting in the

4   entire state of New Hampshire. The beautyful artwork stretches

5   across the inside walls of the buildding, over the bookcases, and

6   around the corners of the room. This huge mural is nameed *An*

7   *Epic of American Civilization.* Students are truely fascinated by

8   Orozco's larger-than-life figures who work carefuly at puting

9   together a modern nation. The largeest figure in the mural is

10   takeing a break from his work. He has layed down his hammer

11   and is readding a book. An idea occured to me when I lookked at

12   that figure in Orozco's painting. Perhaps this figure is busyly

13   building a modern nation, too. After all, learnning and

14   educateion can be more powerrful tools than hammers.

Frank & Ernest reprinted by permission of NEA, Inc.

PLURALS OF NOUNS

25k   To form the plurals of most nouns, add –s.

SINGULAR	hill	plea	hoe	bird	turkey	Turner
PLURAL	hills	pleas	hoes	birds	turkeys	Turners

25l   To form the plurals of nouns ending in *s, x, z, ch,* or *sh,* add –es.

SINGULAR	bus	box	waltz	bunch	wish	Gómez
PLURAL	buses	boxes	waltzes	bunches	wishes	Gómezes

EXERCISE 9   Spelling the Plural Forms of Nouns

On your own paper, write the correct plural form of each of the following words by adding – *s* or – *es.*

EX.   1. gas

1. brush	14. fiddle	27. breakfast	40. latch
2. desk	15. Mackintosh	28. hanger	41. Bendix
3. lunch	16. Rodríguez	29. thrush	42. emerald
4. donkey	17. pick	30. cure	43. toothbrush
5. harness	18. buzz	31. Martínez	44. rake
6. window	19. toss	32. topcoat	45. crunch
7. tax	20. sea	33. dustpan	46. Parnell
8. Thomas	21. hunch	34. index	47. eye
9. Washington	22. crease	35. splash	48. robin
10. class	23. bush	36. Hsing	49. sign
11. dash	24. loss	37. laser	50. Marsh
12. radio	25. mouth	38. Dempsey	
13. batch	26. face	39. Wauneka	

25m To form the plurals of nouns ending in *y* preceded by a vowel, add –*s*.

SINGULAR	boy	display	donkey	guy	Shay
PLURAL	boys	displays	donkeys	guys	Shays

25n To form the plurals of nouns ending in *y* preceded by a consonant, change the *y* to *i* and add –*es*.

SINGULAR	county	baby	dairy	dolly	lily
PLURAL	counties	babies	dairies	dollies	lilies

EXCEPTIONS   For proper nouns, add –*s*.

EXAMPLES   Codys   Reillys

25o To form the plurals of some nouns ending in *f* or *fe*, add –*s*. For others, change the *f* or *fe* to *v* and add –*es*.

SINGULAR	leaf	chief	roof	wife	knife
PLURAL	leaves	chiefs	roofs	wives	knives

NOTE   When you are not sure how to spell the plural of a noun ending in *f* or *fe*, look in a dictionary.

EXERCISE 10   Spelling the Plural Forms of Nouns

On the line after each noun, write its correct plural form.

EX.   1. cherry _____cherries_____

1. pony _____
2. life _____
3. daisy _____
4. valley _____
5. bay _____
6. gulf _____
7. half _____
8. city _____
9. reef _____
10. Bally _____

11. strawberry _____
12. key _____
13. shelf _____
14. loaf _____
15. tray _____
16. Wednesday _____
17. journey _____
18. staff _____
19. fly _____
20. giraffe _____

25p **To form the plurals of nouns ending in *o* preceded by a vowel, add –s. For nouns ending in *o* preceded by a consonant, add –es.**

SINGULAR   rodeo   ratio   Romeo   potato   cargo
PLURAL   rodeos   ratios   Romeos   potatoes   cargoes

EXCEPTIONS   For musical terms and proper nouns ending in *o* preceded by a consonant, add –s.

soprano—sopranos   Makito—Makitos

NOTE   To form the plurals of some nouns ending in *o* preceded by a consonant, you may add either –s or –es (*dominos* or *dominoes*; *banjos* or *banjoes*, for example). When you are not sure how to spell the plural of a noun ending in an *o* preceded by a consonant, look in a dictionary.

25q **The plurals of a few nouns are formed in irregular ways.**

SINGULAR   foot   tooth   child   deer   man   ox   goose   mouse
PLURAL   feet   teeth   children   deer   men   oxen   geese   mice

25r **For most compound nouns, form the plural of the last word in the compound.**

SINGULAR   football   five-year-old   mouthwash   playing card
PLURAL   footballs   five-year-olds   mouthwashes   playing cards

25s **For compound nouns in which one of the words is modified by the other word or words, form the plural of the word modified.**

SINGULAR   brother-in-law   man-of-war
PLURAL   brothers-in-law   men-of-war

EXERCISE 11   Spelling the Plural Forms of Nouns

On your own paper, write the correct plural form of each word below.

EX.   1. piano
      1. pianos

1. tomato
2. woman
3. studio
4. ox
5. cello
6. patio
7. Nakamoto
8. mountain lion
9. two-year-old
10. gentleman
11. moose
12. city hall
13. solo
14. bolo tie
15. cameo
16. fishing rod
17. banjo
18. car pool
19. baseball
20. sheep

EXERCISE 12   Writing Sentences with Plural Nouns

On your own paper, write ten sentences. Use the plural form of each of the following nouns in a sentence.

EX.   1. sister-in-law

    1. I have no sisters-in-law.

1. alto

2. runner-up

3. basketball

4. flamingo

5. bulldog

6. cowbell

7. piano

8. sweat shirt

9. video

10. great-aunt

EXERCISE 13   Proofreading a Paragraph for Misspelled Words

Underline the twenty misspelled words in the paragraph below. Write the correct spelling above each word.

EX.   [1] Many amber *pieces* piece contain insects.

[1] Million of year ago, sticky yellow sap oozed from prehistoric trees. [2] When ancient insectes stepped into the gooey sap, their foots became stuck, and they were trapped. [3] The sap hardened into amber, enclosing creatures and gasses bubbls. [4] Sand flys that are one hundred thirty millions years old also have been perfectly preserved. [5] Today, scientistes study those piece of amber in order to learn about ancient ecologys. [6] They have gained clues about the lifes of extinct mosquito and dragonflys. [7] Fadi Acra and his father have collected one of the world's largest supplys of ancient amber.   [8] These mans began collecting amber in Lebanon in 1962. [9] Since then, they have continued their searchs in other countries. [10] Their pieces of amber, stored in plastic boxs, wait like hundred of tiny times capsules.

CHAPTER REVIEW

A. Correcting Spelling Errors in Sentences

Underline the misspelled words in each sentence below. Then write the words correctly on the line before the sentence.

EX. ___height; weight___ 1. The doctor measured the <u>hieght</u> and <u>wieght</u> of the baby seal.

_____ 1. Heros of Greek mythes include Ajax and Theseus.

_____ 2. One of the largest countrys in the world, Indonesia, is made up of more than thirteen thousand islandes.

_____ 3. If they follow the recipes carefuly, even beginers can prepare most of the dishes presented in this cookbook.

_____ 4. The band members prefered playing waltzes rather than marchs.

_____ 5. We carried our trays to the picnic table and began to eat our lunchs.

_____ 6. Did you follow your consceince, or is this action just conveneint?

_____ 7. The baseball team succeded in makeing the most errors ever recorded in a game.

_____ 8. Many kindes of potatos grow in Peru.

_____ 9. Is the nineth wave always larger than the eight waves preceeding it?

_____ 10. The word _recieve_ is frequently mispelled.

B. Proofreading a Paragraph for Spelling Errors

The following paragraph contains twenty misspelled words. Underline each misspelled word, and write the correct spelling above it.

EX. [1] There are fifteen major <u>librarys</u> in the city of Istanbul.
                  libraries

[1] Throughout history, Istanbul, the largest city in Turkey, has

been one of the world's cheif citys. [2] Its advantagous location is
partialy responseible for its importance. [3] For hundred of years, it
was the capital of the Byzantine Empire. [4] Then, after many feirce
battles, the Ottoman Turks captureed the city in 1453. [5] The
Ottomanes remained in power in Istanbul for more than four
centurys. [6] During World War I, Allyed forces defeatted the
Ottoman Empire. [7] From 1918 to 1923, the Allies occupied Istanbul.
[8] Freedom from outside rule occured for Istanbul in 1923, when
Turkey succeded in becomeing a wholely independent republic.
[9] Istanbul remains Turkey's greatest center for industrys, culture,
and foriegn trade. [10] As a result, Istanbul is famous for the shoping
at the Covered Bazaar.

C.   Working Cooperatively to Create a Word Puzzle

Find the word *SPELL* in this hidden-word puzzle. Its letters might run
across the puzzle, down a column of the puzzle, or even in a diagonal line
that slants from one corner of the puzzle to another. When you find the
word, circle it.

```
L  S  R   I   S  P
P  P  S   S   E  E
E  E  P   E   L  L
S  L  E  M  L  P
M  L  S   S   E  P
```

Now work with a partner to create your own hidden-word puzzle. First,
work together to form the plurals of the words listed below. Write each
plural on the line after the word. Next, on a piece of graph paper, hide all
the words in a puzzle like the one above. Once you have placed all the
words in the puzzle, fill in the remaining spaces with other letters. When
you have finished your puzzle, trade papers with another set of partners.
Work with your partner to solve the hidden-word puzzle that you receive.

1. radio _____   3. zoo _____

2. subway _____   4. toy _____

SPELLING WORDS

50 Commonly Misspelled Words

ache	country	laid	tear
across	doctor	meant	though
again	does	minute	through
always	don't	often	tired
answer	early	once	tonight
blue	easy	ready	trouble
built	every	said	wear
busy	friend	says	where
buy	half	shoes	which
can't	hour	since	whole
color	instead	straight	women
cough	knew	sugar	
could	know	sure	

250 Spelling Words

abandon	against	argument
absolutely	aisle	article
acceptance	amount	assistance
accidentally	analysis	authority
accommodate	anticipate	awful
accompany	anxiety	basis
accomplish	apology	beginning
achieve	apparent	believe
acquaintance	appearance	benefit
acquire	application	boundary
actually	appreciation	bouquet
advertisement	approach	bulletin

250 Spelling Words (continued)

business	defense	explanation
canceled	definite	fascinating
capacity	definition	favorite
careless	describe	February
carrier	description	finally
ceiling	desirable	flu
challenge	despair	forty
choice	develop	fourth
choir	diamond	friendliness
chorus	difficulties	generally
circuit	disappointment	governor
colonel	discipline	grammar
column	discussion	gratitude
coming	distinction	guarantee
commercial	distribution	guardian
committees	doctrine	gymnasium
competition	duplicate	hatred
completely	economic	height
conceive	eighth	heroine
condemn	eligible	hesitate
congratulations	embarrass	humorous
conscience	engineering	ignorance
conscious	enthusiasm	imagination
control	eventually	immediately
convenience	exactly	incidentally
courteous	exaggerate	individual
criticism	excellent	inferior
cylinder	existence	initial
dealt	experience	inspiration
decision	experiment	intelligence

250 Spelling Words (continued)

interfere	opinion	recommend
interrupt	opponent	referring
involve	opportunity	regularly
jealous	orchestra	relieve
judgment	originally	repetition
knowledge	paid	research
laboratory	parallel	response
leisure	parliament	restaurant
lengthen	patience	rhythm
license	performance	satisfied
lieutenant	personal	saucer
loneliness	personality	schedule
majority	persuade	scissors
manufacture	philosopher	sense
marriage	picknicking	sentiment
mechanical	planned	separate
medieval	pleasant	sergeant
military	possess	shepherd
mourn	precede	similar
multiplication	preferred	solemn
muscular	prejudice	source
mystery	privilege	souvenir
naturally	probably	sponsor
necessary	procedure	straighten
nickel	professor	subscription
nonsense	pursuit	success
numerous	qualified	sufficient
obvious	realize	suggest
occasionally	receipt	surprise
occurrence	reechoing	suppress

250 Spelling Words

surround	tradition	utilized
suspense	tragedy	vacuum
suspicion	transferred	variety
tailor	tries	various
temperament	truly	vein
tendency	unanimous	view
theory	unnecessary	villain
therefore	unsatisfactory	violence
thorough	until	warrant
tobacco	useful	weird
tonsils	using	wholly